Italian Americans on the Page

SUNY series in Italian/American Culture

Fred L. Gardaphé, editor

Italian Americans on the Page

Revisiting the Classics and
Exploring New Voices

Edited by

R YAN C ALABRETTA -S AJDER AND
A LAN J. G RAVANO

Cover credit: Galliciano panorama photo by Juliet Grames. Galliciano is a living Greco city, complete with a Greek Orthodox church.

Published by State University of New York Press, Albany

EU GPSR Authorised Representative:
Logos Europe, 9 rue Nicolas Poussin, 17000, La Rochelle, France
contact@logoseurope.eu

For information, contact State University of New York Press, Albany, NY
www.sunypress.edu

Library of Congress Cataloging-in-Publication Data

Names: Calabretta-Sajder, Ryan, editor. | Gravano, Alan J., editor.
Title: Italian Americans on the page : revisiting the classics and exploring new voices / edited by Ryan Calabretta-Sajder and Alan J. Gravano.
Description: Albany : State University of New York Press, [2025] | Series: SUNY series in Italian/American culture | Includes bibliographical references and index.
Identifiers: LCCN 2025007526 | ISBN 9798855803990 (hardcover : alk. paper) | ISBN 9798855804010 (ebook) | 9798855804003 (pbk. : alk. paper)
Subjects: LCSH: American fiction—Italian American authors—History and criticism. | Canadian fiction—Italian authors—History and criticism. | Italian Americans in literature.
Classification: LCC PS153.I8 I83 2025 | DDC 810.9/851—dc23/eng/20250508
LC record available at https://lccn.loc.gov/2025007526

This volume is dedicated to Doug Steward
(June 22, 1970–Nov. 5, 2020),
Director of the Association of Departments of English
Modern Language Association

Contents

Acknowledgments

First and foremost, the editors would like to thank all the contributors for their hard work and dedication to the project. This project was born out of an MLA Working Group Session at the 2019 MLA@Seattle Convention. We asked participants to prepare their papers ahead of time, share and comment on them, and then, at the convention, workshop each paper. Thus, the process was tiring but worthwhile, as we are finally publishing this rich volume. Much appreciation goes to Karin Bagnell and Dierdre Henry from the MLA, who have always been such amazing collaborators over the years. They always oriented us when we were lost or needed a favor. We appreciate the various readings from Anthony Julian Tamburri and Fred L. Gardaphé on diverse pieces in the volume, particularly the introduction. As always, they continue to be our "Virgils," mentoring us in the world of Italian American studies. We would also like to recognize the mentoring of William Boelhower and Mark Pietralunga, who have always been generous with their time and feedback.

Ryan: I would like to acknowledge Peter Bondanella, the first person to academically engage with me on the topic of Italian Americana at the university. Bondanella had just published *Hollywood Italians* when I arrived at Indiana University Bloomington; "Hollywood Italians" was my first graduate-level course and inspired me to embrace my *Italianità* in a scholarly and critical manner. I would also like to thank Rebecca West for her insight into Italian Americana and continuous support over the years. Last in the chronology, but certainly not least, Anthony Julian Tamburri, who has always challenged me to be a more engaged reader, a savvy thinker, a critical scholar, and an inspirational teacher. A heartfelt thank you goes to Sandra Celli Harris, with whom I had hours of conversations about the representation of Italian Americans in literature and cinema. Our conversations have led to much of my scholarly production and curricular creation.

To my cherished editors, Alan J. Gravano, Donnamarie Kelly, and Mercedes Rooney, I appreciate the time you have dedicated to challenging my work and making it better. As much as I love receiving those edits, I dread the "ding" of the email when they arrive. Thanks to my Italian American family, especially my mother, aunt, and grandparents, for teaching me what it means to be "Italian American" culturally, emotionally, and linguistically. To the next generation—Carson, Tristan, Arden, Skylar, Teagan, and Collette—I hope to be instrumental in teaching you about your *Italianità*.

Alan: I would like to express my deepest gratitude to my mentors at the University of Miami, Professors John Paul Russo and Robert Casillo, whose unwavering guidance, insightful feedback, and scholarly rigor have profoundly shaped my academic journey. Their mentorship has been invaluable, providing a solid academic writing and research foundation. Additionally, I am profoundly thankful for the collaborative relationship with Ryan Calabretta-Sajder, which has resulted in five enriching projects. Ryan's creativity, dedication, and collaborative spirit have greatly enhanced our work together. Last, I extend my heartfelt thanks to Tamara Gravano, whose unique perspective and thoughtful critiques have significantly improved the quality and depth of my academic writing. Her contributions have been instrumental in refining my research and scholarly expression.

Finally, we would like to thank Dr. Adam Pope at the University of Arkansas, Fayetteville, and his rhetoric course for providing a final edit of the complete manuscript. We truly appreciate the students' insights and are happy they collaborated with us.

Introduction

Rethinking the Past and Bridging the Future
of Italian American Studies

RYAN CALABRETTA-SAJDER AND ALAN J. GRAVANO

Overview: From *Italian Americans on Screen* to
Italian Americans on the Page

Italian Americans on the Page has been a discussion in the works for numerous years, yet the editors only put pen to paper for the first project, *Italian Americans on Screen*, in 2018 when we submitted a working group special session to the Chicago MLA convention (2019). We intended to provide attention to lesser-studied Italian American texts and topics from the working group's inception, such as film and media projects in the first collection, since much Italian American film research revolves around certain directors, mainly Michael Cimino, Francis Ford Coppola, and Martin Scorsese. In fact, few manuscript-length studies exist in Italian American cinema. The earliest is *Screening Ethnicity: Cinematographic Representations of Italian Americans in the United States,* edited by Anna Camiati Hostert and Anthony Julian Tamburri (Bordighera 2002), and the only comprehensive single-authored study is Peter Bondanella's *Hollywood Italians: Dagos, Palookas, Romeos, Wise Guys, and Sopranos* (London: Continuum/Bloomsbury 2004).[1] To be more inclusive in our project, we incorporated Media Studies and a piece on Italian Canadian cinema in *Italian Americans on Screen* (Lanham: Lexington Press 2021).

Following a model used by the American Comparative Literature Association (ACLA) and the MLA's working group, we combined philosophical working paradigms and asked our contributors to complete an article-length paper by December. The group spent the conference time workshopping and offering feedback. We furnished a timeline for submitting revisions and prepared a book proposal. Soon after, we found a series, "Media, Culture, and the Arts," that fit the theme of the edited collection and published *Italian Americans on Screen: Challenging the Past, Re-Theorizing the Future* with Lexington Books in 2021. While not exhaustive, the collection excels in bridging past and present studies in Italian American and Canadian cinema and media, offering new critical approaches to the field.

For our second project, we turned our attention to Italian American literature. We decided to concentrate on several genres of literature, such as memoirs, novels, poetry, and theater; therefore, for the Seattle MLA convention (2020), we submitted another working group, but this time engaging with Italian American literature. While focusing primarily on understudied works, we additionally consider some "so-called" canonical works through a new theoretical lens.

Always conscious of the category Italian "American," we return to the question of primary texts; one challenge that the field of Italian American studies faces is inclusivity outside North American texts targeting US-centered authors and their works. In our volumes, we attempt to consciously move beyond the confines of Italian American studies to embrace more Italian Canadian texts and attempt to recognize concepts revolving around the Italian diaspora whenever possible. Italian American and Italian Canadian studies are academic disciplines that study the experiences, contributions, cultural identities, and evolution of Italian communities in North America. These fields of study have evolved, reflecting the diverse histories and contexts of Italian immigrants and their descendants in the United States and Canada, respectively.

The shared, yet incredibly unique, historical foundations of Italian American and Italian Canadian studies are rooted in the migration of Italians to North America, particularly in the late nineteenth and early twentieth centuries. These studies explore Italian immigrants' challenges: adaptation to a new culture while trying to integrate, yet often remaining outside the norm, forming distinct Italian neighborhoods and communities. Both fields examine the maintenance and evolution of Italian cultural identity in the diaspora. This involves preserving language, traditions, religious practices, and culinary heritage within Italian communities in the United States and Canada. Scholars investigate the social and cultural impact of Italian communities and those of Italian descent on the broader North American society, including contributions to arts, film, literature, politics, theater, and the overall fabric of multicultural societies.

While Italian immigration to the United States and Canada occurred in significant numbers, the timing, scale, and regional origins of immigrants differ. Italian Americans primarily trace their roots to the mass migration of the late nineteenth and early twentieth centuries. By contrast, Italian Canadians have experienced waves of immigration at different points, including post–World War II and more recent periods. The geographical context significantly influences the experiences of Italian communities. Italian American studies often considers the dynamics of Italian communities in cities like New York, Chicago, and Boston, while Italian Canadian studies may concentrate on cities such as Toronto, Montreal, and Vancouver, each with its unique social, political, and cultural landscape.

In *Italian Americans on Screen,* Jessica Leonora Whitehead and Paul S. Moore contributed "Cinema Paradiso: Toronto's Italian Language Cinemas and Distribution Networks." Whitehead and Moore documented the importance of Italian-language films in Toronto and surrounding areas concentrating on Italian Canadians. Giuseppe Sorrentino examined Italian cinema and television, discussing the Italian American experience through the perspective of Italians. Sorrentino analyzes the films *Vacanze in America* (Carlo Vanzina 1984) and *My Name Is Tanino* (Paolo Virzi 2001).

Opening Thoughts:
Dreaming the Past, Charting the Future

Continuing the importance of studying Italian Canadians,[2] in *Italian Americans on the Page,* we include Domenico A. Beneventi, a comparative literature professor at the Université de Sherbrooke. Beneventi's "Queer Intimacies in Italian Canadian Literature" addresses Salvatore Antonio's play *In Gabriel's Kitchen* (2007) and Christopher DiRaddo's novel *The Geography of Pluto* (2014). Colleen Ryan's "(En)gendering an American Dream: Mother-Daughter Relationships in the Plays of Italian American and Italian Canadian Women Playwrights" investigates plays by two lesbian Italian Canadian playwrights: Mary Melfi's *My Italian Wife* (1996) and Michaela De Cesare's *Eight Ways My Mother Was Conceived* (2012). Underscoring how Italian Americana reaches beyond the borders of the United States, we document and illustrate similarities in the Italian diaspora across space and time by including Italian Canadian texts in our analysis.

Even though *Italian Americans on the Page* does include a few traditionally foundational texts, depending on how one defines the canon, our overarching goal is to celebrate the rich literary tradition of less-read Italian American voices.[3] Although Don DeLillo is one of the most recognizable novelists in twentieth-century American literature, Bryan Santin builds on the work of Fred L. Gardaphé, Amy Hungerford, Josephine Gattuso Hendin, and John Paul Russo, situating DeLillo in an Italian American context.[4] There is also a chapter dedicated to Helen Barolini's *Umbertina*, a canonical text within Italian American studies. However, Leonardo Buonomo and John Paul Russo have argued that it may be premature to define an Italian American canon: "A few caveats: at present it may be more accurate to speak of a collection of writings rather than a canon; hence, the qualifier 'emerging'" (2010–2011, 77). In "An Idea and Ideal of a Literary Canon," Charles Altieri argues that "any desire to put literature to work as a social force would require us self-consciously to build canons that serve our concrete, 'political' commitments" (39). Altieri continues with a philosophical approach to questioning the confines and future of the canon. Most recently, Sabrina Vellucci has contested that an Italian American literary canon has been solidified: "For, indeed, a canon had already been charted, as Rose Basile Green's *The Italian-American Novel* (1974) testifies" (2018, xiv). Although the question of the canon persists, our goal remains the same—to reread essential texts in a new light, unveil lesser-known Italian American authors, and help establish their opus within the field.

Thus, a plethora of Italian American/Italian Canadian authors, such as Salvatore Antonio, Giovanna Capone, Theresa Carilli, Nicole Antonia Carro, Peter Covino, Donna de Matteo, Louise DeSalvo, Christopher DiRaddo, Juliet Grames, Michele Linfante, Kim Ragusa, and Karen Tintori never seem to make the syllabi, or at least the research agendas, of those studying multi-ethnic literature. Most primary texts studied are only known and studied if a student has a faculty member publishing on Italian Americana. Some of this omission may be due to questions of the canon, while another obstacle to this quandary is the need for an academic home for Italian American studies. As Tamburri has mentioned, Italian American studies are often viewed as too "American" for Italian departments/programs and not "American" or "ethnic" enough for the English department. Even within American studies, it usually fares as not "ethnic" enough to be considered for multi-ethnic literature.[5] Thus, we aim to bring further attention to lesser-known critical voices while unearthing newfound attention to canonical pieces. By illustrating these unheard voices, we hope to contribute to novel discussions on Italian American literature, which are also in dialogue with similar ethnic/migratory literary experiences. In doing so, we join other literary traditions with unique yet applicable critical lenses, including but not limited to queer and gender studies, cultural studies, Latino/Latinx studies, and Black studies, to mention only a few.

Considering the contemporary political moment, we situated our work among the many essential scholars of Italian American studies; in so doing, we decided to ground our project by acknowledging the importance of the many women who paved the way for us, such as Olga Peragallo's *Italian American Authors and Their Contribution to American Literature* (1949), Hendin's *Vulnerable People: A View of American Fiction since 1945* (1979), Micaela di Leonardo's *The Varieties of Ethnic Experience: Kinship, Class, and Gender among California Italian-Americans* (1984), Helen Barolini's *The Dream Book: An Anthology of Writings by Italian American Women* (1985), Lucia Chiavola Birnbaum's *Black Madonnas: Feminism, Religion, and Politics in Italy* (1993), Mary Jo Bona's *Claiming a Tradition: Italian American Women Writers* (1999) and *By the Breath of Their Mouths: Narratives of Resistance in Italian America* (2010), Edvige Giunta's *Writing with an Accent: Contemporary Italian American Women Authors* (2002), Ilaria Serra's *The Value of Worthless Lives: Writing Italian American Immigrant Autobiographies* (2007), Chiara Mazzucchelli's *The Heart and the Island: A Critical Study of Sicilian-American Literature* (2015), and Suzanne Manizza Roszak's *Intersecting Diasporas: Italian Americans & Allyship in US Fiction* (2021). Within the genre of Italian American female poetry, much significance is indebted to Daniela Gioseffi, who published her poetry collections in 1971 (*Care of the Body* and *The Sea Hag in the Cave of Sleep*) but has also organized associations revolving around Italian American poetry. In 2007, she was recognized for her dedication and passion for poetry with the John Ciardi Award for Lifetime Achievement in Poetry.

Beginnings of Italian American Thought

As mentioned earlier, one of the oldest pioneers, Olga Peragallo, began her study in 1949 and died before completing her research. Although encyclopedic in nature, the work solidifies the significance of Italian American studies within the US canon. Within this anthology, fifty-nine Italian American authors are profiled; eleven are women, almost 20 percent. Considering the study period, 1949, 20 percent is a decent representation of female Italian American writers. Of the most notable, we have Frances Winwar (Francesca Vinciguerra), known to many as the "Virgil" for the young Joseph Tusiani, and Rosa Zagnoni Marinoni, the first female poet laureate of the state of Arkansas and founder of the University-City Poetry Club in 1926.[6] Twenty-five years after Peragallo's original research, Rose Basile Green published the first critical study of Italian American literature, *The Italian-American Novel: A Document of the Interaction of Two Cultures* (1974), focusing on the significance of the Italian American novel within the American canon, based on her PhD dissertation *The Evolution of Italian-American Fiction as a Document of the Interaction of Two Cultures* (1962).

As early as 1969, the American Italian Historical Association (AIHA) celebrated the Italian American Novel at its Second Annual Conference. In his introduction to *The Italian American Novel: The Literary Value and Social Significance of The Italian American Novel*, AIHA President Rudolph J. Vecoli states, "At the time of the meeting, an Italian-American novel was leading the best-sellers list throughout the country."[7] This early attention to the Italian American novel promoted an entire conference dedicated to the genre and resulted in a scholarly volume that illustrates the relevance of multi-ethnic literature. The fact that the American literature scholar Basile Green was invited to give a keynote lecture at the 1969 conference, predominantly run and hosted by a board of men, demonstrates her significance as a pioneer in the field. Critical to note, Vecoli and Basile Green's sentiments were never forgotten. Justly, Tamburri argues in *A Semiotic of Ethnicity: In (Re)cognition of the Italian/American Writer*, the AIHA proceedings, which include Basile Green's keynote address, "constitute a base of knowledge and documentation which should now prove most useful for a further theorization of issues" (125).[8] These conferences served as annual engagements for critical thought and debate, producing volumes of invaluable insight into the field.

In *The Italian-American Novel: A Document of the Interaction of Two Cultures* (1974), Basile Green challenges the confines of the American literary canon, particularly concerning the conceptualization of the novel. She opens her introduction strongly prepared to argue against the "absolute egalitarian" who "will insist that an American novel is an American novel, and that it matters *not* whether the materials are of Jewish, Negro, Italian, Lithuanian, or whatever reference" (1974, 17, emphasis ours). In fact, she continues, confronting the limits of the academy: "Furthermore, assured by an established formula in institutional scholarship and by fixed popular promotion, the devotee of an accepted tradition will probably maintain that an Italian or any other ethnic-American writer is successful only insofar as he meets the criteria for successful writing in the past" (Basile Green 1974, 17). In her opening paragraph, Basile Green overtly evidences the difficulty of even considering the Italian American novel's subgenre, not to mention creating a field of Italian American studies. As her book's subtitle rightly underscores, Italian Americanness explores the "interaction" between US and Italian cultures. The *Oxford English Dictionary* highlights the "reciprocal" nature that the word "interaction" suggests, accurate not only as a description of her work but as a cornerstone for exploring the field. The Italian American experience offers a "push-and-pull" relationship regarding the struggle of leaving one culture to integrate with another and all the added difficulties that come with the exilic experience, whether voluntary or involuntary. Consciously or unconsciously, the migrant artist carries their experiences, culture, and language with them, and these cultural artifacts often resurface without purpose. Thus, being "migrant" or even "other" naturally constructs layers of compilation and frustration when exploring the phenomena of integration.[9]

In 1996, twenty-two years after Basile Green's keynote lecture, Fred L. Gardaphé points out that "there are close to 200 Italian American novels that depict the immigrant struggle, second-generation conflicts between American-born children and their parents, and the third generation's search for a cultural heritage" (10). Basile Green and Gardaphé represent the earliest scholarship on Italian American literature, specifically fiction, from the perspective of single-authored works aside from *A Semiotic of Ethnicity*. Noteworthy, however, for charting a *filone* from Green to the present are the works of Robert Viscusi and Helen Barolini. Viscusi's 1981 article "*De vulgari eloquentia*: An Approach to the Language of Italian American Fiction," republished and expanded for his manuscript *Buried Caesars* as "*De vulgari eloquentia*: Ordinary Eloquence in Italian America," discusses how Dante's goal of a "italiano volgare" could be (or not) developed for Italian American studies. Through both linguistic and literary considerations, which include several writers, such as Louis Forgione, Garibaldi M. La Polla, Jerre Mangione, Rocco Fumento, Mario Puzo, and Joseph Arleo, Viscusi concludes with the hope that the third generation of Italian Americans "will hear a new complexity . . . this traveler will find in the ancient sounds echoes that the natives never hear, and will discover then, it may be, as Irving, Stein, and James before this, another music of paradox, policy, and hesitation (Viscusi 1981, 57–58). Meanwhile, in *The Dream Book* (1985), Barolini challenges

Richard Gambino's *Blood of My Blood* by concentrating on Italian American women writers Grazia Deledda, Rosemary Terrango, Louise DeSalvo, Valentine Rossilli Winsey, and Rosemarie Caruso. She employs these women to refute Gambino's claim about "the Ideal of Womanliness" and celebrates the intersectionality of Italian American women writers, underscoring not only their constant presence but also their worth (1985, 10). Leonardo Buonomo and John Paul Russo stress that "Italian American poetry has not yet received a single comprehensive study" (2010–11, 90); however, several poets such as John Ciardi, Gregory Corso, and Diane di Prima have received monographic attention as American poets, but not as Italian Americans authors. Rodolfo Pucelli's *Anthology of Italian and Italo-American Poetry* (1955) represents the first collection of poets born in Italy and those of Italian descent in the United States. As the #MeToo and #BLM (Black Lives Matter) movements gain support from students and faculty, both within the United States and abroad, we are reminded of how Basile Green illustrates that shared experiences cross ethnic boundaries, as well as unique ones, for which "ethnic groups are actively seeking recognition" (1974, 17). The ultimate purpose of her book, as she later articulates, "is to present the contribution of the Italian American novelist to the mainstream of American literature" and explore how Italian Americans have influenced the canon (1974, 25). Almost fifty years after her book's publication, literature by Italian Americans still struggles for recognition and legitimacy.

Pen to Page: An Overview of *Italian Americans on the Page*

This volume builds on the works of William Boelhower, Mary Jo Bona, Peter Carravetta, Luigi Fontanella, Fred L. Gardaphé, Josephine Gattuso Hendin, John Paul Russo, Anthony Julian Tamburri, and Robert Viscusi.[10,11] More specifically, we situate Italian American/Canadian literature within the contemporary and intersectional debates concerning ethnic identity. Given the ever broader, competing, and sometimes conflicting concepts and representations of migration in culture and literature—from exile and diaspora, page to stage, theory to application—this book links past scholarship to theoretical underpinnings with new hermeneutical literary approaches. *Italian Americans on the Page* represents one of the first edited collections focused on literature by applying theoretical models based on race, class, gender, and sexuality, demonstrating this subject's relevance today. Gardaphé, Giordano, and Tamburri's *From the Margin: Writings in Italian Americana* (1991), and later Giordano and Tamburri's *Beyond the Margin: Readings in Italian Americana* (1998) serve as two cornerstones for Italian American literature and film studies. These two volumes brought together numerous "new" and understudied voices to the forefront.[12] Sabrina Vellucci and Carla Francellini's *Re-Mapping Italian America: Places, Culture, Identities* (2018), stemming from a conference of the same name (May 2016), provides a variety of fresh perspectives on the current and future realities of Italian American studies, newfound literary analyses, and innovative views on performance and gender.

Although the field of Italian American studies showcases many Italian American/Canadian writers, a small number of publications address Italian American/Canadian identity in literature. Most research to date concentrates on individual novelists, such as DeLillo, and their opus or individual works, affording minimal attention to questions of ethnicity and their potential influence on ethnic identities and values. In our volume, by contrast, we invert the dominant paradigm in two ways: 1) placing in first position variations on the concept of ethnicity through more intersectional approaches to the question of identity, and 2) forging new modes of interpretation across writers and genres by integrating a variety of contemporary critical theories.

The book's organization reflects the following thematic arrangement: 1) Rereading the Italian American Canon: Intersectionalizing the Narrative, 2) Confessionalism in Italian American Poets: Moving Beyond Categories, 3) Blurring the Past, Redefining the Future: Italian Americans and Memoir, and 4) From Page to Stage: Italian Americans and Italian Canadians.

Part one's contributions redefine and expand the concept of diaspora, particularly from the perspective of Kim D. Butler. In "Defining a Diaspora, Refining a Discourse" (2001), Butler calls on scholars to stop and consider the various definitions of "diaspora" and create, at the very least, a series of characteristics needed to be called "diaspora." In the piece's first section, "Diaspora as Concept," she accepts the ethnographic approach, citing William Safran and his list of five principal characteristics:

1. dispersal to two or more locations

2. collective mythology of homeland

3. alienation from the host land

4. idealization of return to the homeland

5. ongoing relationship with the homeland (Safran in Butler 2001, 191)

She then adds Robin Cohen's importance on "'ethnonational consciousness'—and, importantly, on whether a group not living in its homeland had the option of choosing between returning and making a permanent home in diaspora" (Cohen in Butler 2001, 192). Butler concludes by arguing the three main characteristics need to exist for a diaspora: 1) a minimum of two destinations, 2) "some relationship to an actual or imagined homeland," and 3) "self-awareness of the group's identity," and she adds a fourth, "its existence over at least two generations" (Butler 2001, 192).[13] Thus, the Italian American experience conforms to Butler's definition.[14]

In this first section of the volume, all four of Butler's characteristics are present, exploring aspects of affect theory and how exactly diaspora forms and impacts family, neighborhood, and identity. Francesco Ferrari, in "'Who Will Buy My Marriage Spread?' Trading Affects and Yearning for Tomorrow in Italian American Diaspora," explores the affective and economic significance of the dowry's (*corredo*) transgenerational nature in Helen Barolini's *Umbertina*. Through a gendered perspective, he analyzes the *trousseau*'s role in reproducing home spaces, the sense of nostalgic detachment deriving from its sale, and the costs and benefits that the trade implicates. Such a trade, albeit painful, can be read as a form of negotiation to construct a new transnational subjectivity. In "*Dietrologia*: Italian American Masculinity and the Conspiracy of Postwar Whiteness in DeLillo's *Underworld*," Bryan Santin questions DeLillo's half-century–spanning magnum opus with a related theoretical lens that is germane to his fiction, though rarely employed in relation to it: Cold War–era racialized ethnicity. By focusing on the novel's "half-Italian" protagonist, Nick Shay, and its minor black characters, he demonstrates how DeLillo traces a complex relationship of competing identities between Italian Americans, African Americans, and ostensibly "race-less" white Americans. While eschewing a historically naive "wop to white" narrative, DeLillo nevertheless tells an illuminating story about how Italian Americans emerged from an ambiguous, anxious form of whiteness in the midcentury into a more stable, normative form by the century's end. In "The Very Queer Truth: Ben Piazza's Italian Southerner," Douglas Steward and Tracy Floreani explore the little-known text, *The Exact and Very Strange Truth*, the 1964 novel by Ben Piazza, which occurs in both Arkansas and Georgia. They demonstrate that, although the novel follows specific motifs and characteristics of more famous Southern writers like Carson McCullers and Flannery O'Connor, it breaks from the typical "Southern grotesque" and displays the trope of "freakishness" to consider ethnic identity within the realm of gender and sexuality studies.

Part two centers around women and queer poets, bridging the diaspora theme to the context of poetry. In "Hidden Roots: Mary Jo Paradise Salter and the Subtle Presence of Italian-ness," Alan J. Gravano investigates elements of *Italianità* in Salter's "Libretto," "Dead Letters," "Poppies," and "Mary Cazzato, 1921." Even though previous scholarship has focused on Salter's poetry, no article or book examines her Italian descent on her mother's side; Lormina Paradise Salter is Italian American. Like Don DeLillo, who considers himself an American writer, even though he is Italian American and has Italian American characters in his works, most scholars recognize Salter as an American poet because many are unaware of her family origins. Her poems incorporate *Italianità,* and the characters struggle with their sense of identity. Salter's poetry uses Homi Bhabha's concept of "in-between," the interstitial spaces within and among individuals and cultures, which do not maintain a single position but form identities in an ongoing process. In "Queering Italian American Poetry: Peter Covino's *Cut Off the Ears of Winter:* Psychoanalysis, Performativity, and Language," Ryan Calabretta-Sajder explores the concept of identity through a gendered lens, analyzing how Covino confronts the traumatic world of familial abuse, both physical and emotional, and approaches gender in his poetry as a verb. Calabretta-Sajder uses Lacan's mirror stage to examine the Imaginary and the Real in Covino's autobiographical moments and explores the performative nature of his early homosexuality. He charts the evolution of the volume through psychoanalysis and queer theory, demonstrating how the narrator of the volume himself evolves as a "confident," or at the very least "aware," homosexual male.

Part three studies nonfiction and memoirs by women. In "Memoir and the Invention of the Italian American Working-Class Feminist: Louise DeSalvo's *Vertigo* and *Adultery,*" John Champagne argues that DeSalvo's oeuvre challenges any naive understanding of writing about the self. Rather than what Robyn Wiegman calls "impoverished understandings of the work of memory, narrative, identification, and desire," we find a rich exploration of this labor in DeSalvo (317). In her memoirs, DeSalvo shares the story of how her step-grandmother was penned dark when referring to her skin tone by an anonymous bureaucrat on her naturalization application. In doing so, the writer posits Italian American identity not as the grounds of experience but as constitutive. Champagne, a former student of DeSalvo, delivers a unique memoir-like chapter; however, he interweaves theoretical underpinnings in discussing the importance of writing oneself into a piece, in this case, a chapter. Although DeSalvo passed away in 2018, Champagne's contribution eulogizes her and sits between three other women writers, Kym

Ragusa, Juliet Grames, and Karen Tintori, as an interesting counterpoint. Mary Jo Bona and Jessica Maucione's "Criminalizing Desire: An Intersectional Approach to Patriarchy's Monsters in Tintori's *Unto the Daughters: The Legacy of an Honor Killing in a Sicilian American Family* and Grames's *The Seven or Eight Deaths of Stella Fortuna*" propounds that the generic hybridity used by the authors enables an elaborate and deliberate representation of gendered domestic violence in Italian and Italian American families. They place Tintori and Grames into the larger tradition of Italian American women's writing and deploy feminist intersectional theories to enlarge a critique of how these authors criminalize women's desire in heteronormative ways that also reinscribe an Old World/New World binary imaginary that consequently limits the authors' critiques of gender and ethnicity under transatlantic modes of patriarchy.

Part four's contributions highlight queer and gendered Italian American and Italian Canadian playwrights. In "Queer Intimacies in Italian Canadian Literatures," Domenico A. Beneventi examines the queering of the Italian Canadian family in Salvatore Antonio's play *In Gabriel's Kitchen* (2007) and Christopher DiRaddo's novel *The Geography of Pluto* (2014). Taking into consideration the work of Jack Halberstam, Jose Esteban Muñoz, and Lee Edelman on queer geographies and temporalities, he analyzes how the gay or queer characters in the works of Antonio and DiRaddo open up spaces of "utopic longing" that are both real, physical, and lived spaces (such as the immigrant home, the city, and the suburb, and the body itself) and imaginary spaces on which memory, affect, and life narratives are written. He demonstrates that in their desire to negotiate a space of belonging in the city and the family, the queer protagonists imagine and experience time and space in ways that are different from their heteronormative and ethnically prefigured surroundings. Colleen Ryan considers lesbian playwrights in "(En)gendering an American Dream: Mother-Daughter Relationships in the Plays by Michele Linfante, Chris Cinque, Theresa Carilli, Mary Melfi, and Michaela Di Cesare." She showcases how Italian American and Italian Canadian women dramatists have critically examined the self-perpetuating cycle of gender codes and gender roles in second- and third-generation Italian American/Canadian families. Through her study of dramas by Linfante, Cinque, Carilli, Melfi, and Di Cesare, Ryan explores how grandmother-granddaughter, mother-daughter, and sister-sister relationships are, for these authors, the locus of revised, gender-conscious American Dreams.

Italian Americans on the Page fills a lacuna in critical approaches to Italian American studies. Although the book starts with the examination of iconic novelists such as DeLillo and Barolini, who reveal that the liminal racial space once inhabited by Italian Americans can function as a privileged aperture from which to view the construction of whiteness, our innovative contributions include a focus on underexplored artists such as Italian American women and queer writers whose subjects are not necessarily Italian, Italian American, or Italian Canadian but who nevertheless probe the diasporic experience regarding family, gender roles, and sexuality.

Returning to Basile Green, her abandoned study of Italian American novels furnishes the foundation for the literary study of writers of Italian descent. Additionally, one cannot overlook the importance of her work published in the 1970s in the context of today's #MeToo movement. Not only has her research magnified the significant role Italian American literature currently boasts within American studies, but her critical framework, which manifests itself within a cultural studies foundation, also embraces what we now call affect theory and aspects of sociology. In *By the Breath of Their Mouths*, Bona concludes, "as we continue to shape the field, resurgent voices of Italian American acquire value and significance as their histories, cultural backgrounds, and artistic strategies are clarified by creative scholarship able to meet this rich body of writing on its own, multilayered terms" (2010, 234). This edited collection represents voices—some old, some new—hoping that this scholarship adds to the ever-growing field of Italian American studies aimed at enriching the knowledge of today so that the next generation of scholars continues to nurture and expand the field.

Notes

1. While Peter Bondanella's *Hollywood Italians* was truly a tour de force for its breadth and reach, especially when originally published, it lacks an in-depth analysis of individual films. What Bondanella's works succeeds in, beyond other aspects, is presenting a broad audience with a rich variety of Italian American films, as well as discussing them within particular categories providing unique insight to the numerous representations of Italian Americans on the big screen.

2. For a wider scope of Italian Canadian studies, consider Licia Canton's *Here & Now: An Anthology of Queer Italian Canadian Writing* (2021) and volume 2 (2024) and her film *Creative Spaces* (2021), the rich and diverse work of Michaela Baldo, particularly on queer Italian Canadians, as well as the journal *Italian Canadiana*.

3. For the rich history of writing on the American canon, please see Barbara Herrnstein Smith, "Contingencies of Value," *Critical Inquiry* 10, no. 1 (September 1983): 1–35; Jane Tompkins's *Sensational Designs: The Cultural Work of American*

Fiction, 1790–1860 (Oxford: Oxford University Press, 1985), Paul Lauter, *Canons and Contexts* (Oxford: Oxford University Press, 1991); John Guillory, *Cultural Capital: The Problem of Literary Canon Formation* (Chicago: University of Chicago Press, 1993); David Palumbo-Liu, "Introduction," in *The Ethnic Canon: Histories, Institutions and Interventions* (Minneapolis: University of Minnesota Press, 1995), 1–27; Fred L. Gardaphé, "Left Out: Three Italian American Writers of the 1930s," in *Leaving Little Italy* (Albany: State University of New York Press, 2004), 53–65; Mary Jo Bona and Irma Maini, *Multiethnic Literature and Canon Debate* (Albany: State University of New York Press, 2006); Bona, "Revival/Risorgimento—Stories Continue: Shaping U.S. Italian American Writing," in *By the Breath of Their Mouths: Narratives of Resistance in Italian America* (Albany: State University of New York Press, 2010), 211–34.

4. Please see James Perricone, "DeLillo's *Underworld*: Towards a New Beginning for the Italian American Novel." *VIA: Voices in Italian Americana* XI, no. 1 (2000): 141–58, and John Duvall, *Don DeLillo's* Underworld: *A Reader's Guide* (London: Continuum, 2002).

5. For a complete discussion of this topic, see Anthony Julian Tamburri, *Italian Diaspora Studies and the University*, where he not only discusses the issues of Italian American studies not having a home, but also the challenges the current situation as well as provides suggestions to remedy it. Additionally, within the history of *MELUS: Multi-Ethnic Literature of the United Staties*, a prestigious journal focusing on ethnic American literature, only one volume has even been "dedicated" to Italian American literature (volume 28, issue 3 [September 2003]).

6. Ethel C. Simpson and June Baker Jefferson, "Rosa Zagnoni Marinoni (1888–1970), Encyclopedia of Arkansas, https://encyclopediaofarkansas.net/entries/rosa-zagnoni-marinoni-1705/.

7. Rudolph J. Vecoli, "Introduction," in *The Italian American Novel*, ed. John M. Cammett (Philadelphia: American Italian Historical Association, 1970).

8. For later and expanded reference to Basile Green's influence on theorizing Italian American literature, see Tamburri, *Re-reading Italian Americana: Specificities and Generalities on Literature and Criticism* (2015) and *Signing Italian/American Cinema: A More Focused Look* (2021).

9. See Hamid Naficy, *An Accented Cinema: Exilic and Diasporic Filmmaking* (Princeton, NJ: Princeton University Press, 2001). In *Divergenze in celluloide: Colore, migrazione e identità sessuale nei film gay di Ferzan Özpetek*, Calabretta-Sajder has argued for the need to use Naficy's theoretical construction even in literary texts as the exilic/migrant artist rarely is able to completely lose their accent.

10. William Boelhower, *Through a Glass Darkly, Ethnic Semiosis in American Literature* (Oxford: Oxford University Press, 1986); Mary Jo Bona, *By the Breath of Their Mouths: Narratives of Resistance in Italian America* (Albany: State University of New York Press, 2010); Peter Carravetta, *Prefaces to Diaphora: Rhetorics, Allegory,*

and the Interpretation of Postmodernity (Lafayette, IN: Purdue University Press, 1991); Luigi Fontanella, *Migrating Words: Italian Writers in the United States* (New York: Bordighera Press, 2012); Fred L. Gardaphé, *Italian Signs, American Streets: The Evolution of Italian American Narrative* (Durham, NC: Duke University Press, 1996); Josephine Gattuso Hendin, *Heartbreakers: Women and Violence in Contemporary Culture and Literature* (London: Palgrave Macmillan, 2004); John Paul Russo, *The Future Without a Past: The Humanities in a Technological Society* (Columbia: University of Missouri Press, 2005); Anthony Julian Tamburri, *To Hyphenate or Not to Hyphenate?: The Italian/American Writer: An Other America* (Hamilton, Ontario: Guernica, 1991); Robert Viscusi, *Buried Caesars, and Other Secrets of Italian American Writing* (Albany: State University of New York Press, 2006).

11. William J. Connell and Stanislao G. Pugliese, *The Routledge History of Italian Americans* (New York: Routledge, 2017) and Edvige Giunta and Kathleen Zamboni McCormick, *Teaching Italian American Literature, Film, and Popular Culture* (New York: Modern Language Association, 2010).

12. It is also important to note that both anthologies were published by university presses, bringing Italian American studies into a new "political" light.

13. For a well-rounded discourse on diaspora from definition to methodology, see Rainer Bauböck and Thomas Faist's *Diaspora and Transnationalism: Concepts, Theories and Methods.* For a discussion of diaspora from a more Italian-centric or European perspective, see Sandra Ponzanesi's work, particularly, Sandra Ponzanesi and Gianmaria Colpani, *Postcolonial Transitions in Europe: Contexts, Practices and Politics.*

14. For an extended study of the Italian Diaspora, consider enrolling in Italian Diaspora Studies Summer Seminar (IDSSS), launched in the summer of 2015 by Fred Gardaphé, Anthony Julian Tamburri, and Margherita Ganeri. Its current home is at Università degli Studi Rome Tre, directed by Gardaphé, Tamburri, and Sabrina Vellucci. The summer seminar analyzes the global dispersion of Italian communities beyond Italy. The seminar fosters interdisciplinary research, collaboration, and a deeper understanding of the experiences of Italians and their descendants worldwide. The program investigate the cultural, social, and historical aspects of the Italian diaspora, acknowledging the diverse contexts and contributions of Italian communities in various regions.

The seminar allows participants to engage in meaningful discussions, share research findings, and collaborate on projects that contribute to the broader field of diaspora studies. Faculty involvement in the IDSSS varies from year to year, but it includes renowned scholars and experts in the field. These faculty members guide participants through lectures, workshops, and discussions, offering their expertise and insights to enhance the overall learning experience. The interdisciplinary nature of the seminar allows participants to benefit from the diverse perspectives of faculty members with backgrounds in history, sociology, literature, cultural studies, and related fields.

Works Cited

Altieri, Charles. 1983. "An Idea and Ideal of a Literary Canon." *Critical Inquiry* 10 (1): 37–60.

Basile Green, Rose. 1974. *The Italian-American Novel.* Madison, NJ: Fairleigh Dickinson University Press.

Boelhower, William. 2021. *Immigrant Autobiography in the United States: Constantine Panunzio, Pascal D'Angelo, Emanuel Carnevali, Jerre Mangione.* 2nd ed. New York: Bordighera Press.

Bona, Mary Jo. 2010. *By the Breath of Their Mouths: Narratives of Resistance in Italian America.* Albany: State University of New York Press.

Buonomo, Leonardo, and Russo, John Paul. 2010–2011. "Introduction to Forum: The Emerging Canon of Italian American Literature." *RSA Journal* 21–22, 90–94.

Butler, Kim D. 2021. "Defining Diaspora, Refining a Discourse." *Diaspora: A Journal of Transnational Studies* 10 (2) (2021): 189–219.

Calabretta-Sajder, Ryan and Alan J. Gravano. 2021. *Italian Americans on the Screen: Challenging the Past, Re-Theorizing the Future.* Lanham, MD: Lexington Press.

Connell, William J., and Stanislao G. Pugliese. 2018. *The Routledge History of Italian American.* New York: Routledge.

Gardaphé, Fred L. 1986. "Oral Traditions Live in Italian American Novels." *Expressions* 2 (1): 5, 10.

Gardaphé, Fred L., Paolo Giordano, and Anthony Julian Tamburri. 2000. *From the Margin: Writings in Italian America.* 2nd ed. West Lafayette: Purdue University Press.

Giordano, Paolo, and Anthony Julian Tamburri. 1998. *Beyond the Margin: Readings in Italian Americana.* Madison, NJ: Fairleigh Dickinson University Press.

Naficy, Hamid. 2001. *An Accented Cinema: Exilic and Diasporic Filmmaking.* Princeton, NJ: Princeton University Press.

Peragallo, Olga. 1949. *Italian-American Authors and Their Contribution to American Literature.* New York: Vanni.

Pucelli, Rodolfo. 1955. *Anthology of Italian and Italo-American Poetry.* Boston: Bruce Humphries.

Simpson, Ethel C., and June Baker Jefferson. "Rosa Zagnoni Marinoni (1888–1970). https://encyclopediaofarkansas.net/entries/rosa-zagnoni-marinoni-1705/.

Tamburri, Anthony Julian. 1998. *A Semiotic of Ethnicity: In (Re)cognition of the Italian/American Writer.* Albany: State University of New York Press.

———. 2014. *Re-reading Italian Americana: Specificities and Generalities on Literature and Criticism.* Madison, NJ: Fairleigh Dickinson University Press.

———. 2021. *Signing Italian/American Cinema: A More Focused Look.* Ambler, PA: Ovunque Siamo Press.

———. 2022. *Italian Diaspora Studies and the University.* New York: Bordighera Press.

Vellucci, Sabrina, and Carla Francellini. 2018. *Re-Mapping Italian America: Places, Cultures, Identities.* New York: Bordighera Press.

Viscusi, Robert. 1981. "*De vulgari eloquentia:* An Approach to the Language of Italian American Fiction." *Yale Italian Studies* 1 (3): 21–38.

———. 2006. *Buried Caesars, and Other Secrets of Italian American Writing.* Albany: State University of New York Press.

von Hallberg, Robert, ed. 1984. *Canons.* Chicago: University of Chicago Press.

Wiegman, Robyn. 2019. *Object Lessons.* Durham, NC: Duke University Press.

Rereading the Italian American Canon

Intersectionalizing the Narrative

1

"Who Will Buy My Marriage Spread?"

The Economy of Affects and the Construction of a Diasporic Domesticity in Helen Barolini's *Umbertina*

Francesco Ferrari

Migrant Objects and Homes in Motion

For those who migrate, it is maybe the departure, more than the arrival, that marks a moment of painful objecthood: What before departing had only been a long-imagined eve, filled with hope, fear, and foretasted nostalgia for the home and the affectivities, now turns into a tangible reality. This feeling is made more acute by the physical and affective proximity between the migrants and their belongings the moment when they decide what to leave behind and what to bring with them in their journey across the ocean. Their meager "treasure" typically consists of a trunk, a bundle of clothes, some toiletries, and a good pair of shoes, tied together with lace and hanging around their necks, to wear only once off-board.[1] In other words, practical things, functional artifacts to be used in everyday life but with little or no monetary value. Yet their worth transcends the principle of functionality and the economic potential, as they are entrusted with the task of compensating for the imminent loss and bridging the distance—at least in part—between the homeland and the new place. In that sense, they guarantee continuity between past and future.

This is particularly true for a certain class of artifacts such as those included in the trousseau, an important component of women's dowry, which the young bride would bring into her new household after the marriage. Handmade linens, towels, bed sets, handkerchiefs, and tablecloths with refined floral embroidered motives represented a foundational stone in the creation of a new domestic space. In addition, they were meant to be passed down to the future generation, via maternal lineage, from mother to daughter. In this light, these objects can be seen as genealogical devices, as they guarantee the transmission of familial ties, traditions, and memories to posterity by virtue of their cross-generational potential.

The question of genealogy is crucial in the context of migration, where the transnational subject is often caught in a constant tension between continuities and discontinuities in the symbolic and material relationship with their native culture. In *Transnationalism and Genealogy*, Philip Yang illustrates the importance of these two categories to understand "the impact of immigrant transnationalism on family relations; [. . .] the effect of immigrant transnationalism on family lineage; [. . .] transnational family arrangements; transnational motherhood, fatherhood, and childhood, and their differences from traditional motherhood, fatherhood, and childhood" (Yang 2020, 2). The importance of migrants' belonging, in particular artifacts involved in genealogical transmission or items entrusted with preserving a sense of homeliness in the new land, can help us observe the continuities and divergences between the traditional configurations of home and the organization of domestic roles, and their diasporic double.

When the time comes to leave her remote village in the Calabrian Mountains, the eponymous heroine of Helen Barolini's novel (1979), *Umbertina*,[2] gathers the few things she wants to bring with her, as many have done previously. Among these are some rosemary twigs whose scent filled her little stone house: "She dug a root and carefully wrapped it close to the dampness of Paolo's swaddling clothes. Just to be sure, she would take her own with them" (48). The metaphor of the root establishes a clear symbolic connection between the plant and the migrant, both uprooted and replanted into foreign soil. But it also encapsulates the promise of a future sense of homeliness formulated by the familiar aromatic atmosphere of rosemary's herbaceous hints.[3] Therefore, home, the home of the future, will preserve the scent—this is the hope, or the promise—of the home of the past. Here, too, just as in the case of genealogical relations, the preoccupation is to establish a continuity between past and future in the face of the disaggregating forces. In other words, it is a negotiation that alters not only the organization of the domestic space but also the notion of domesticity itself.

What transnational and diasporic contexts reveal is that home cannot be seen anymore as a space of stability and immutability. Geographical and cultural displacement, as conditions of permanent passing, exposes the home to transience and change, which, however, do not necessarily translate to a precarious existence. Instead, the reconfigurations of the domestic space mirror the re-subjectification of its inhabitant, who becomes a transnational individual embodying both the rupture and the continuity between past and future, old world and new world. In the introduction to the collected volume *Uprootings/Regrounding,* the editors challenge "the presumptions that movement involves freedom from grounds, or that grounded homes are not sites of change, relocation or uprooting" (Ahmed et al. 2018, 1). Conversely, the concepts of uprootings/regrounding provide an interpretive tool for "rethinking home and migration in ways that open up the discussion beyond oppositions such as stasis versus transformation, or presence versus absence" (1). Migrant narratives, such as Barolini's novel, compel a radical rethinking of these oppositions by showing a redefinition of living and urban spaces. This contribution demonstrates how the experience of loss, displacement, and nostalgia can generate new domesticities and, subsequently, new subjectivities—and how material objects coming from the old world provide the symbolic and physical material for mobilizing future-making practices in the new world.[4] This specific form of yearning results in a seemingly paradoxical mode of inhabiting that I call a "diasporic domesticity"[5]—a new configuration of dwelling that partially reproduces and partially subverts the original domestic models. I focus my analysis on material objects, keeping in mind Walter Benjamin's notion of the interior as the result of a certain organization of human and non-human elements, both in a mutual relation of care and both participating in the construction of the same affective network that we call home. "To feel at home is to know that things are in their place and so are you" (Boym 2001, 251), but when things are not exactly in their place anymore, when the order of affective ties is altered, home becomes a porous space of negotiation between nostalgia and hope, loss and reconstruction. It is not just the melancholic receptacle of bittersweet memories, nor is it a shell where one's original identity can be preserved and kept unaltered. On the contrary, the home reveals itself as an always-in-the-making space inhabited by an always-in-the-making subjectivity.

Such a new, yet familiar-looking, model of domesticity emerging from the uprooting configures what Homi K. Bhabha would call an "almost the same but not quite" (1994, 89) that challenges the traditional notion of home space as structured on binary oppositions, such as proposed by the theories of the separate spheres and the hostile worlds.[6] The socioeconomic approaches famously illustrate the supposed irreducibility of the public to the private and the unbridgeable hiatus between the domain of economics and that of the affects. The dualistic construction of traditional domesticity mirrors the dualistic organization of gender roles, inside and outside the domestic space. As Bart Verschaffel highlights, "the house is the proper place for the pre-modern, female labor," which he defines as the specific form of "work that is done neither for profit and growth, nor for developing or inventing the new, but that essentially aims at making life possible and at passing it on" (2002, 288). This analysis summarizes a long-standing tradition epitomized by the Victorian cult of domesticity, which establishes an inescapable connection between home and femininity, ideally embodied by a motherly figure whose work consists of nurturing and reproducing affects. In that way, domestic space is placed outside the processes of modernization. However, migration makes the gender divisions that articulate the spaces of social and labor activities more fluid, blurring the distinction between the sphere of the private and the sphere of the public, traditionally imposed and protected by domestic walls.

That is because leaving the native home is no longer a male prerogative, and the increasing number of women moving to America turns what was considered a transitory experience into a lifetime choice. On the one hand, such regrounding demands the construction of more stable social and domestic spaces. That means a higher involvement of women in the sphere of economic production while still being largely entrusted with affective labor.

Therefore, the boundaries that separate the spaces of production, progress, and transformation from home, the space of tradition, preservation, and reproduction of the biological, affective, and cultural patrimony, begin to blur. Indeed, part of domestic labor is the perpetuation of traditions and customs that must be preserved and passed on to the future household. Yet the transmission always implies a multiplicity of readjustments and relocations, and therefore transformations, changes, and ruptures with the past. In fact, Hilde Heynen and Gülsüm Baydar describe the construction of modernity in similar terms: "modernity means change and rupture, it seems to imply, necessarily, the leaving of home" (2005, 2). Such a condition leads to what the author defines as a metaphorical "homelessness," which bolsters the equation between modernity and masculinity: "It seems as if the vicissitudes of modernity are cast into a scenario which ascribes the active and generative roles to the masculine qualities of reason, dominance, and courage, while leaving the more passive and resistant roles to the feminine capacities of nurturing and caring. Agency, consequently, is most of all located with predominantly male heroes venturing out to conquer the unknown, whereas it is generally the role of women to embody modernity's "other"—tradition, continuity, home" (ibid.). Under this light, narratives focusing on the female migration tell a different story in which domestic labor participates in the construction of modernity and its spaces. For instance, *Umbertina* shows how displacement intervenes to alter the equilibrium between the two separate spheres and redesigns the topography of domesticity. Nevertheless, what can be considered an achievement is based on sacrifice.

This chapter addresses the question of how loss can give momentum to a generative or regenerative process; how nostalgia provoked by the detachment from the house, homeland, and affective objects can be the driving force of future-making practices. The notions of uprooting and regrounding define the two steps of the process migrant subjects undergo to reposition themselves within a new space: reestablish a domestic order inspiring a sense of "being-in-there," and provide an anchorage in the new soil.

The idea of being-in-there connects to one last polarization included by the editors of *Uprootings/Regrounding* in their list of opposites, that is, presence versus absence. Perhaps migration can be described as a continuous struggle to regain a presence within a place that feels foreign and unhomely. Regardless of whether such a sense of presence is achieved, and the unhomely space finally domesticated, migrants' lives are nonetheless haunted by the spectral images of what they have lost. In a certain way, being migrant subjects means precisely building up a presence among and with the absences: what was lost or left behind. Material objects, in particular, affective belongings, confer a sense of tangibility to an experience characterized by the imminence of loss and absence, and at the same time, a coveted sense of presence. In the novel, an absent object, the "coperta matrimoniale" that Umbertina is forced to sell represents the perfect materialization of the tension between mourning the past and yearning for a future regrounding. In that sense, a Derridean "hauntological" reading will help to illuminate the power exerted by an absent object, the bedspread, that counterintuitively gives the former possessor a direction toward the future. Undoubtedly, the bedspread is also an object of nostalgia, but a particular configuration of such a structure of feeling that might be better rendered by the term of longing whose gerundive voice more efficaciously unfolds the potentialities of a future-oriented nostalgia.

The Time-Crossing Potentials of the *Corredo*

The feeling of longing permeates the novel just as the *corredo* spectrally casts its shadow throughout its pages, especially in part 1, where Umbertina's story is unfolding. Since the beginning of the novel, the *corredo* was for the young Calabrian "goat girl" the absent object of a quest that she first obtained, and successively gave away, to overcome the financial hardships faced upon her arrival in America. Thanks to her sacrifice, she and her family could find a way out from the wretchedness of the overcrowded New York City's Lower East Side and have a fresh start in Cato, far from the abject poverty of the Italian slums. Nonetheless, this loss opens a void replenished by nostalgic feelings.

Before discussing the hauntological nature and analyzing in detail the implications of yearning triggered by this object, it would be useful to explain the social and anthropological importance that the *corredo* has in traditional Italian culture. To this end, *Embroidered Stories* provides an insightful account. The volume presents a vast collection of contributions by authors from different fields of expertise, essays, poems, memoirs, and biographical fragments, displaying the profound connection that links Italian immigrant women to the trousseau. "Italian women," Edwige Giunta and Joseph Sciorra highlight in the introduction, "saw these items as beautiful objects, examples of their skill and resourcefulness; they also regarded their needle arts as a potential source of wealth and an epitome of womanhood" (Giunta and Sciorra 2014, 3). Hence, not only are the embroidered items the very cornerstone of the household because of their metonymical connection to womanhood, but they also identify the junction between the economic and the affective. The *corredo* indeed attests the status of eligibility of a woman to a good marriage; thus, it determines de facto the possibility of starting a new family and creating a new household. As a fundamental component of the dowry, the embroidered items were an indicator of the economic status of the bride's family. The more refined the pieces of the set, the higher the prestige and the monetary benefits brought by the bride to her new family. The pieces in the set varied in number from six to twelve bedsheets or even twenty-four for the richest families. Wealthier families were often able to include tablecloths, underskirts, and robes. The fabric and the designs were also telltales of the bride's status. Linen, for instance, was considered one of the most exquisite fabrics used to sew the *corredo*.

The most interesting aspect of this object, however, lies in its time-crossing potential. There is an old Calabrian proverb, "daughter in nappies, dowry in the glory box"[7] ("a figghia inta a fascia, a doti inta a cascia"), that remarks on the centrality of concern over the dowry, especially the embroidered items that practically predate its future recipients. Also, the life of these specific artifacts is supposed to be longer than the biological life of their possessors, as it is meant to survive them. Traditionally, daughters inherited the trousseau from mothers to provide them with the necessary means to maintain social respectability and a minimum economic asset to contract marriage.[8] This specific aspect illuminates the importance of domestic labor to be intended as a female responsibility and prerogative to guarantee a future and a continuity to the domestic universe. As Hwei-Fen Cheah explains in *Precious Traditions: Biancheria in American Australian Women's Lives*, all of the items included in the *corredo* had to be saved and kept pristine for future generations. Therefore, perpetuating social respectability—of not only the present but also the future household—depended on maintenance of practices such as laundering, ironing, folding, and storing linens. The importance accorded to the endurance of *corredo* originates in the concern of preserving and transmitting to posterity the traditions and values that this object encapsulates. The "embroidered biancheria," Cheah writes, "represented a tangible link between traditions of their homeland and the immediate needs of the present: settling and making home" (2014, 41). Moreover, considering these items from their everyday functional dimension, they speak directly of the woman's role "as homemaker and keeper of tradition" (41). Cheah highlights the peculiarity and the tension between settling and preserving, uprooting and regrounding, the same tension between past and future that characterizes the sentiment of nostalgia as well as the construction of diasporic domesticity. This tension resonates in Umbertina's words when she says that her bedspread "was to be the traditional design of the countryside" (44). Ilaria Vanni, in "From Domestic Craft to Contemporary Arts," recalls the words that the artist Graziella del Popolo uses as a commentary to her project *Belongings*. About her linens, she claims: "These sheets were in one of the trunks. They are mine now and were very precious to my mother because they had been a wedding gift from her own mother [. . .]. These special bed sheets get used only occasionally now. They could never be replaced. They're an heirloom, irreplaceable today. They are stored safely in my cupboard" (Vanni 2014, 121). Consequently, it becomes apparent that "Maintaining and passing [. . .] *biancheria* to the future generations [. . .] represents the sustenance of lineal ties" (Cheah 2014, 53), which can be kept only through treasuring this precious object. We can better understand now what this loss means to Umbertina, how the subsequent sense of longing transcends the limits of the individual experience and why it cannot be defined merely as a yearning for the past.

The longing originating in the physical absence of the bedspread involves a broader range of social relations, for it determines not only the status of the bride to whom it belongs, but also that of the following generations that are meant to inherit it. Rather than the connection to her homeland, what the immigrant woman yearns for, after losing her *corredo,* is the possibility of a future regrounding. Likewise, Umbertina, who, belonging to a less fortunate family, had grown up without a dowry, decided that the bedspread given by her betrothed, Serafino, "was the one thing she would bring to her new home [America], and she wanted it beautiful and strong, to last forever" (Barolini 1999, 44). In that way, she would be able to preserve and perpetuate a certain model of domesticity even far from her home of origin.[9] If, at first glance, the act of preserving and maintaining a tradition could be read as a form of regressive nostalgia[10] looking back at the birthplace, this is not the case with Umbertina, who is not emotionally attached to the myth of a national origin.[11] Nostalgia then must reside somewhere else and cannot be explained only in terms of geographical displacement. Rather, the trading of this affective object reveals the multidirectionality of longing: It surely mourns the failed potentialities of yesterday conjugated in the past conditional (what could have been), but it also interrogates the possibilities of tomorrow. According to the anthropologist Purnima Mankekar, "tradition does not indicate nostalgia for past modes of living"; on the contrary, it "indexes futurity rather than the past" (2015, 15). The *corredo,* which ideally is meant to be treasured, has to be understood precisely as a compound of affective and economic potentialities whose trajectories interweave a texture of memories, patrimonies, and roots that are deeply grounded in the future.

The Nostalgic Costs of Trading Affects

The miserable conditions in which Umbertina and her family live during their first years in America prevent, however, the woman from treasuring her *corredo*. In her case, the object perfectly fulfills its practical functions, even though, at the same time, it exceeds them: "From the first Umbertina had kept her marriage bedspread on the one bed of that room. It not only kept them warm in winter, but it was also her one thing of beauty in all that squalor; it was her remembrance of leaves and flowers and the sun overhead" (Barolini 1999, 67). Traditionally, the value of an artifact can be determined by its exchange potential in the market or by its functionality. But what is the function of a bedspread? It is surely meant to keep one warm during the winter nights, but, as we can read, such a function is transcended and ends up coinciding with the emotional labor, at least for what concerns the construction of a domestic space. The bedspread acquires a consolatory function by enlightening the sufferings of Umbertina, and more importantly, by giving a homey atmosphere to an otherwise completely unwelcoming house ("it was her one thing of beauty in all that squalor"). In other words, it provides what Kathleen Stewart defines as an "atmospheric attunement" (2011, 452). In articulating this notion, the author overly reprises Martin Heidegger's notion of "worlding" that she describes as a "compositional process of dwelling in spaces" where "things matter not because of how they are represented but because they have qualities, rhythms, forces, relations, and movements" (Stewart 2011, 445). In the order of the domestic universe, the *corredo* is an integral part of the system of meanings that we call home, as it is a material marker of our being-in-there. In that sense, the forces exerted by the *corredo* and the relations built around this object engender worlding. Unfortunately, this is only a fragile and vicarious sense of domesticity that was not meant to last. Umbertina, who had always refused to give away her *corredo*, eventually agreed to a sacrificial trading to escape the purgatorial space where she had been living:

> "Signorina," she said, "do you know anyone who will buy my marriage spread?" Anna Giordani had raised her eyebrows in surprise [. . .] "Why, yes, yes . . . I might know someone. There is a Quaker lady, I know very refined and cultured, who has traveled to Italy and collects things of this rustic nature as well as fine things. She had both shawls and embroideries and things of that kind from Italian immigrants over here. But why do you want to sell it? Don't you have anything else? She knew what the spread meant to Umbertina [. . .] Umbertina makes this sacrifice in order to better her lot.
> "Nothing" said Umbertina. (Barolini 1999, 75)

This fragment presents some significant expressions such as "to sell," "to buy," "collection," and "sacrifice." The first couple of verbs belong to the field of economics, while the verb "sacrifice" instead casts light on the emotional costs of trading affects: a transaction that results in a financial gain but entails an affective loss that gives way to a pervasive nostalgia. Finally, "collection" evokes a topical expression of modernity that reaches its peak at the height of the nineteenth century and is also deeply intertwined with nostalgia as a historical and collective form of yearning. As such, it is experienced, although in different ways, by both the seller and the buyer. The latter embodies a form of nostalgia that presides over the bourgeois collection mania of the time, a result of modern capitalism, based on the circulation of mass-produced goods and serial objects specifically designed for immediate consumption. In the novel, American society epitomizes this aspect of modernity seen through the gaze of Umbertina, who cannot understand the fascination that her poor bedspread exerts over the rich woman. When the newly arrived immigrant asks the reason for the wealthy Quaker woman's interest in this item, Anna Giordani, who is mediating the purchase, gives a significant response: " 'It is very beautiful, signora' said Anna, 'it is all hand-done on hand-loom fabric. You cannot find something like this in the cities, and no tourist goes to places like your village. This is a unique spread, an individual spread not made in batches for the shop' " (Barolini 1999, 75). The woman's longing for handcrafted items is a historically determined sentiment, not separate from a patina of exoticism that emerges in the fashion of a quest for authenticity. Yearning for more refined and unique handmade objects perfectly aligns with the exquisitely modern ambivalence between preservation and consumption. With the rise of mass culture, when the sense of detachment and loss seeps into everyday life, a collection urge spreads in late nineteenth-century society.[12] The scene puts two specular forms of nostalgia in a dialectical confrontation: One is triggered by the rise of mass culture in which nostalgia unfolds as a fashionable trend; the other, instead, is situated at the level of individual loss. Umbertina yearns for her world of origin, remembered and envisioned as a world of affectivities ("it was her remembrance of leaves and flowers and the sun overhead") as opposed to the world of cold and inhumane economic reasons to which the Quaker lady belongs. When Umbertina reconsiders her decision and wants to buy back her *corredo*, the polarization between these two worlds and these two mindsets reaches its peak: "I can pay for cleaning," Umbertina protests, "and whatever else she wants extra. The spread is something of my life and nothing to her" (Barolini 1999,

78). Even so, the answer she receives does not admit replies whatsoever: "You people shouldn't be so attached to showy things but should work to get ahead and then buy things that are more practical" (78).

Described as just a "showy thing," her matrimonial bedspread therefore is something whose refinement mismatches Umbertina's social status. This passage reveals the fracture between different classes because beauty—this response implies—is a form of luxury that does not find any use in her social condition. Functionality, instead, is what would fulfill her needs, and thus what she should seek. Hence, Anna Giordani's reaction exacerbates not only the frictions of classes but also the polarization between functional and affective value, as well as that of between the spheres of intimacy and economics: "This is a country without a heart [. . .] only buying and selling is understood here" (1999, 78), as Umbertina bitterly acknowledges.

The misconception of beauty—which, drawing from Stewart, I could formulate at this point as the attunement potentials of the bedspread—does not mismatch her condition. On the contrary, it fulfills a crucial function, especially within a diasporic context,[13] that is, to foster a relationship between individuals, objects, and environment to convey to the protagonist a semblance of domesticity even amid her wrecked economic conditions.

The traumatic aspect of such trading consists then in the loss of the only device that can grant the preconditions for a worlding and attunement, although only partial and precarious. Therefore, the question would be what happens when this object gets *un-worlded*, that is, when a transaction alienates the object from the system of meanings on which the regrounding depends? Eventually, what happens to the futurity that this object promises once it is sacrificed?

The *Un-worlded* Object

In the previous paragraphs, I have shown how this particular object exceeds the binarism of economic and emotional labor, functionality, and affective value. Yet two more categories need to be singled out: presence versus absence. In this case, although disjointed from the system of meanings to which it originally belongs, the object never ceases to be a fundamental signifier of the domestic order and Umbertina's identity as a transnational subject. The fabric of present and potential future relations established through the possession and transmission of the *corredo* does not fray even when the object is not there anymore. This paradoxical property of the artifact is already preluded in the passage where Umbertina parts with her bedspread: "'Ah America!' said Umbertina, taking the spread from the bed and folding it carefully, caressingly, passing her hands over its richness to smooth it and feel it, as if to impress forever into her memory the raised embroidery of its design. She gave the spread to Anna Giordani" (Barolini 1999, 76). The woman ritualistically prepares the separation by carefully folding and caressing the *corredo* until she intakes the object in the phantasmatic form of tactile memory. This passage marks another crucial moment of tangibility where the imminent absence is already experienced right before its actualization through touch. Her touch also provides some sort of compensatory treasuring of the *bedspread*—the only form of treasuring that Umbertina can afford—and announces the transformation of the artifact into a specter. In *Specters of Marx,* Jacque Derrida, who famously engaged with ghosts throughout his work, writes, "The metamorphosis of commodities was already a process of transfiguring idealization that one may legitimately call spectropoetic" (1994, 56). In the novel, the spectropoetic moment is marked by a significant centrality of the human body whereby the absent object, now spectralized, finds a surrogate body in the skin of its former owner. In that way, the specter reveals the specificities of its "paradoxical phenomenality" consisting of "the tangible intangibility of a proper body without a flesh" (6), which in the novel also assumes a gendered nuance. The process of embodiment activated by Umbertina's touch reinforces the link between womanhood and the *corredo* as if it were a nonhuman appendix of its possessor. By virtue of this connection inscribed on the epidermic memory of the woman, the absent object realizes its paradoxical presence and, subsequently, the paradoxical nostalgia for something that it is lost and yet still there. Precisely because of the hauntological nature of the nostalgic object, which involves different temporalities, nostalgia cannot index only backward modes of yearning. However, this manifestation of longing is no stranger to the novel. For instance, even from her deathbed, the image of the lost *corredo* keeps haunting Umbertina's visions: "Nearly eighty, as she lay dying, her vision dimmed [. . .] and then a sudden brightening came to her eyes as in a vision of light she saw the lost *coperta* of her marriage bed with all the intensity of its colors and bright twining of leaves and flowers and archaic designs in its patterns. 'Ah' she gasped at its beauty" (Barolini 1999, 146).

The return of the ghost signals the end of Umbertina's existence as a transnational subject in America, as its first apparition had signaled the beginning: "I want a *coperta matrimoniale* for the wedding bed," said Umbertina, "such as I have seen hanging from balconies in Soveria Mannelli on Corpus Christi day" (1999, 44). Drawing again from Derrida, spectrality is a "question of repetition: a specter is always a *revenant*. One cannot control its comings and goings because it begins by coming back" (1994, 11). These passages evidence how, in the novel, different regimes of temporality the characters encounter—childhood memories that flow back from the past and spring into the present—give a boost to future-making practices. As a child, the blankets, with their brilliant colors and designs of flowers and leaves, exposed on the balconies of the town to honor the procession of Corpus Christi, left a profound mark on Umbertina's memories. Ever since, "she knew that they were part of what she wanted too" (1999, 33): not only a *corredo*, but also a proper house, a social status that would fulfill her womanhood and the worlding that this object promises. However, its first appearance in the narrative is given in absentia, something that the protagonist can only desire from afar but that she cannot get. Hence, since the beginning, the *corredo* occupies a borderline position between presence and absence, appearing as an *un-worlded* object: displaced, abstracted, and alienated from a consistent system of meanings, but nonetheless capable of promising possible future *worldings*. Such a "virtual agency of the no longer" (Fisher 2014, 18) originates a specific form of nostalgic desire that can take the fashion of an aspirational future being-in-there, denied today but still achievable tomorrow. Reprising the notion of hauntology, Mark Fisher writes, "the future is always experienced as a haunting: as a virtuality that already impinges on the present, conditioning expectations and motivating cultural production" (16). This interpretation of the future explains that even its ghostly manifestations are generative forces that orient practices of cultural construction, and certainly domesticity is one of those. In the experience of migration, we should also add the notions of origin and end. The origin and the arrival are absent and immaterial objects of nostalgia, yet agentic to the point that they give a direction to the process of resubjectification. Similarly, in the migrant experience, the place of origin is absent and immaterial; it marks a point of no return where the process of detachment from the old self and the desubjectification of the migrant begins. But positively, it is also the point from which the reconfiguration of one's identity gets underway.

The phantasmatic, *un-worlded*, object inspires a longing for a reworlding. Therefore, it is the conduit of a nostalgic feeling but not as oriented toward the reestablishment of a previous condition or for restoring a supposed authenticity located somewhere in the past. Likewise, Umbertina does not aim to reproduce faithfully the same model of domesticity and familiar life of her birthplace. Conversely, her parable testifies to the constant renegotiations and transformations of the original models. Rather than rejecting or struggling to preserve them, she incorporates, reuses, and relocates these models within the new context, balancing and negotiating between the symbolic material provided by her culture of origin and the one offered by the new world. The creation of diasporic domesticities relies precisely on balance, and mediation between these two reference points and the trousseau—along with other affective objects—is the fulcrum of such a balance. Even years after the selling, the *corredo* still mediates between the old and the new world, between Umbertina's past and the future of her daughter's households: "Imperturbable in her convictions and in the revenge, she plotted over the loss of her tenement days, she continued to buy and store up linens for her daughters and send out the sheets and pillowcases to be hand-monogrammed by her countrywoman, old Vincenzina, who had been taught handwork in a convent" (Barolini 1999, 132). Anthony Julian Tamburri describes Umbertina's parable as a "financial Cinderella story, not only for her immediate family but likewise the generations to follow" (1991, 54), and that is precisely because the bedspread is situated in the interstitial space between presence and absence, yesterday and tomorrow. This idea seems to be reinforced by evoking the traditional, hand-monogrammed designs made by old Vincenza, the depositary of an ancient art protruding in the new world, which reveals the mediatory function of the *corredo* stitching together two antipodes: her hometown, Castagna, and Cato. Discussing the function of sewing and the economic emancipation of migrant women in America, Mary Jo Bona observes that "the needle both returns the sewer to her *paese* (hometown) and connects her to an increasingly transnational identity that situates her to some degree of the 'regime of nationalism,' while also reinforcing her status as a laborer in a capitalistic market" (2014, 144). Although the novel does not focus on the economic resourcefulness of sewing, Umbertina's case is not that different. By trading the bedspread, she too participates in a market that is changing women's labor, "altering their roles in the family economy" (Bona 145) and transforming the former "goat girl" into the manager of a familial business, the *Longobardi & Sons* wholesale. The painful and sacrificial trade that she is compelled to deal with brings about a long and successful chain of commercial enterprises that strongly contrasts with her condition as a young girl in Calabria, perfectly rendered by the dialogue with her brother Beppino. "It's not your part to interfere in the bargaining," he had scolded, trying to intimidate her, though he was younger. "When I set terms for the sale of the goats that's what it is. I am the man" (Barolini 1999, 31). The comparison of this passage with the representation of Umbertina's role in her household in Cato provides additional evidence of how trade, sacrifice, and loss can also be read as forms of negotiation for the construction of a new transnational subjectivity that, besides her traditional emotional labor, participates in the economic production and represents the connection between these two domains. "The literary works emerging from the Italian diaspora'" Bona asserts, "persuasively demonstrate the relationship between the Italian female immigrant, industrial work and a complex transformation of domestic codes during the twentieth century" (2014, 144). In that respect, the novel offers a vivid description of the place where Umbertina's family lived, worked, and enjoyed an unhoped-for wealth: "The ground floor would house the grocery on one side and the ticket agency and the bank on the other; the first and second floor would have two apartments each on either side of the stairway. It would be under Umbertina's direction, the Longobardi's last endeavor to practice thrift and plain living" (Barolini 1999, 118). The boundaries separating the space of intimacy and the space of purchase are crossed, and the home opens up to a new space at the intersection of affects and the modern economy. At the same time, the shifting of the domestic paradigm accompanies the radical transformation of Umbertina's subjectivity. Thus, to a reconfiguration of the domestic environment—once the barriers between economic and affective sphere are broken—corresponds a reconfiguration of the role of women's labor, as well as the rise of diasporic domesticity and a female transnational subject.

Conclusions

By focusing on the genealogical functions, affective values, and monetary potentials of the *corredo,* we can see how the experience of displacement is never just the displacement of subjects but also the displacement of their affective objects. This brings about a radical alteration of the network of symbolic ties and relations of care and practices to which I referred with the term *worlding.* We have also seen that the core element of this system, the bedspread, is for the most part in the novel an *un-worlded* object, meaning a material entity taken from the environment to which it is supposed to belong and relocated into an unhomely space, such as the tenements in New York. To this first displacement follows another; in fact, it becomes an object of trading that metaphorically displaces the *corredo* from its proper function, turning it into a commodity. Yet being *un-worlded* does not necessarily mean losing its attunement potential consisting of its ability to guarantee a continuity of the household through its permanence. The *corredo* fulfills this expectation thanks to its hauntological phenomenality. Its absence traumatically alters the order of the original domesticity. Still, its ghostly presence fosters a fertile rearticulation of the domestic space, inevitably affecting the way the individuals, in particular women, conceive their position and their role within the new environment.

As with many migrant objects, the *corredo* has the double function of preserving the affective link with the origins and allowing the construction of new domesticity in the new land. That implies not only a reuse but also a resignification of the original modes of domesticity to create new ones without pursuing the illusion of its faithful reproduction. The reemployment and refunctionalization of symbolic and physical material (objects and belongings brought into the new country) imply a deviation from the original model, originating what I defined as diasporic domesticity.

A balance between preservation and reconstruction characterizes such a transnational mode of dwelling. In that way, the house truly becomes a space of tradition in the etymological sense of *tradere*, both spatially and temporally. It becomes the space where values, affective relationships, and social roles are taken from their original environment and regrounded in a new world. In the previous pages, I referred, for instance, to the theory of the separate spheres and the hostile worlds. One of the transformations concerns the binary opposition of home precisely as a space of intimacy opposed to the outside, to the space of economics and the public life. The diasporic home breaks this neat separation to become a space of transience between the spheres: affect and trading, public and private. For instance, Umbertina's house is exposed to a permanent porosity where the economy encroaches on the affective, but where such porosity is not a threat anymore. It just signals the fictiveness of the separate spheres and the hostility of the two supposedly irreconcilable worlds. Umbertina represents a paradigmatic model of a woman who resituates her subjectivity between tradition and mutation. On the one hand, she performs traditional care labor within the domestic walls; on the other hand, she is also an active subject within the circuit of economic production located outside the sphere of intimacy.

Nonetheless, the construction of transnational subjectivities requires a painful sacrifice, which requires her to give up the most precious, affectively and economically, thing she owns. Such a detachment unavoidably leads to a sense of nostalgia, which, however, does not result in a static contemplation of the loss. On the contrary, it turns into a generative force that allows the protagonist to move forward. Overall, hers is a successful parable that has a high price to pay. Unwillingly forced by economic circumstances, she finds herself being an active, albeit successful, subject within a capitalist economy. For her family, herself, and the generations to follow, she will never forget, or forgive, the loss of her bedspread. Umbertina's memories are indeed haunted by the phantasmatic presence of the trousseau, and its absence creates an empty space filled by a sense of manqué that, on the one hand, turns the lost *corredo* into the object of an unachievable quest. Its specter becomes the conduit of an alternative form of nostalgia, a generative nostalgia, that yearns for tomorrow, and instead of longing for an illusionary restoration of the past, pursues the dream of creating alternative domestic spaces and new forms of subjectivity.

Notes

1. In *Sull'Oceano*, the Italian writer Edmondo DeAmicis offers a vivid portrays of the emigrants: "molti erano scalzi, e portavan le scarpe appese al collo." Edmondo DeAmicis, *Sull'Oceano*, Kindle.

2. As a general overview on the different critical approaches on Barolini's novel, I would like to mention the following contributions: Anthony J. Tamburri, "Umbertina: The Italian/American Woman's Experience," in *From the Margin: Writings in Italian Americana*, ed. Paola A. Giordano, Fred L. Gardaphé, and Anthony J. Tamburri (West Lafayette: Purdue University Press, 1991); Carol Bonomo Albright, "From Sacred to Secular in Umbertina and a Piece of Earth," *MELUS* 20, no. 2 (1995): 93–103; Mary Ann Mannino, "In Our Ears, a Voice: The Persistence of the Trauma of Immigration in Blue Italian and Umbertina," *Italian Americana* 20, no. 1 (2002): 5–13; Laura Salsini, "Voicing a Gendered Ethnicity: Tarantella's Cinematic Re-presentation of Umbertina," *Italian Culture* 21, no. 1 (2003): 133–48; Maria Kotsaftis, "Barolini's Umbertina: A Female Odyssey in Quest of the Self," in *Adjusting Sites: Essays in Italian American Studies*, ed. William Boelhower and Rocco Pallone (Stony Brook, NY: Forum Italicum, 1999), 163–79.

3. Margherita Ganeri devotes a section of her book *Italian America: Epos and Story Telling in Helen Barolini* to the symbology of rosemary. The author observes that "rosemary is loaded with connotations, which historically allude both to fidelity (also in marriage) and to immortality: in fact in ancient and medieval time it was traditionally used at weddings as much as in funerals. For Umbertina, the plant is a symbol of continuity with the past, and therefore, also of journey, loss and death. [. . .] the persistence of the plant presupposes death, mourning, grief—about

the past but also the future, although rosemary is a sign of strength and hope of regeneration." Margherita Ganeri, *Italian America: Epos and Story Telling in Helen Barolini* (Milan: Mimesis, 2015), 67.

4. In another writing, Helen Barolini reflects on the significance of a cabinet, which stores objects linking the author to her Italian grandparents: "they came with almost nothing—one grandmother with a tin heart [. . .], the other with a pair of coarsely knit russet and cream cotton stockings [. . .] woven for her wedding day by some relatives in Sicily. And I could not speak to any grandparent I remember as a child for we had no language in common. And I do not think they could have furnished me with any kind of past lineage. Nevertheless, I managed to have a presence of them in the angolino." Helen Barolini, *The Curio Cabinet* (2009), 570.

5. I draw from Svetlana Boym's notion of diasporic intimacy discussed in her article "On Diasporic Intimacy: Ilya Kabakov's Installations and Immigrant Homes." Here, Boym writes that "a diasporic intimacy is not opposed to uprootedness and defamiliarization but constituted by it" (1998, 499).

6. Viviana Zelizer engages with these theories in *The Purchase of Intimacy* where she writes, "The nineteenth-century ideology of domesticity provided further, powerful justification for the separate spheres doctrines. Despite some feminists' critiques, social theorists upheld separate spheres and hostile worlds views as essential for preserving the sacredness of the family. In this deeply gendered scheme, households, women and children needed protection from the dangerously encroaching and aggressive masculine market." Viviana Zelizer, *The Purchase of Intimacy* (Princeton, NJ: Princeton University Press, 2005), 24.

7. This proverb seems to be quite diffuse in Italy at least in the central and southern regions. A version of it is reported by Jane Schneider in her famous essay *Trousseau as Treasure: Some Contradictions of Late Nineteenth-Century Change in Sicily* (1988).

8. Although the *corredo* is meant to be stored and passed on to future generations, its trading is a very common practice, but as Schneider notes in the abovementioned essay: "selling or pawning [it] was the last resort—a desperate, almost immoral necessity" (104). Moreover, if in literature the relation between embroidery and womanhood is well documented, less can be found about the transaction of embroidered items. A very famous example of sacrificial trading is however provided in Vittorio DeSica's *Bicycle Thieves* (1948), where the protagonist's wife pawns the linens to provide her husband with the money that he needs to purchase a bike and finally get a job.

9. On the importance of genealogies in women's writings and in particular in Italian American culture, I refer to Eva Pelayo Sañudo, "Elegies and Genealogies of Place: Spatial Belonging in the Italian/American Culture and Literature," *Miscelánea: A Journal of English and American Studies* 62 (2020): 125–46; Anna Maria Torriglia, "From Mother to Daughter: The Emergence of a Female Genealogy in Anna Banti's Artemisia and Alba De Cespedes's Dalla parte di lei," *Italica* 73, no. 3 (1996): 369–87; Alys Eve Weinbaum, "Writing Feminist Genealogy: Charlotte

Perkins Gilman, Racial Nationalism, and the Reproduction of Maternalist Feminism," *Feminist Studies* 27, no. 2 (2001): 271–302.

10. In *The Future of Nostalgia*, Svetlana Boym traces a distinction between two forms of nostalgia, namely restorative and reflective nostalgia. "Restorative nostalgia manifests itself in total reconstruction of the past, while reflective nostalgia lingers on ruins, the patina of time and history, in the dreams of another place and another time" (XVIII).

11. See Anthony Julian Tamburri's *A Semiotic of Ethnicity: In (Re)Cognition of the Italian American Writer* (Albany: State University of New York Press, 1998).

12. See Svetlana Boym, *The Future of Nostalgia*.

13. To this end, I want to recall Mary Jo Bona's words when she analyzes Bernardi's Openwork: "Beyond its utilitarian value as a source of economic support, cloth-work's aesthetic value as represented openwork embroidery illuminates the enduring nature of social ties" (111).

Works Cited

Albright, Carol Bonomo. 1995. "From Sacred to Secular in Umbertina and A Piece of Earth." *MELUS* 20 (2): 93–103.

Amicis, Edmondo de. 2015. *Sull'oceano*. n.p.: Nobel. Kindle.

Arendt, Hannah. 2018. *The Human Condition*. Chicago: University of Chicago Press.

Ahmed, Sara, Claudia Castada, Anne-Marie Fortier, and Mimi Sheller. 2018. *Uprootings/Regroundings: Questions of Home and Migration*. Oxford: Berg.

Barolini, Helen. 1999. *Umbertina: A Novel*. New York: Feminist Press at the City University of New York.

———. 2009. "The Curio Cabinet." *Southwest Review* (94): 570–76.

Bhabha, Homi. 1994. *The Location of Culture*. New York: Routledge.

Benjamin, Walter. 2002. *Arcades Project*. Cambridge, MA: Harvard University Press.

Boym, Svetlana. 1998. "On Diasporic Intimacy: Ilya Kabakov's Installations and Immigrant Homes." *Critical Inquiry* 24 (2): 498–524.

———. *The Future of Nostalgia*. 2001. New York: Basic Books.

Bona, Mary Jo. 2014. "'A Needle Better Fits?': The Role of Defensive Sewing in Italian American Literature." In *Embroidered Stories: Interpreting Women's Domestic Needlework from the Italian Diaspora*, edited by Edvige Giunta and Joseph Sciorra, 144–64. Jackson: University Press of Mississippi.

———. 2015. *Women Writing Cloth: Migratory Fictions in the American Imaginary*. Lanham, MD: Lexington.

Cheah, Hwei-Fen. 2014. "Precious Traditions: Biancheria in Italian Australian Women's Lives." In *Embroidered Stories: Interpreting Women's Domestic Needlework from the Italian Diaspora*, edited by Edvige Giunta and Joseph Sciorra, 41–61. Jackson: University Press of Mississippi.

Cosmini-Rose, Daniela, Maria Palaktsoglou, Eric Bouvet, and Diana Glenn. 2016. "Tales of Glory Boxes, Suitcases and Dreams: An Investigation of Cultural and Social Changes in the Dowry Practices of Greek and Italian Post-War Migrants in South Australia." *Modern Greek Studies* (Australia and New Zealand) 16 (17): 215–36. https://openjournals.library.sydney.edu.au/index.php/MGST/article/view/11057/10657.

Derrida, Jacques. 1994. *Specters of Marx. The State of the Debt, the Work of Mourning and the New International.* London: Routledge.

Fisher, Mark. 2014. *Ghost of My Life. Writings on Depression, Hauntology and Lost Futurity.* London: Zero Books.

Ganeri, Margherita. 2015. *Italian America. Epos and Story Telling in Helen Barolini.* Milan: Mimesis.

Edvige Giunta and Joseph Sciorra, eds. 2014. *Embroidered Stories: Interpreting Women's Domestic Needlework from the Italian Diaspora.* Jackson: University Press of Mississippi

Heynen, Hilde, and Baydar Gülsüm. 2005. *Negotiating Domesticity. Spatial Production of Gender in Modern Architecture.* Abingdon, UK: Routledge.

Kotsaftis, Maria. 1999. "Barolini's Umbertina: A Female Odyssey in Quest of the Self." In *Adjusting Sites: Essays in Italian American Studies*, edited by William Boelhower and Rocco Pallone, 163–79. Stony Brook, NY: Forum Italicum.

Mankekar, Purnima. 2015. *Unsettling India: Affect, Temporality, Transnationality.* Durham, NC: Duke University Press.

Mannino, Mary Ann. 2002. "In Our Ears, a Voice: The Persistence of the Trauma of Immigration in Blue Italian and Umbertina." *Italian Americana* 20 (1): 5–13.

Salsini, Laura. 2003. "Voicing a Gendered Ethnicity: Tarantella's Cinematic Representation of Umbertina." *Italian Culture* 21 (1): 133–48.

Schneider, Jane. 1988. "Trousseau as Treasure: Some Contradictions of Late Nineteenth-Century Change in Sicily." In *The Marriage Bargain: Women and Dowries in European History*, ed. Marion A. Kaplan, 81–119. New York: Institute for Research in History and Haworth Press.

Stewart, Kathleen. 2007. *Ordinary Affects.* Durham, NC: Duke University Press.

———. 2011. "Atmospheric Attunement." *Environment and Planning D: Society and Space* 29: 445–53. https://journals.sagepub.com/doi/10.1068/d9109.

Tamburri, Anthony J. 1991. "Umbertina: The Italian/American Woman's Experience." In *From the Margin: Writings in Italian Americana*, edited by Paola A. Giordano, Fred L. Gardaphé, and Anthony J. Tamburri. West Lafayette: Purdue University Press.

———. 1998. *A Semiotic of Ethnicity. In (Re)Cognition of the Italian American Writer.* Albany: State University of New York Press.

Vanni, Ilaria. 2014. "From Domestic Craft to Contemporary Arts: Needlework and Belonging in Two Generations of Italian Australian Artists." In *Embroidered*

Stories: Interpreting Women's Domestic Needlework from the Italian Diaspora, edited by Edvige Giunta and Joseph Sciorra, 121–35. Jackson: University Press of Mississippi.

Verschaffel, Bart. 2002. "The Meanings of Domesticity." *Journal of Architecture* 7: 287–96.

Yang, Philip Q. 2020. *Transnationalism and Genealogy*. MDPI—Multidisciplinary Digital Publishing Institute.

Zelizer, Viviana A. 2005. *The Purchase of Intimacy*. Princeton, NJ: Princeton University Press.

2

Dietrologia

Italian American Heritage and the Conspiracy of Postwar Whiteness in Don DeLillo's *Underworld*

Bryan M. Santin

Introduction: The White (Ethnic) Voice of America

A sprawling, half-century literary representation of postwar American life, Don DeLillo's *Underworld* begins with a sentence composed in the disorienting ambiguity of the grammatical second person: "He speaks in your voice, American, and there's a shine in his voice that's halfway hopeful" (DeLillo 1997b, 11). This sentence foregrounds the enigmatic question of "American-ness" through subtle intertextual means, for it alludes to the final sentence of Ralph Ellison's *Invisible Man*, in which Ellison's nameless black narrator addresses a presumed white audience and makes the provocative claim that he may "speak" for them: "Who knows but that, on the lower frequencies, I speak for you?" (Ellison 2004, 581). At first glance, it may seem like DeLillo aims to replicate the black/white thematic racial binary embedded in Ellison's novel, since DeLillo's opening sentence refers to the reoccurring character Cotter Martin, a black teenager through whom DeLillo focalizes significant portions of the novel's prologue set in New York City on October 3, 1951, as the New York Giants beat the Brooklyn Dodgers to capture the National League pennant. When considering the intertextual linkage between *Underworld* and *Invisible Man*, the literary scholar David Witzling assumes this thematic racial binary when he writes that it is unclear "[w]hether *Underworld* marks the successful achievement of hybrid [black/white] cultural consciousness or a sentimental return to a Cold War–era vision of racial integration" (Witzling 2008, 25). However, in a novel that emphasizes not only postwar constructions of race but also the shifting nature of seemingly white ethnic identities, particularly the racial "in-between-ness" of Italian American ethnic identity in the early to mid-twentieth century, DeLillo's opening sentence certainly echoes *Invisible Man*, but ironically, for DeLillo disrupts the familiar, black/white framework of the Cold War-era United States. DeLillo begins the novel in this way, I argue, to catalyze a nearly 900-page interrogation of what it means to be an American in the second half of that century and to speak in a distinctly "American" voice—a voice shorn of an ethnic Italian-ness that had once been more explicitly racialized. Exploring how this seemingly objective, authoritative voice erases racial and ethnic otherness, DeLillo uses various tropes of Italian American ethnicity to critique the hollow postmodern numbness of certain configurations of postwar whiteness, but without succumbing to either romanticized racism or a simulacrum of ethnic nostalgia. In short, DeLillo thematizes an older, racialized Italian ethnicity as a form of (nearly) forgotten cultural waste that reveals the paradoxical plasticity of race as a category in the post–World War II United States.

To discern the specificity of my argument, one must first appreciate how, for most of DeLillo's career, scholars have tended to place *Underworld* into a few well-established categories: the "systems novel" and its derivative tropes of conspiratorial plots and premeditated political violence; the poststructuralist novel rooted in the televisual hyperreality of Baudrillardian simulacra and the semiotic undecidability of Derridean deconstruction; more recently, the postmodern religious novel wherein mystical literary language is read as a staging ground for implicit theological rituals, beliefs, and practices; and finally, the major Italian American novel of the late twentieth century that finally solidified DeLillo's reputation as a serious Italian American author indisputably interested in conceptions of *Italianità*.[1] Drawing from these previous scholarly frameworks, I analyze *Underworld* with a related theoretical lens that is germane to DeLillo's fiction, though rarely employed in relation to it: Cold War–era racialized ethnicity.[2] By focusing on the novel's "half-Italian" protagonist, Nick Shay, and a selection of its minor black characters, I demonstrate how DeLillo traces a complex relationship of competing identities between Italian Americans, African Americans, and ostensibly "race-less" white Americans. While eschewing a historically naive "wop to white" narrative, DeLillo nevertheless tells an illuminating story about how Italian Americans emerged out of an ambiguous, anxious form of whiteness at midcentury into a more stable, normative form by century's end. Moreover, DeLillo implies that this identity-forming shift was neither culturally neutral nor politically benign; instead, DeLillo narrates it as a kind of *dietrologia*—that is, the Italian word meaning roughly "conspiracy theory"—motived by a masculine-coded agency panic that feared the perceived socioeconomic "bottom" of American society. Ultimately, as a distinctly "Italian American novel," DeLillo's *Underworld* reveals that the liminal racial space once inhabited by Italian Americans can function not only as a privileged aperture from which to critique the construction of postwar whiteness, but also as an imaginative, metaphysically groundless form of ethnic heritage and personal meaning.

Underworld: "Italian American Novel" Disguised as "Great American Novel"

What is at stake in labeling *Underworld* an Italian American novel? For scholars of Italian American literature and culture, the notion that *Underworld* is an Italian American novel has been a truism since its publication in late 1997. In his influential, turn-of-the-century piece "DeLillo's *Underworld*: Towards a New Beginning for the Italian American Novel," James Periconi captured the importance of DeLillo's book to Italian American literary studies: "More than any other Italian American writer living or dead, DeLillo can rightly lay claim to literary greatness at the same time that, against all expectation, he seeks to recover his personal and literary Italian past" (Periconi 2000, 142). For the purposes of my argument, classifying *Underworld* as an Italian American novel has little to do with the relatively trivial academic interest of categorical genre accuracy, and even less to do with any quasi-mystical celebration of some reified ethnic Italian-ness; rather, I insist on the label because it illuminates the novel's deepest themes—notably, the fraught nature of postwar American identity—through a kind of calculated, formally modernist misdirection on DeLillo's part: For first-time readers, what looks like a bid for the "Great American Novel" is, by the end of the reading experience, an Italian American novel interrogating the plasticity of whiteness in Cold War–era American culture.

Drawing on his own early experiences growing up in the midcentury Bronx in a working-class Italian neighborhood to Italian immigrant parents, DeLillo focalizes significant passages of *Underworld* through the first-person perspective of Nick Shay, originally named James Nicholas Costanza, the half-Italian, half-Irish American protagonist born (like DeLillo) in the Bronx in the late 1930s. Nick, abandoned as a young boy by his Italian father, the small-time numbers runner James Costanza, adopts his mother's Irish last name (Shay) and grows up to be an angry teenager who accidentally shoots and kills an older man, the heroin-addicted gambler George Manza, a problematic, surrogate father figure for Nick. After the accidental murder, Nick is sent to a correction facility for juveniles run by a Jesuit Catholic priest, Father Paulus, who profoundly influences Nick's spiritual orientation to language and life. However, when readers first encounter Nick in part 1 of the novel, set in 1992, none of this backstory has been made available yet. By strategically omitting explicit details about Nick's Italian ethnicity—although small hints are dropped, such as Nick putting sunscreen on his "olive-dark skin, dark as my father was"—DeLillo introduces Nick as a generic, fifty-seven-year-old (white) everyman amid a midlife crisis (DeLillo 1997b, 64). A waste management executive who lives in a standard suburban house in Phoenix, Arizona who feels a nagging, and eventually vindicated, suspicion that his wife, Marian, has cheated on him with his good friend, Nick seems like an alienated protagonist drawn from a John Updike novel or John Cheever short story who is stricken with middle-class ennui, that familiar malaise of postwar white male fiction.[3] When traveling on business, for instance, Nick says that he has perfected a deadpan comic line to tell service workers at hotels and rental companies, which reveals him as a man moving through life with quiet, Thoreauvian desperation: "I live a quiet life in an unassuming house in a suburb of Phoenix. Pause. Like someone in the Witness Protection Program" (66). DeLillo also shrouds in narratological mystery the trigger event of Nick's midlife crisis, since readers are introduced to Nick after he has read an article about Klara Sax, an avant-garde artist who specializes in massive outdoor installations—the most important of which is the painting of rows upon rows of decommissioned B-52 bombers in the Nevada desert. What readers do not find out until the end of the novel, though, is that Klara is the young, unhappy housewife married to Albert Bronzini in the Bronx, with whom Nick had a short-lived affair when he was seventeen. Without this knowledge, it is tempting to read the opening scenes of part 1, in which Nick drives a rental car through the desert to see Klara and her vast landscape art, as indicative of the hollowness of Nick's postmodern, ethnically unmarked life. However, after a thorough reading of the novel, it becomes clear that Nick is not looking to regain Klara so much as the feeling of authenticity that he associates with his younger self, a nostalgic ethnic identity bound up with the postwar Italian American Bronx. In the novel's epilogue, which returns readers to the 1990s after long flashbacks through earlier decades, Nick finally admits this point in an emotionally climactic moment: "I long for the days of disorder. I want them back, the days when I was alive on the earth, rippling in the quick of my skin, heedless and real. I was dumb-muscled and angry and real. This is what I long for, the breach of peace, the days of disarray when I walked real streets and did things slap-bang and felt angry and ready all the time, a danger to others and distant memory to myself" (DeLillo 1997b, 810). Recapturing the formal temporality of high modernism, DeLillo portrays a chronological collision between history's linear path and Nick's backward glance. "Thus, the novel contains two journeys," writes John Paul Russo, "Nick's life-story outward from the Bronx; and the internal story, moving in the opposite direction, from the American world back to the remembered Little Italy" (Russo 2003, 83).[4] Moreover, Russo argues that the novel's denouement, which juxtaposes the postmodern present with the ethnically marked past, is undoubtedly a plunge into a rich world of communally binding Italian American values: "The oppositions between the technological milieu and the ethnic neighborhood include such features as speed and efficiency vs. natural rhythms and ritual; over-consumption vs. scarcity; suburban solitude vs. community; silence vs. sound; surface and screen values vs. a plenum of sensation" (76–77). Russo's astute analysis throws into relief the problematic urge for some scholars to read *Underworld* as a "Great American Novel" underpinned by a universalizing, default discourse of whiteness. That kind of interpretive premise is foundational for comparative misreadings that assume a one-to-one correspondence between Nick Shay and other classic white male American protagonists, such as Lawrence Buell's characterization of "1990s Nick [Shay] as a warier, wearier update of Sinclair Lewis's George Babbitt" because of their mutual despair over the vacuous nature of white middle-class life (Buell 2016, 453).[5] Conversely, the novel's two journeys that Russo outlines are also two different journeys of whiteness: the chronological historical journey from "wop to white" that Nick undergoes and the nostalgic imagined journey from hollow whiteness to an older, more invigorating ethnic heritage.

This ethnically attuned analytical plot summary sheds new light on critics' impulse to coronate *Underworld* immediately upon its publication as the latest incarnation of the "Great (White) American Novel."[6] Similarly, in the sphere of academic literary studies, even though DeLillo's works were already well-known objects of analysis following his breakout novels

The Names (1982) and *White Noise* (1985), it helps us reevaluate the way in which *Underworld* became an exemplary text for indexing the status of the novel as a genre in the era of late postmodernism. In *The Dream of the Great American Novel*, a genealogical monograph that traces the formal and critical evolutions of the "Great American Novel," Lawrence Buell identifies *Underworld* as perhaps the most likely candidate for that honorific in the second half of the twentieth century after Pynchon's *Gravity's Rainbow* (453). Even in scholarly accounts that highlight white male authorial angst surrounding the novel-form's cultural decline, as Kathleen Fitzpatrick argues in *The Anxiety of Obsolescence*, *Underworld* functions as an epic work that registers novelistic prestige as such, the quintessential late-twentieth-century novel in which DeLillo supposedly casts the novel form as " 'other' in a culture ruled so pervasively by television" (Fitzpatrick 2006, 232). However, I draw attention to these critical and scholarly discourses not because I wish to adjudicate the contentious, angels-dancing-on-a-pinhead debate about the ontological status of the "Great American Novel," but to point out a curious fact: These claims of aesthetic quality or scholarly utility are often premised on deemphasizing the book's ethnic Italian (though not necessarily racial) themes and tropes. Buell's evaluation of *Underworld* as a "systems novel" in agonistic dialogue with Pynchon's *Gravity's Rainbow* typifies this tendency. For Buell, both novels are postmodern, media-obsessed representations "of a world in which humans can no longer be separated from machines, in which extremes of order produce extremes of chaos and vice versa, in which the world of preterite souls that seems about to collapse somehow keeps turning" (Buell 2016, 453). Such readings of *Underworld* emerge from, and at times appear catalyzed by, the critical consensus regarding DeLillo's pre-*Underworld* literary project as one undertaken by a novelist who had strived for most of his career to be ethnically "unmarked."[7] In a December 1997 interview, DeLillo admitted that this critical consensus of his career up to that point could appear persuasive. Aside from a handful of early, novice fictional vignettes he had set in the Bronx, DeLillo noted that his first novel was "a kind of journey into the broader culture," which in retrospect functioned like a "curious unintentional form of repetition of my own parents' journey, my immigrant parents who came to the U.S. from Italy" (DeLillo 1997a, E5). As a younger writer, DeLillo continued in the same interview, "that [his ethnic Italian] background and those narrow [Bronx] streets seemed to be a bit constricting in terms of what I could get out of them as a writer because I hadn't yet developed a perspective, a maturity as a writer" (E5). Significantly, DeLillo frames the autobiographical return to his childhood experiences in *Underworld* as commensurate with achieving a newer, more mature authorial viewpoint. While DeLillo's words suggest that Italian ethnicity is a foundational trope in his magnum opus and that any thorough exegesis of the novel must account for, and indeed foreground, DeLillo's ethnic turn, he does not prepare unsuspecting, first-time readers for how Italian American heritage constitutes the novel's thematic core.

In *White Flights: Race, Fiction, and the American Imagination* (2019), Jess Row shrewdly points out that default-white readings (like Buell's) of *Underworld*—that is, as an enormous "social novel" directed from above by an omniscient, tacitly race-less, consciousness that roams freely over Cold War America to make its cultural ennui legible—is premised on "a deeply rooted belief in what might be called the white autonomy of the imagination" (Row 2019, 82). These readings, Row continues, miss the ethnic Italian tropes at the heart of Shay's supposedly white identity. Nick moves through life "in a state of toxic exaltation over [his] own inherent falseness," Row claims, less because Nick is an empty postmodern subject and more because he is "gripped by a paralyzing, obsessive nostalgia" for his teenage experiences in the Italian American Bronx (88–89). Row rightly asserts that critics of DeLillo's *Underworld* note the Italian American context as supplemental: Since the novel "vibrates with an ethnic consciousness that . . . is all the more powerful for being so powerfully repressed," *Underworld* is "an Italian-American novel just as much as Gish Jen's *Typical American* is a Chinese American novel or Oscar Hijuelos's *The Mambo Kings Play Songs of Love* is a Cuban American novel" (88). Essentially, DeLillo has pulled off a literary sleight of hand: *Underworld* is a deeply Italian American novel concealed in the ostensible whiteness of the "Great American Novel." To grasp the political implications of placing *Underworld* into such an unfamiliar—perhaps even bizarrely antiquated—ethnic literary category, one must understand how DeLillo subversively aestheticizes the twentieth-century shift in cultural perceptions of Italian Americans from a suspect racial people to indisputably, "invisibly" white. Ultimately, labeling *Underworld* an Italian American novel clarifies, more than obscures, DeLillo's aim to rediscover the nourishing parts of midcentury Italian American culture without romanticizing a Cold War–era cultural paradigm that either disparagingly racialized Italian ethnicity or uncritically celebrated Italians' shift into "full" whiteness.

Racialized Italian Ethnicity as Waste:
The Underworld of Cold War Whiteness

Though DeLillo utilizes a variety of tropes in *Underworld*, from televisual technology to nuclear bombs, the central trope of the novel is waste. DeLillo highlights the significance of the trope not only within major scenes (e.g., the confetti-like pieces of paper described as "happy garbage" in the prologue that fans shower down onto the field after the Giants-Dodgers baseball game, Klara Sax's artistic recycling of decommissioned bombers, Nick's visit to a nuclear waste site in the former Soviet Union) or just through key characters (e.g., Sister Edgar and J. Edgar Hoover's obsession with cleaning or eliminating social rubbish and personal garbage; salvage artists such as Klara Sax, Simon Rodia, and the graffiti artist Moonman 157; Nick and his colleagues as waste management engineers), but in the very organizational logic of the novel's structure (DeLillo 1997b, 44). The novel's incantatory refrain, "everything is connected," manifests the theme of connectedness itself in the underground networks through which the dark, wasteful excesses of the Cold War, Western capitalism, and liberal democratic ideologies are futilely hidden away. The novel's preoccupation with waste, then, is essentially a preoccupation with the ideas and materials that mainstream culture would rather conceal, forget, or ignore. However, for as insightful as critics have been in their various analyses of waste in the novel, one thematic implication that they have tended to overlook is the crucial notion of racialized ethnicity, specifically Italian American ethnicity, as a form of waste.[8] One exception is Josephine Gattuso Hendin, who notes briefly in her essay "Italian American Insights and the Nineties" that waste management for DeLillo "is the capacity to recycle the used, depleted ethnic, past into a vantage point on mainstream culture" (Hendin 2000, 51). Building on Hendin's passing remark, we can see how DeLillo does not indulge in cheap, feel-good colorblind liberalism, which would equate racialized ethnicity with waste to suggest that ethnicity is no longer a resonant identity category and should be cast into the proverbial dustbin of history. Instead, anticipating Ta-Nehisi Coates's trenchant analysis of the construction of whiteness, DeLillo interrogates how and why "the history of civilization is littered with dead 'races' (Frankish, Italian, German, Irish) later abandoned because they no longer serve their purpose—the organization of people beneath, and beyond, the umbrella of rights" (Coates 2015, 115). When focusing especially on Nick, who orients his entire professional life around waste and his entire personal life around the ambivalent meaning of his Italian American heritage, it becomes clear that Italian American ethnicity is a constitutive gap, a seemingly obsolete form of waste at the core of Nick's identity, an aporia even in the American Cold War–era notion of whiteness.[9]

DeLillo's construction of Nick as an ostensibly generic white male character who is half proud, half ashamed of his Italian ethnic past is politically significant because it complicates the white/black racial binary that structured Cold War public discourse, transforming Nick's semi-repressed Italian-ness into a discarded identity that critically illuminates postwar whiteness. Throughout the novel, Nick's ethnic pride manifests in the way he repeatedly invokes media-generated Italian American stereotypes, usually to entertain business partners who themselves are only dimly aware of his Italian heritage. Sometimes "speaking a few words in a movie gangster's growl," Nick says, "I picked up the phone in the middle of a meeting and pretended to arrange the maiming of a colleague, a maneuver that drew snide laughter from the others in the room" (DeLillo 1997b, 87). In a scene depicting Marian Shay's affair with Nick's colleague, Brian Glassic, she tells Brian that Nick is "half Italian" (165). Although Brian does not see "it in [Nick's] face," he does "hear it in that voice [Nick] does," Brian tells Marian, a "gangster voice making threats" at work, "Expert, stereotyped, pretty funny" (165). The notion that Nick's Italian heritage is physically undetectable implies that Nick's Italian-ness is less an embodied presence than a set of performative routines that closely track the shifting perceptions of Italian Americans as "gangsters" in the wake of Italian American novels and films, especially Francis Ford Coppola's influential films *The Godfather* (1972) and *The Godfather Part II* (1974). In one of Nick's more introspective moments, set significantly in 1978 only a few years after Coppola's *Godfather* movies, he describes his detached identity and affective blankness by combining an Italian word meaning "distance" (*lontananza*) and a cinematically influenced ethnic term (the "made man") drawn directly from the vocabulary of Italian American gangster movies: "Distance or remoteness, sure. But as I use the word [*lontananza*], as I interpret it, hard-edged and fine-grained, it's the perfected distance of the gangster, the syndicate mobster—the made man. Once you're a made man, you don't need the constant living influence of sources outside yourself. You're all there. You're made. You're handmade. You're a sturdy Roman wall" (DeLillo 1997b, 275). Nick's identification with the "made man" invokes the historically unique form of Italian American ethnic pride that emerged as a result of what film critics commonly refer to as "the Godfather effect"—that is, the notion that *The Godfather* films transformed the life stories of first- and second-generation Italian Americans into gripping "American Dream" narratives worthy of dignity and respect. "Suddenly, mobsters or not, Italians were no longer caricatures worthy of derision," writes Tom Santopietro in *The Godfather Effect*, but "figures fit for admiration" (Santopietro 2012, 6). As Joel Dinerstein points out in *The Origins of Cool in Postwar America*, the Italian mafia figure that catalyzed "the Godfather effect" became one of the most prominent manifestations of "coolness" in post-1945 American popular culture. "American cool," Dinerstein writes, echoing Nick's imagined self-image precisely, "became synonymous with a certain stylish stoicism: emotional self-control carried off with a signature style" (Dinerstein 2017, 9). Far from a depoliticized personal style, Dinerstein argues, "coolness" was above all a tactic for "the valorization of the individual against larger dynamic forces," ultimately making "cool" a "myth invested in the recuperation of individual agency" (25–26). The profound irony of Nick's appropriation of Italian American "gangster cool," as Tim Engles notes in his critical reading of the same passage in *Underworld*, is that the "individualizing 'distance' [Nick] feels and enacts springs more from his whitening residential and vocational movement, away from that which he evokes to explain his psychic and emotional distancing, his Bronx-Italian heritage" (Engles 2015, 200). Significantly, although Nick appears to ethnicize his coolness by tracing its origins back to his Italian father (e.g., "There's a certain distance in my makeup, a measured separation like my old man's," Nick says), his "made man" fantasy stems not from cultivating actual mafia connections, but from climbing the white corporate ladder (DeLillo 1997b, 275).

Nick's seemingly contradictory tactic of claiming a hypermediated, though somehow still authentic, ethnically cool identity makes more thematic sense when readers realize the depth to which he is conflicted about his father, and thus the meaning of his Italian American heritage, because of his father's disappearance when Nick was a young boy. A romanticizer of the Italian American gangster, Nick constructs an elaborate melodramatic story in which his father was killed by the mob. In one scene set in 1974 and focalized through Nick's younger brother, Matthew, DeLillo writes that "Nick believed their father was taken out to the marshes and shot, and . . . this became the one plot, the only conspiracy that big brother could believe in" (454). Although Matt was convinced that "his brother was guilty of emotional delusion," he also realized that Nick "could not afford to succumb to a general distrust. He had to protect his conviction about what happened to Jimmy" (454). What Matthew implies with the word "protect" is that for most of Nick's life, he cannot admit the more plausible, mundane, and painful story that his father abandoned the family. Once the brothers grow up, Matthew's disenchanted view of their father collides with Nick's romanticized story, revealing Nick's biggest fear: dishonorable abandonment. In one scene in the late 1980s, in the face of Nick's repeated denials that their father "didn't walk out" and that "they [i.e., mafia hitmen] came and got him," Matthew looks Nick square in the eye and delivers the painful truth: "He did the unthinkable Italian crime. He walked out on his family. They [i.e., midcentury Italian Americans] don't even have a name for this" (204). The notion that their father's abandonment constitutes a specifically ethnic transgression so terrible that it must remain nameless not only fuels Nick's rage during his teenage years, contributing to his murder of the father-like figure, George Manza, but it also reveals the racialized anxiety Nick feels throughout his life and that helps propel him towards whiteness.

Partly ashamed of his Italian American heritage because it reminds him of his father, this explains why Nick spends most of his life distancing himself from his real Bronx-Italian upbringing: He cannot help but associate his father's abandonment with racist stereotypes of blackness. As Nick realizes with dismay, and as DeLillo reveals through the perspectives of other supporting characters, the most readily available language for abandoned, fatherless sons in the postwar United States was found not in Italian American immigrant discourse, but rather in the racist discourse of African American cultural pathology.[10] DeLillo focalizes this black pathological discourse through Sister Edgar, who, while volunteering in the worst crime-ridden area of the South Bronx in the late 1980s, looks at the robed monks also volunteering and thinks that the monks stood out in that environment because they "were men in a place where few men remained" (240). Unwittingly describing Nick's past life of teenage delinquency and crime, Sister Edgar concludes that the "teenage boys in clusters" are the only "men of the immediate streets," and that no one knew "where the others had gone, the fathers, living with second or third families" (240). Conversely, in Italian American immigrant discourse, as DeLillo illustrates in the extended 1950s flashback section, the family is sacrosanct, which buttresses Matt's claim as an adult that their father's desertion was a specifically "Italian" crime. In one scene, after Jimmy has already abandoned his wife, Rosemary, and their two young sons, Rosemary hears the Italian women in her apartment building calling in their husbands for dinner. "It was a special summons, a call to family duty," Rosemary thinks, sorrowfully listening to the Italian families gathering in the surrounding apartments. "The family requires the presence of every member tonight. Because the family was an art to these people and the dinner table was the place it found expression" (698). DeLillo's depiction of the complicated matrix of moral problems related to the Italian family, race, crime, fatherlessness, and cultural decay can be understood better when thrown against the backdrop of *The Godfather* films. As Chris Messenger trenchantly points out in *The Godfather and American Culture: How the Corleones Became "Our Gang,"* the popular appeal of *The Godfather* films was underpinned by an intelligible moral universe in which the men of the Corleone family, a patriarchal kinship unit characterized by a curious "mixture of extreme violence and domestic warmth," committed crimes in the ruthless protection of the family (Messenger 2002, 9). In these films, Messenger argues, "crime, violence, and narrow ethnicity are rechanneled and shown to produce unimaginable American wealth and power *within the very text of the family itself,* which *The Godfather* asks us to read as both the ground and reason any action is sanctioned" (46). Without the welfare of the Italian family as a foundational moral justification, Messenger implies, organized crime and violence in themselves become inexcusable, which one well-known scene in *The Godfather* alludes to directly. When Don Giuseppe Zaluchi advocates for keeping drug sales "in the [neighborhoods of the] dark people, the colored, [because] they're animals anyway, so let them lose their souls," the film uses racist tropes of blackness to tacitly suggest that when a crime is not committed with the larger, exculpatory sacred interest of the family in mind, it contributes to the (racialized) deterioration of the communal fabric (*The Godfather*).[11]

If readers of *Underworld* are aware of this cultural discourse, they can see that Nick's lifelong racial prejudices are rooted less in a typical account of masculine white supremacy—that is, one in which a racially "pure" subject emphasizes a fictitious, unbridgeable metaphysical chasm between white and black racial essences—than in Nick's anxiety about his own historically uncomfortable proximity to blackness as a trope of racial denigration. Nick's prejudices began during his teenage years as Nick grew up in an immigrant community, which paradoxically saw African Americans as both weakly inferior and powerfully menacing because the dreadful prospect of residential "mixing" with black people served as a key threat to Italian American respectability. DeLillo sketches this environment in an extended passage exposing the collective racist unconscious of Nick's midcentury Italian Bronx:

> There was always the neighborhood and who was leaving and
> who was moving in, showing up on the fringes. Tizzoons . . . A
> southern dialect word, a corruption, a slur, an invective, from

> *tizzo* . . . a firebrand or smoldering coal, and broadened to human dimensions in *tizzone d'inferno*, scoundrel, villain. But the word they [i.e., Italian Americans] used suggested a hellishness, a fiendishness that made it more unspeakable, in a way, than nigger. But they spoke it, of course, these men, these immigrants or sons of immigrants, the hordes who threaten society's peaceful sleep, who are always showing up and moving in. (DeLillo 1997b, 768)

Significantly, in the final lines of this passage, DeLillo structures the sentence with grammatical vagueness purposefully—as "hordes" could refer to the Italian immigrants themselves or the perceived black interlopers. Ironically, Italian Americans, DeLillo's formally sophisticated sentence implies, redeploy the same anti-immigrant "threatening hordes" label once hurled at them to denigrate their assumed racial inferiors, a cycle of hatred that manifests in real-world violence when a teenage Nick punches a black teenager who doesn't realize, from Nick's skewed perspective, that "It's better . . . if you [i.e., Nick's black victim] stay where you belong" (762–63). These scenes recapitulate the fraught definitional struggles over "race" and Italian-directed prejudice that raged in the wake of increased European immigration between the late nineteenth century and the early twentieth century.[12] As Jennifer Guglielmo writes in *Are Italians White? How Race is Made in America*, generations of immigrants arrived from Italy, usually totally unaware of the politics of the American "color line," and were thrust into a complex racial reality: On the one hand, they were "white" in the legal eyes of the United States government (enjoying access to citizenship, the voting franchise, property ownership, jury duty, and inter-ethnic marriage); but on the other hand, Italians Americans were stigmatized for working in black-coded occupations, which led to the American culture industry "bombard[ing] Americans with images of Italians as racially suspect" (J. Guglielmo 2003, 11). Corroborating these insights, Thomas A. Guglielmo's research shows that, although Italians immigrants did not need to "become white" and were essentially "white on arrival," they still faced historically distinctive forms of racial discrimination (T. Guglielmo 2003, 7). "[W]hile Italians suffered greatly for their putative *racial* undesirability as Italians, South Italians, and so forth," Guglielmo concludes, "they still benefited in countless ways from their privileged *color* status as whites" (9). In *Underworld*, as Tim Engles argues in the context of this Italian American historiography, DeLillo uses Nick's long character arc to allegorize midcentury Italian Americans as "an ever-expanding 'white' group whose collective, fearful, identity-forming movement has always entailed a negatively relational ontology, conceiving of themselves less as white and more as 'those who are not non-white' " (Engles 2015, 201). In short, Nick's ethnic identity has always been unstable and anxious because, in Roediger's memorable words, he has been part of an immigrant group for much of his life that was only "conditionally white" (Roediger 2005, 144).

Throughout the novel, this practice of Italian Americans identifying as "not non-white" manifests in the anxious indexing of skin color. From childhood to adulthood, Nick and Matt both remain dark-skinned and appear, at various times in their lives, to occupy a liminal racial zone. "Back in the Bronx, people said [Matt] looked like a little of everything. Mexican, Italian, Japanese even," DeLillo writes, "A police sketch made from seven different descriptions—that was Matt" (DeLillo 1997b, 409). Nick's angst about his less-than-fully-white teenage identity surfaces anew when his then-teenage son, Jeff, begins to dress like the late-twentieth-century black "gangsta rap" group N.W.A. after the 1992 Los Angeles riots, wearing "an L.A. Raiders hat and an ultralong t-shirt" that suddenly turns Jeff, in Nick's eyes, into a "social being with a ghetto strut" (104–5). For Nick, Jeff's sudden visibility as a "social being" exposed to police surveillance stems from Nick's own deeply entrenched fear of being mistaken as black, for he laments with Marian that "if people ever saw our son in the commission of a crime they wouldn't know how to describe him except for skin color" (120). Since this passage appears relatively early in the novel, first-time readers will be unaware not only of Nick's past fear of being perceived as a dark racial Other in America but also of the identity work that Nick himself undertakes (roughly 500 pages into the novel) in a juvenile corrections facility in upstate New York after killing George Manza. At first, Nick befriends members of a street gang from Harlem who told him they had been "doing nigger time" for most of their lives, coming "up through Youth House and a number of reformatories, raised on the felony alphabet" (502). But Nick, quickly realizing that incarceration coupled with his skin color associates him with the menacing specter of blackness, commits himself seriously to "the stern logic of correction" (502). Since Nick does not feel especially responsible for George's murder, the deeper reason for his turn to the harsh discipline and rigor of the juvenile prison system is bound up with a desire to shed his older, ethnically marked, liminal racial self, to complete "a homicide by whatever name" against himself (503). At one point, Nick is relieved to feel "the dead soul slowly drain out of me, the sedimentary stuff of who I was" (502). During his first winter as a juvenile prisoner, Nick relishes the ritualistic repetition of shoveling snow and reading books, two twin metaphorical plunges into whiteness that he remembers as "how I began to build an individual [self]" (502). Nick's experiences in the juvenile corrections facility highlight the tension famously identified by Werner Sollors between descent (ascribed hereditary identity) and consent (chosen achieved identity) at the heart of American identity: "the conflict between contractual and hereditary, self-made and ancestral, definitions of American identity—between *consent* and *descent*—[is] the central drama in American culture" (Sollors 1986, 5–6). What DeLillo shows in this crucial moment, to quote Sollors, is that the "concepts of the self-made man and of Jim Crow had their origins in the same culture at about the same time," revealing the intimate relation between "two systems of widely shared [celebratory] consent bias and severe de jure discrimination of totally descent-defined groups" (38). Although Nick remains consciously unaware of why he is so attracted to these forms of discipline and punishment, DeLillo suggests that Nick was in the process of transforming the shame of inferior, descent-defined racial association into the social capital of freely chosen white individuality.

Once Nick has left behind his previous, liminal racial subject position, DeLillo juxtaposes the transformation process of Nick's (nearly forgotten) ethnic identity with the novel's minor black characters to create a privileged aperture from which to view the odd, quasiconspiratorial logic of postwar whiteness. In one tense scene about the racial politics of baseball that features Nick and other mostly white waste management consultants, their black colleague Simeon Biggs, nicknamed Sims, challenges Nick's justification for buying Bobby Thompson's famous home-run baseball from the 1951 Giants-Dodgers game. When Nick claims that the ball represents "the mystery of bad luck, the mystery of loss" because it was thrown by the pitcher Ralph Branca, Sims points out that Thompson and Branca appear at sports dinners together. "Branca's a hero," Sims theorizes, "Because he's white . . . Because the whole thing is white. Because you can survive and endure and prosper if they let you. But you have to be white before they let you" (DeLillo 1997b, 97–98). What Sims omits, though it lurks beneath the surface, is that the "half-Italian, half Hungarian" Branca was somehow chosen for a cultural redemption narrative not only because he was perceived as white, but also because Branca's whiteness was so axiomatic that his failed pitch, signified by the now-sacred souvenir baseball, could take on an aura of, in Sims's words, "melancholy junk from yesteryear" (99). Nick's melancholic feeling of loss, DeLillo implies, is bound up with the loss of (a mythical) ethnicized authenticity in exchange for hollow white individuality. Paradoxically, such an exchange makes Nick long for that feeling of being a teenager who was "dumb-muscled and angry and real," even though it also triggers that other shameful feeling of being a racialized orphan abandoned by his father (810). For Nick, this loss (or set of losses) feels ostensibly inevitable, like a conspiracy that coerces him into identifying with whiteness to enjoy the rights promised within the paradigm of possessive liberal individualism. In a later conversation between Nick and Sims, DeLillo deepens this thematic point when Sims half-jokingly wonders whether the waste management company they both work for is "mob-owned," speculating that the Italian mafia is "a silent partner. Or they own us outright" (280). Instead of answering directly, Nick explains, "There's a word in Italian. *Dietrologia*. It means the science of what is behind something. A suspicious event. The science of what is behind an event" (280). Essentially, Nick is providing a belated answer to the previous conversation he had with Sims about the Thompson-Branca home-run ball and the "mystery of loss," deploying an Italian word to adumbrate the very Italian-ness he was seemingly compelled to discard.

Although he does not grant Nick a life-altering epiphany here, DeLillo does depict—for readers, especially—the embryonic beginnings of an ideological framework that illuminates postwar whiteness as a kind of paranoid conspiracy, a predestined plot that many racially ambiguous immigrants had little choice (from their ideological subject positions) but to play out over the second half of the twentieth century. These later scenes recast Nick's sarcastic joke toward the beginning of the novel about how living in an inconspicuous Phoenix suburb makes him feel "like someone in the Witness Protection Program" (66). As Samuele F. S. Pardini notes in his aptly titled essay "From Wiseguys to Whiteguys [sic]," Nick Shay is, on some level, a highbrow "literary version of *Goodfellas'* Henry Hill, an empty subject who is existing but no longer living" (Pardini 2016, 256). The difference between Nick Shay and his fellow "half Italian, half Irish" counterpart Henry Hill, of course, is that Hill works as a real mobster in Martin Scorsese's film *Goodfellas* (1990), and Hill is coerced into the Witness Protection program because of actual threats to his life. Nick, on the other hand, is not forced into his white middle-class suburban life, even though he senses a kind of soft, unnamable coercion operating in the background, a *dietrologia* (or "science of dark forces") that leaves him feeling both comforted and uneasy (DeLillo 1997b, 280). In one exemplary moment, while Nick drinks soy milk and ponders the Velcro wallet he straps to his ankle each morning before jogging, he thinks, "The ankle wallet answered a need. It spoke directly to a personal concern. It made me feel there were people out there in the world of product development and merchandising and gift cataloguing who understood the nature of my little nagging needs" (86). The lived experience of Nick's adulthood reads less like the sinister conspiracies operating in earlier postmodern novels than like a sterile parody of John Updike's oft-quoted quip: "America is a vast conspiracy to make you happy" (Updike 2013, 774). The massive conspiracy at the heart of a postmodern novel like Pynchon's *Gravity's Rainbow*, as Samuel Chase Coale argues, teases readers by claiming "to reveal a more or less linear explanation of events that embodies rather than reduces paranoia, taking comfort ironically in the notion that there is human agency behind hidden agendas, as opposed to impersonal global forces: Someone somewhere is pulling the strings [and usually for malevolent purposes]" (Coale 2019, 212). For Nick Shay, though, the conspiracy is an ostensibly benevolent plot that transforms him into an unquestionably "white" liberal subject and materially enriches his life, despite draining it of existential meaning.

Nick's paranoid feelings of an inescapable trajectory into whiteness dovetails with what David R. Roediger has called the "deep tragedy" of the Italian American immigrant experience: "that proximity to oppression could also lead new immigrants to distance themselves from black Americans" (Roediger 2005, 32). That trajectory, Roediger argues, was buttressed by explicitly racist political policies and practices, since upward mobility for Italian Americans was inseparable from their ability to take advantage of the materialist privileges of whiteness, such as whites-only job opportunities and mortgage loans for suburban housing outside of "stigmatized 'mixed race' areas" (231).[13] Ironically for Nick, some of the most influential, behind-the-scenes actors behind the conspiracy of Italian American whiteness were, and always had been, Italian American immigrants themselves. As Peter Vellon documents in *A Great Conspiracy Against Our Race: Italian Immigrant Newspapers and the Construction of Whiteness in the Early 20th Century*, Italian immigrants vigorously policed the boundary between blackness and whiteness, using their newspapers to support Italian imperialism in northern Africa and to accuse anyone in the United States who linked Italian Americans and African Americans through skin color as guilty of perpetuating a "conspiracy" against the "great [Italian] race" (Vellon 2014, 11, 122). This historiography helps explain why malevolent conspiracies reminiscent of Pynchonian postmodernism are still active interpretive options in *Underworld*, but almost exclusively for black characters such as Sims and Cotter Martin's father, Manx. When Sims floats the paranoid idea that the US census undercounts millions of African Americans deliberately, for instance,

Nick rejects the theory as just one of Sims's "cheap and easy delusions" that American society has been systematically arranged to disadvantage black people (DeLillo 1997b, 335–36).

Similarly, Manx Martin knows that he cannot sell the famous home-run baseball to a black man because he would "look [Manx] down with that saucy eye he's got for outrageous plots against his person" (642). The crucial upshot for Nick's character is that romantic interracial identification between blacks and whites—epitomized by Jack Kerouac's romanticized racist fantasies in *On the Road* or Norman Mailer's patronizing racial primitivism in "The White Negro"—seems almost unthinkable; instead, Nick's racialized ethnic identity looks more like the intraracial psychodrama of a black writer like Richard Wright's, whose experience of upward mobility allowed him to glimpse the hollowness of white bourgeois society only to feel an ambivalent longing for the poor, black oppressed communities of his youth.[14] As someone who once belonged to a racialized ethnicity that now seems like an obsolete form of cultural waste by century's end, Nick cannot help but experience "complex longings," DeLillo writes, referring to both actual waste and metaphorical waste: "Nostalgia for the banned materials of civilization, for the brute force of old industries and old conflicts" (286).

Conclusion: DeLilloian Italian-ness as Text, Not Essence

By focalizing the sociological trajectory of Italian Americans through Nick and the forgotten, nearly discarded "waste" of his midcentury racialized Italian American heritage, DeLillo reveals that the damaging psychic motivations that drove Nick's *dietrologia* into whiteness—that is, the masculine-coded agency panic that feared the perceived socioeconomic "black" bottom of American society—are not part of an inevitable, sinister plot, but rather an underworld of Cold War whiteness, an "underhistory" [sic] that can be unearthed and rewritten in the twenty-first century (DeLillo 1997b, 791). In other words, once readers become aware of Nick's relationship to the conspiratorial feeling of postwar whiteness, DeLillo leaves open the possibility of a specific materialist solution: Nick can embrace a "recycled," anti-foundationalist vision of his Italian American heritage. This rhetorically powerful, though metaphysically groundless, vision of ethnicity shares certain similarities with what recent scholars describe as DeLillo's quasi-secularized conceptualization of Roman Catholicism. Influentially, Amy Hungerford argues that DeLillo formally deploys "belief absent of doctrine," since DeLillo's fiction "imagines how religion that is abandoned in most respects can persist in a literary form, and how it can do so without ceding religious experiences or meanings to secular versions of the same" (Hungerford 2010, 74). Just as DeLillo empties religion of its metaphysical essence while retaining its textual existence in literary form, DeLillo also registers Italian American heritage as a hopeful, life-giving set of textual practices and concrete rituals without turning Italian-ness into a racialized ethnic essence.[15]

As scholars working on the intersection of DeLillo's *Underworld* and Italian American culture have long argued, DeLillo salvages these elements of his Italian American heritage through various embodied linguistic practices and a fundamentally aesthetic orientation toward life. In his memorialization of Little Italy, John Paul Russo points out, "DeLillo's prose comes alive as the plenum of sensation," conjuring up a feast for the senses in both English and Italian (Russo 2003, 89). Using language in this way as a "retaining medium," Hungerford claims, "frees the person from the strictures of reason to reach a mystical relation to the material world and to what transcends the material world," meaning that it allows characters to gain existential sustenance via language without reifying its source (Hungerford 2010, 73). Regarding the religious "belief without doctrine" trope, Hungerford argues that this is also the point of Nick's Jesuit education: "Father Paulus teaches him to name the parts of a shoe, and through the act of naming to see 'the depth and reach of the commonplace' represented by that 'gorgeous Latinate word,' 'quotidian'" (73). Likewise, DeLillo uses the language of food—for example, the "autumnal pink Parma ham, sliced transparently thin" or the smell of "rolled beef, meatballs, basil"—to achieve a similar effect in relation to the "ethnicity without essence" trope (DeLillo 1997b, 672, 699). Both patterns of language usage, DeLillo suggests, contribute to a certain aesthetics of Italian American existence: "The Italians. They sat on top of the stoop with paper fans and orangeades. They made their world. They said, Who's better than me? . . . They knew how to sit there and say that and be happy" (DeLillo 1997b, 207). This passage represents a healthy nostalgia that "is corporeal in the Mediterranean fashion, a repository of the humanism of the immigrants and their communitarian ways of being, a collective subject that defies assimilation in the heart of modernity, the city of New York" (Pardini 2016, 256). Ultimately, though, DeLillo manages to celebrate his Italian American heritage without fetishizing or reifying it because of the way Nick comes to terms with his father's abandonment at the end of the novel. Finally letting go of any heroic, movie-like mafia myth about his father, Nick admits, "I don't think he [i.e., Jimmy] wanted a fresh start or a new life or even an escape . . . He lived day-to-day and step-to-step and did not wonder what would become of us or how she [i.e., Nick's mother] would manage or how tall we grew or how smart we became . . . The failure it brought down on us does not diminish" (DeLillo 1997b, 808–9). By the end, somewhat ironically, Nick sees that the person who most fulfilled the ethnic Italian role in his life was his mother, Rosemary Shay, who is not ethnically Italian at all, but Irish. After Rosemary dies, Nick elegizes her influence on his life: "I felt suffused with her truth, spread through, as with water, color or light. I thought she'd entered the deepest place I could provide, the animating entity, the thing, if anything, that will survive my own last breath, and she makes me larger, she amplifies my sense of what it is to be human" (804). On the surface, this passage reads like a profound ode to the transcendent, life-sustaining power of *Italianiatà*. On a deeper thematic level, though, it presents a creative, novel mingling of descent (mother-to-son) and consent (Irish-to-Italian), recycling the metaphysical "waste" of racialized Italian ethnicity into a dynamic, aesthetic form of Italian American heritage.

Notes

1. While I cannot fully summarize the prodigious amount of extant scholarship on DeLillo's *Underworld*, the critical works germane to my argument include: the "systems theory" analysis in Tom LeClair's seminal book *In the Loop: Don DeLillo and the Systems Novel* (1988); David Cowart's poststructuralist approach in *Don DeLillo: The Physics of Language* (2002); the tracing of religious practices and theological themes in *Underworld* found in John A. McClure's *Partial Faiths: Postsecular Fiction in the Age of Pynchon and Morrison* (2007) and Amy Hungerford's *American Literature and Religion since 1960* (2010); and the interrogation of Italian American tropes and themes beginning with Fred Gardaphe's foundational work *Italian Signs, American Streets: The Evolution of Italian American Narrative* (1996) and then followed by scholars such as John Paul Russo, James Periconi, Josephine Gattuso Hendin, and Samuele F. S. Pardini (all of whom are cited throughout this chapter).

2. My usage of the term "racialized ethnicity" is drawn primarily from the sociologist Ramón Grosfoguel's work, which interrogates the ambiguous intersection between "ethnicity" (a fluid word for cultural identity) and "race" (a biologically or culturally essentialist word). If one is aware of the discursive power relations involved in many American social contexts, Grosfoguel argues, the notion of "racialized ethnicity" is an illuminating concept (315–16), which is to say that in certain discourse formations "ethnicity" is, for all intents and purposes, used as a

code word for "race," and vice-versa in other discourse formations. In the early and mid-twentieth century, "Italian" often functioned as a racialized ethnicity.

3. In his first novel, *Americana* (1971), DeLillo utilizes this "white male alienation" trope when he portrays the novel's white protagonist David Bell as someone feels like his "whole life was a lesson in the effect of echoes, that [he] was living in the third person" (58). As Gardaphe points out in *Italian Signs, American Streets*, DeLillo's strategically places minor Italian American characters in *Americana* to "set up ways of being that challenge the WASP experience in [David Bell's] America" (134).

4. Although *Underworld* is frequently read as a postmodern novel, is worth noting that my identification of a distinctly modernist temporality accords with DeLillo's own view of *Underworld*. "I don't see *Underworld* as post-modern," DeLillo told an interviewer for the *London Guardian* in 1998, "Maybe it's the last modernist gasp" ("Everything under the Bomb"). I do not mean to imply that "modernism" and "postmodernism" are mutually exclusive categories or that scholarship on *Underworld* as a postmodern novel is deficient, but merely that the novel is just as indebted to specific elements of modernism as it is to postmodernism.

5. When one performs a closer, comparative reading of Lewis's *Babbitt* (1922) and DeLillo's *Underworld* with the latter's Italian American context in mind, the different uses of racialized ethnic tropes are thrown into stark relief. First, whereas George Babbitt fantasizes about a white female "fairy child" to reinvigorate his life in the future, Nick Shay fantasizes about a lived ethnic past (Lewis 1922, 4). Secondly and more importantly, George Babbitt lumps together African Americans, Jews, and ethnic Italians as non-white Others, even calling Italian Americans "wops" and dago[s]" (Lewis 1922, 77, 156). In *Babbitt*, then, the boundaries of whiteness are implicitly defined against all other forms of racial impurity, including the racial "in-between-ness" of first- and second-generation Italian immigrants.

6. For an extended analysis of the "Great American Novel" label being pinned on *Underworld* by various critics—including David Wiegand (*San Francisco Chronicle*), Andrew Pyper (*Montreal Gazette*), and Christopher Bigsby (*London Telegraph*)—see John Duvall's chapter "The Novel's Reception" in *Don DeLillo's Underworld: A Reader's Guide* (2002). In the decades after its publication, the novel only grew in critical esteem. Among a host of awards and honors, two seem especially noteworthy: *Underworld* won the William Dean Howells Medal in 2000 (a major literary prize awarded by the American Academy of Arts and Letters that recognizes "the most distinguished work of American fiction published in the previous five years"), and it finished in second place (behind Morrison's *Beloved*) in the 2006 competition conducted by the Book Review section of the *New York Times*, which asked several hundred critics and writers to name "the best work of fiction in the last 25 years" (Duvall 2002, 77).

7. In a succinct, clinical analysis of Italian ethnicity in DeLillo's pre-*Underworld* novels, Daniel Aaron, a noted Americanist scholar and founding president of the

Library of America, epitomized this consensus view in language that could not have been clearer: "I think it's worth noting that nothing in [DeLillo's] novels suggests a suppressed 'Italian foundation'; hardly a vibration betrays an ethnic consciousness . . . [T]here's nothing particularly 'ethnic' about his dark comedy unless we imagine that traces of the uneasy alien or of ethnic marginality are discernable in his brand of grotesque parody, his resistance to the American consensus (1991, 67–68). Published five years before the emergence of *Underworld*, Aaron's analysis appeared well grounded in that moment. From his first novel published in 1971 (*Americana*) to his last novel published before *Underworld* in 1991 (*Mao II*), DeLillo omitted major, though not minor, characters with Italian American heritage from his fiction. For a trenchant reading of the Italian American tropes in DeLillo's pre-*Underworld* fiction, see Gardaphe's perennially useful *Italian Signs, American Streets*.

8. For a range of literary scholars, the "waste" trope—and the related trope of "recycling"—in *Underworld* has been a popular, multivalent point of focus. To explore a variety of critical perspectives (though not an exhaustive list) on this related set of tropes, see Ruth Helyer's " 'Refuse Heaped Many Stories High': DeLillo, Dirt, and Disorder" (1999); Todd McGowan's "The Obsolescence of Mystery and the Accumulation of Waste in Don DeLillo's *Underworld*" (2005); Paul Gleason's "Don DeLillo, T.S. Eliot, and the Redemption of America's Atomic Waste Land" (2002); Sarah L. Wasserman's "Ephemeral Gods and Billboard Saints: Don DeLillo's *Underworld* and Urban Apparitions" (2014); Rachele Dini's " 'What We Excrete Comes back to Consume Us': Waste and Reclamation in Don DeLillo's *Underworld*" (2019).

9. For an extensive analysis of Cold War–era racial discourse in the United States, especially regarding the reification of the black/white rhetorical paradigm in American political discourse, see Mary L. Dudziak's *Cold War Civil Rights: Race and the Image of American Democracy* (2011). While the "full story of civil rights reform in U.S. history cuts across racial groups," Dudziak writes, "U.S. policymakers . . . saw American race relations through the lens of a black/white paradigm. To them, race in America was quintessentially about 'the Negro problem' " (14).

10. For a wide-ranging survey on the controversial discourse of black cultural pathology, see Daniel Geary's *Beyond Civil Rights: The Moynihan Report and Its Legacy* (2017). In his infamous 1965 report "The Negro Family: The Case for National Action," Daniel Patrick Moynihan "worried that achieving full racial equality [in the United States] would be hindered by what he viewed as the 'crumbling' and 'deteriorating' structure of many African-American families," Geary writes; "Family structure stood at the heart of what he notoriously labeled a 'tangle of pathology' evident in high rates of juvenile delinquency, drug abuse, and poor educational achievement among African Americans" (2).

11. Although outside the purview of my core argument, perhaps a latent connection exists between the condemnation of drugs as soul-destroying in *The Godfather* and Nick's murder of George Manza, the drug-addicted bachelor (DeLillo 1997b, 724–26).

12. For two excellent, recent summaries of these definitional debates about race and prejudice in Italian American history, see Peter G. Vellon's "Italian Americans and Race During the Era of Mass Immigration" and Salvatore J. LaGumina's "Discrimination, Prejudice and Italian American History," which both appear as chapters in *The Routledge History of Italian Americans* edited by William Connell and Stanislao Pugliese (2017).

13. Roediger's seminal analysis casts light on the different strategies for performatively embodying "coolness" deployed by Nick (who idolizes Italian mafia figures) and Nick's son, Jeff (who idolizes black rappers). In Joel Dinerstein's typology of "cool," Nick associates blackness with degradation and thus embodies the white, working-class male version of "Euro-American cool," whereas Jeff seeks to embody an "African-American cool" that repudiates white racism and grew out of jazz music, the Civil Rights Movement, and eventually, rap and hip-hop culture (Dinerstein 2017, 31).

14. I am referring to the reflective passages in Wright's autobiography *Black Boy* (1945) where he laments: "The essence of the irony of the plight of the Negro in America, to me, is that he is doomed to live in isolation while those who condemn him seek the basest goals of any people on the face of the earth. Perhaps it would be possible for the Negro to become reconciled to his plight if he could be made to believe that his sufferings were for some remote, high, sacrificial end; but . . . seeing that a *lust for trash* is what blinds the nation to his claims, is what sets storms to rolling in his soul" (Wright 2007, 273, emphasis added). For a brilliant analysis of Wright's critique of white bourgeois materialism, see Kenneth W. Warren's short book *What Was African American Literature?* (2011).

15. The conclusion of my argument on the relationship between DeLillo and Italian American literature draws inspiration from Henry Louis Gates Jr.'s influential 1988 essay on the relationship between black authors and the African American literary tradition, "Talking Black: Critical Signs of the Times." "The black tradition," Gates argues, "exists only insofar as black artists enact it . . . Race is a text (an array of discursive practices), not an essence. It must be *read* with painstaking care and suspicion, not imbibed" (2249, emphasis in original).

Works Cited

Aaron, Daniel. 1991. "How to Read Don DeLillo." In *Introducing Don DeLillo*, edited by Frank Lentricchia. Durham, NC: Duke University Press.

Buell, Lawrence. 2016. *The Dream of the Great American Novel*. Belknap Press.

Coale, Samuel Chase. 2019 "Conspiracy and Paranoia." In *Thomas Pynchon in Context*, edited by Inger H. Dalsgaard. Cambridge University Press.

Coates, Ta-Nehisi. 2015. *Between the World and Me*. New York: Random House.

Coppola, Francis Ford, dir. *The Godfather*. 1972. Los Angeles: Paramount Pictures.

DeLillo, Don. 1989. *Americana*. Contemporary American Fiction Series. Penguin.

———. 1993. "Don DeLillo: The Art of Fiction CXXXV. Interview with Adam Begley." *Paris Review* 35 (128) (Fall): 274–306.

———. 1997a. "Baseball and the Cold War." Interview with Kim Echlin. *Ottawa Citizen*, 28 Dec. E5.

———. 1997b. *Underworld.* Scribner. 1997.

———. 1998. "Everything under the Bomb." Interview with Richard Williams. *London Guardian*, 10 Jan.

Dinerstein, Joel. 2017. *The Origins of Cool in Postwar America*. Chicago: University of Chicago Press.

Dini, Rachele. 2019. " 'What We Excrete Comes Back to Consume Us': Waste and Reclamation in Don DeLillo's *Underworld.*" *Interdisciplinary Studies in Literature and Environment* 26 (1): 165–88.

Dudziak, Mary D. 2011. *Cold War Civil Rights: Race and the Image of American Democracy*. Princeton, NJ: Princeton University Press.

Duvall, John. 2002. *Don DeLillo's* Underworld: *A Reader's Guide*. Continuum.

Ellison, Ralph. 2004. *Invisible Man*. New York: Random House.

Engles, Tim. 2015. "White Male Nostalgia in Don DeLillo's *Underworld.*" *Postmodern Literature and Race*. Edited by Leon Platt and Sarah Upstone, 195–210. Cambridge University Press.

Fitzpatrick, Kathleen. 2006. *The Anxiety of Obsolescence: The American Novel in the Age of Television*. Vanderbilt Press.

Gardaphe, Fred. 1996. *Italian Signs, American Streets: The Evolution of Italian American Narrative*. Durham, NC: Duke University Press.

Gates, Henry Louis, Jr. 2018. "Talking Black: Critical Signs of the Times." *The Norton Anthology of Theory and Criticism*. 3rd ed., edited by Vincent B. Leitch. W.W. Norton & Company.

Geary, Daniel. 2017. *Beyond Civil Rights: The Moynihan Report and Its Legacy*. Philadelphia: University of Pennsylvania Press.

Gleason, Paul. 2002. "Don DeLillo, T.S. Eliot, and the Redemption of America's Atomic Waste Land." In *UnderWords: Perspectives on Don DeLillo's* Underworld, edited by Joseph Dewey, Steven G. Kellman, and Irving Malin. Newark: University of Delaware Press.

Grosfoguel, Ramón. 2004. "Race and Ethnicity or Racialized Ethnicities?: Identities within Global Coloniality." *Ethnicities* 4 (3): 315–36.

Guglielmo, Jennifer. 2003. *Are Italians White? How Race is Made in America*. Routledge.

Guglielmo, Thomas A. 2003. *White on Arrival: Italians, Race, Color, and Power in Chicago, 1890–1945*. Oxford: Oxford University Press.

Helyer, Ruth. 1999. " 'Refuse Heaped Many Stories High': DeLillo, Dirt, and Disorder." *Modern Fiction Studies* 45 (4): 987–1006.

Hendin, Josephine Gattuso. 2000. "Italian American Insights and the Nineties." *Italian Americana* 18 (1): 46–55.

Hungerford, Amy. 2010. *Postmodern Belief: American Literature and Religion Since 1960*. Princeton, NJ: Princeton University Press.

Lewis, Sinclair. 2005. *Babbitt*. Barnes & Noble Classics Ed. Barnes & Noble Books.

McGowan, Todd. 2005. "The Obsolescence of Mystery and the Accumulation of Waste in Don DeLillo's *Underworld*." *Critique* 46 (2): 123–45.

Messenger, Chris. 2002. *The Godfather and American Culture: How the Corleones Became "Our Gang."* Albany: State University of New York Press.

New York Times. 2006. "What Is the Best Work of American Fiction in the Last 25 Years?" May 21, 2006. http://www.nytimes.com/ref/books/fiction-25-years.html.

Pardini, Samuele F. S. 2016. "From Wiseguys to Whiteguys: The Italian America Gangster, Whiteness, and the Modernity in Don DeLillo's *Underworld* and Frank Lentricchia's *The Music of the Inferno*." *Critique: Studies in Contemporary Fiction* 57 (4): 254–67.

Periconi, James. 2000. "DeLillo's *Underworld*: Towards a New Beginning for the Italian American Novel." *VIA: Voices in Italian Americana* XI (1): 141–58.

Roediger, David R. 2005. *Working Toward Whiteness: How America's Immigrants Became White: The Strange Journey from Ellis Island to the Suburbs*. Basic Books.

Row, Jess. 2019. *White Flights: Race, Fiction, and the American Imagination*. Graywolf Press.

Russo, John Paul. 2003. "Little Italy in DeLillo's *Underworld*." *Culture a contatto nelle Americhe*. Oedipus.

Santopietro, Tom. 2012. *The Godfather Effect: Changing Hollywood, America, and Me*. Thomas Dunne Books.

Sollors, Werner. 1986. *Beyond Ethnicity: Consent and Descent in American Culture*. Oxford: Oxford University Press.

Updike, John. 2013. "How to Love America and Leave It at the Same Time." In *John Updike: Collected Early Stories*, edited by Christopher Carduff. The Library of America.

Vellon, Peter G. 2014. *A Great Conspiracy Against Our Race: Italian Immigrant Newspapers and the Construction of Whiteness in the Early 20th Century*. New York: New York University Press.

Wasserman, Sarah L. 2014. "Ephemeral Gods and Billboard Saints: Don DeLillo's *Underworld* and Urban Apparitions." *Journal of American Literature* 48 (4): 1041–67.

Witzling, David. 2008. *Everybody's America: Thomas Pynchon, Race, and the Cultures of Postmodernism*. Routledge.

Wright, Richard. 2007. *Black Boy (American Hunger): A Record of Childhood and Youth*. Harper Perennial Modern Classics.

Confessionalism in Italian American Poets

Moving Beyond Categories

Hidden Roots

Mary Jo Paradise Salter and the
Subtle Presence of Italian-ness

Alan J. Gravano

Born in Grand Rapids, Michigan, Mary Jo Salter attended Harvard and Cambridge University and studied with Robert Fitzgerald and Elizabeth Bishop as an undergraduate. Her books of poetry include *Henry Purcell in Japan* (1985), *Unfinished Painting* (1989), *Sunday Skaters* (1994), *A Kiss in Space* (1999), *Open Shutters* (2003), *A Phone Call to the Future: New and Selected Poems* (2009), *Nothing by Design* (2013), and *The Surveyors: Poems* (2017). Additionally, she has published a children's book, *The Moon Comes Home* (1989), and a play, *Falling Bodies* (2004).[1] Salter taught for twenty-three years at Mount Holyoke College, "where she was eventually named the Emily Dickinson Senior Lecturer in the Humanities"[2] before joining the faculty at Johns Hopkins University. Her poetry, associated with the New Formalism movement, demonstrates a command of forms such as the sonnet and ekphrasis. Like many contemporary poets, Salter's ekphrastic works find inspiration in works of art. More importantly, this tendency "to limit ekphrasis to descriptions of works of art" begins to take hold at the beginning of the twentieth century and "bear that exclusive meaning" (Preminger and Brogan 1993, 320). Her sources of inspiration include Emily Dickinson, Marianne Moore, and Bishop (Salter 1991, 30).[3] This chapter examines Salter's poems that memorialize mothers. Based on personal communications with the author, the following textual analysis researches the poet's maternal lineage: Lormina Paradise Salter, the mother, and Maria Giuseppe Cazzato, the grandmother.

Besides Salter's formal prowess, numerous examples of Italian-ness or *Italianiatà* surface in her writing, such as a revisioning of Botticelli's *Birth of Venus* in "The Rebirth of Venus," where a street artist recreates the painting on the ground. *Italianità* can be whatever leads "Italian Americans back to the real and mythical images of the land," their ancestors' lifestyle, values, and cultural trappings. This Italian spirit can be "language, food, a way of determining life values, familial structure, a sense of religion"; it can be all of this and much more (Tamburri et al. 2000, 6). This established identity "is composed of the qualities that separate us from Americans of other ethnic backgrounds. If we can isolate these characteristics, then we can begin to identify the ingredients of what goes into *Italianità*, and so we can construct a basis for establishing a distinct Italian / American literature" (Tamburri et al. 2000, 6). This Italian-ness contributes to characters' abilities to connect with Italian audiences, especially "the cultural trappings of their ancestors," while at the same time it symbolizes an ideal for the dominant culture.

Salter fills her collections with geographical spaces throughout Italy, Italian artists, and family members of Italian descent, especially her grand-mother and mother. Her poems highlight interstitial moments for the narrator, who vacillates between the periphery and the center. She imbues certain ones with *Italianità*, which adds another layer of complexity. Yet some reviews situate her place in American poetry: "Salter's first book places her squarely among the new breed of poets who seem to be charting a direction for American poetry" (Corn 1985, 40). Meanwhile, other reviewers fixate on Bishop as a mentor. "Like Elizabeth Bishop," her poems in *Unfinished Painting* (1989) offer "a voice that is relaxed, accessible" (Miller 1989, 73). In reviewing Salter's *New and Selected Poems* (2008), another critic insists that "like her early teacher, Elizabeth Bishop, Salter conjures gold from the seemingly trivial or the overlooked" (Kaufman 2008, 89). Despite these reviews and the fact that she studied with Bishop at Harvard, Salter remains in between. In one sense, she illustrates the center or dominant culture by her academic pedigree, yet little scholarship exists about her poetry.[4]

Tell Me Where the Italian American Poets Are:
In the Heart or the Head

Regarding the American canon of poetry, courses on African American and women poets appear regularly on university syllabi; however, including Italian

American poets or a course on Italian American writers is not commonplace. In "Where Are the Italian American Novelists? (1993),[5] Gay Talese discusses his identity "not as a hyphenated American but as a hybrid American." He questions that "among the nation's most famous novelists and dramatists, there was a conspicuous absence of Americans with Italian surnames." His cover story caused several writers to respond. In an issue of *Italian Americana*,[6] Gioia and others replied, "Italian American writers will be more successful in making a case for individual books and writers than by making categorical demands for wholesale attention" (Gioia 1993, 11). For example, Fred L. Gardaphé's Signet edition of Pietro di Donato's *Christ in Concrete* (1993) and Edward Cifelli's biography of John Ciardi (1997) "will earn Italian American writers more respect in both the scholarly community and general culture than vague general assertions will" (Gioia 1993, 12). Whether intentional or not, Gioia slights Daniela Gioseffi's response. She lists numerous Italian American women authors, such as Mary Jo Bona, Tina De Rosa, Diana Cavallo, Carole Maso, Rosemarie Santini, Susan Caperna Lloyd, and Chris Mazza (28). In his review of Gioia's *Disappearing Ink*, George Guida points out that "by the 1990s . . . scholars had harvested an abundant crop of Italian American writing, including the work of Italian American poets from Emanuel Carnevali to Rose Romano. Unfortunately, critics have written far less about Italian American poetry than they have about other genres" (Guida 2007, 225). Guida identifies an area that, since the publication of his review, has made some headway. Maria Mazziotti Gillan and Jennifer Gillan edited *Unsettling America: An Anthology of Contemporary Multicultural Poetry* (1994). Although not specifically a collection of Italian American poetry, the anthology consists of Lawrence Ferlinghetti, Felix Stefanile, Helen Barolini, Daniela Gioseffi, Vittoria repetto, Rachel Guido deVries, Rose Romano, Michael Palma, and Diane di Prima, among others. More recently, Francesco Durante, Robert Viscusi, and James J. Periconi edited *Italoamericana: The Literature of the Great Migration, 1880–1943* (2014). Published almost fifty years earlier, Rodolfo Pucelli translated and edited the *Anthology of Italian and Italo-American Poetry* in 1955. In section III, *Original English Poems of Italo-American Poets*, he includes John J. Alifano, Vincent D. Calenda, Antonio Crivello, Giuseppe Luongo, Rosa Zagnoni Marinoni, P. S. Moncada, Frank Spadola, Joseph Rizzo Taranletti, and John Tatty; only Crivello and Marinoni appear in *Italoamericana*.

Over the years, there have been several collections that consist of a variety of genres. Helen Barolini's *The Dream Book: An Anthology of Writings by Italian American Woman* (1985) contains memoir, nonfiction, fiction, drama, and poetry. In *Women of the Beat Generation: The Writers, Artists, and Muses at the Heart of a Revolution* (1996), Brenda Knight incorporates selections from Mary Fabilli and Diane di Prima. In 2008, Carol Bonomo Albright and Joanna Clapps Herman edited *Wild Dreams: The Best of Italian Americana*, which consists of poetry and prose. *The Penguin Anthology of Twentieth-Century American Poetry* (2013), edited by Rita Dove, includes one Ferlinghetti and Gregory Corso poem. The seventh edition of *The Heath Anthology of American Literature* (2014) contains two novelists, Pietro di Donato and Don DeLillo; however, Ferlinghetti is the only Italian American poet.

Meanwhile, the sixth edition of *The Norton Anthology of Poetry* (2018) features Ferlinghetti and Dana Gioia (new to the sixth edition). In these multiethnic or Italian American anthologies, only Ferlinghetti made the cut for the *Norton*. Considering Gioia's directive to concentrate on individual poets provides the only practical solution to make the broader audience aware of accomplished writers not represented in the most canonical university texts; one such hybrid poet is Mary Jo Salter.

Italy and *Italianità* in Mary Jo Salter's Poetry

The motifs appear in all of her writing: Italy and Italian-ness. In *Unfinished Painting*, Salter describes Mary as "our other mother, Eve" (14) in "The Annunciation." Even in "Chernobyl," the narrator writes, "As far away as Rome, / unseen through weeks of sun, / the cloud kept children home" (54). In *Sunday Skaters*, she writes about the second-tallest hill: "June: The Gianicolo," where a "million lamps of Rome / light up in rosy approbation" (6). Salter speaks of "holidays in Venice" (31) in "A Benediction." In *A Kiss in Space*, she describes Venice as "sinking imperceptibly / each morning as the sun climbs from a sea" (34) in "The Jewel of the World." In *Open Shutters*, she sets "Trompe l'Oeil" in Genoa. Her father appears in "Erasers" with the mention of "Sister Martha, / like a conductor raising high her chalk" (15). In *Nothing by Design*, Salter references Lake Como in "From a Balcony, Lake Como" and "Unbroken Music."

Thus, this chapter examines elements of *Italianità* in Salter's "Libretto," "Dead Letters," "Poppies," and "Mary Cazzato, 1921." Even though previous scholarship has focused on Salter's poetry, no article or book explores her Italian descent on her mother's side; Lormina Paradise Salter is Italian American. Like Don DeLillo, who considers himself an American writer, even though he is Italian American and has Italian American characters in his works, most scholars recognize Salter as an American poet because many are unaware of her family biography. Indeed, many of her poems incorporate *Italianità,* and the characters struggle with their sense of identity. Salter's poetry makes use of Homi Bhabha's concept of "in-between," the interstitial spaces within and among individuals and cultures, which do not maintain a single position but form identities in an ongoing process. In *The Location of Culture,* Bhabha discusses "gatherings of exiles and émigrés . . . on the edge of 'foreign' cultures; gathering at the frontiers; gatherings in the ghettos or cafes of city centres; gathering in the half-life, half-light of foreign tongues, or in the uncanny fluency of another's language" (139). Salter negotiates her hybrid status by meditating on her mother and grandmother as well as aspects of Italian culture. Indeed, the mother and grandmother's obscured Italian heritage ("foreign tongues") allow the poet to interrogate the past; therefore, eulogizing these women becomes a recurring theme.

In "Libretto," Salter embraces the family's daily life in this "in-between" space, focusing on the confluence linking her mother's divorce from her father and finding a parallel in Puccini's *Madame Butterfly.* Her extended metaphor depicts the child narrator wrestling with the dynamics of marriage through the *Italianità* of language and the Italian opera composer Giacomo Puccini. The mother is second generation, whose parents emigrated from Italy to the United States, and the foreignness of Italian, Puccini, and *Madame Butterfly* represents home and belonging to the child-narrator.

The title is also the first word of the poem: *Libretto* ("little book" in Italian), which means the text or words to which an opera or other extended musical composition is set. In the first octave, the narrator asks, "why are we alone?" The speaker ponders if her father and brothers were "gone / all day" or if her memory had "brushed them from the shot." The scene opens with the narrator as a child with her mother, who has "set aside / just for the two" of them "a lesson." The poet uses "the tall / 'European' drapes" that her mother has "sewn herself." The child informs the reader that this task is "a work of secret weights and tiers." The mother curses "at her own / mother's machine." The record player's needle ties in with the sewing machine's needle and transitions from the "hidden cord" of the drapes to "Puccini's strings." The narrator situates the child in a hybrid position where she does not belong to her mother's Italian culture. Although one can argue that the child-narrator belongs more to US culture than the Italian one, she inhabits a hybrid space on the borderline of both. The narrator, an adult who uses a child's voice, still feels her mother's influence and the importance of the Italian language and elements of the background and identity of her grandmother, Maria Giuseppe Cazzato, in the form of the sewing machine. With the father and brothers absent, Salter emphasizes the mother-daughter bond that shares a cultural and linguistic history.

In the next stanza, Salter embroiders a scene of "shut two-car garages" connecting her home and her parents: "I know / that with two cars, people can separate. / He went away, came back for more." She hears her parents arguing as "operatic scenes" through the wall "as if through a foreign language." Indeed, in stanza three, the speaker includes "Puccini's strings," which have multiple meanings. First, strings are associated with the orchestra's instruments, and Puccini "pulled the strings" by manipulating the characters. Also, the strings connect to the theater's window and stage curtains. String instruments produce a sound that symbolizes the poet's craft and manipulation of the line's rhythm. The separation illustrated by the two cars appears in the caesura of the question: "Who couldn't tell / without the words?" The narrator follows the question with the repetition of "*Libretto.*" The eight-year-old narrator has the English text on her knees, while the Italian one is on her mother's. Rather than the mother bringing the past (i.e., the Italian language) to the present and making a new sense of identity out of them, the child highlights her past studying Italian with her mother. This and other aspects of *Italianità* introduce new identities to Italian Americans, such as familial structure and language.

In an interview, Salter states, "my mother's parents, Francesco Paolo Paradiso (later anglicized to Paradise) and Maria Giuseppe Cazzato, were born in Puglia, in a little town called Castellaneta." Salter explains that "at some point, some of the Castellaneta people headed to Lansing, Michigan, where my mother was born." Although she does not mention why her grandparents emigrated to the United States, it is essential to note the general feeling about southern Italians. For instance, "northern Italians increasingly disparaged southerners in the language of scientific racism" (Gabaccia 2000, 73). These prejudices moved across the Atlantic and permeated American society.

Regarding the courtship of her mother, Lormina Paradise, Salter adds that "my parents met when my father, a recent WWII vet, started classes at Michigan State and got a part-time job as a stock boy for my grandfather's little grocery/florist shop, called Everybody's Market. My mother walked in one day home from her art classes in New York, and they were married just a few months later, on Christmas Day, 1947. (He was 21; she was 23.)" Salter reveals, "when I was a child, we lived in Detroit for a while, and I remember evenings when my grandparents had friends over and spoke in Italian, which nobody taught me. I had to start catching up (or trying to) in college." Consequently, it seems that the narrator's mother knows the Italian language. In this poem, the narrator muses on the mother-daughter dynamics in the form of language, specifically words/*parole* or book/*libretto*—the engagement with English and Italian forges an unbreakable bond between the two. Even with the anecdote of her grandparents and friends speaking Italian, the younger Salter finds herself an outsider, not knowing the language of her *nonni*.

In the fourth and longest stanza, the child-narrator acknowledges, "people interrupting and just plain / not listening, and yet the burden / of the words is simple: Butterfly must die." The poet introduces Puccini's *Madame Butterfly*, and the lines emphasize the importance of words. Even here, "the burden" constitutes the poem's composition, similar to the opera's composition, and "the burden / of the words" underscores the lesson between the mother and daughter and the strife between the mother and the father. Isaac Cates sees the father, Albert Gregory Salter, "as a palpable absence" (313). The child's encounter with Puccini's *Madame Butterfly* works on two levels: First, the American (dominant culture) marrying a fifteen-year-old Japanese bride (the other, as well as East vs. West), and second, the symbolic connection to the absent father in the poem. Briefly, in Puccini's opera, Lieutenant Benjamin Franklin Pinkerton meets Madame Butterfly. She tells him that she earns her living as a geisha. Her uncle curses her for rejecting her religion for her husband's. They consummate their marriage at the end of Act I. In Act II, three years have passed, and Butterfly waits for Pinkerton to return. During this time, she has had Pinkerton's son, who is called Sorrow until his father returns, after which he is named Joy. She receives a letter from Pinkerton. During Act III, Pinkerton returns with his new wife, Kate, and asks to take their son to America. Butterfly agrees. Using the knife that her father used to commit suicide, Butterfly stabs herself.

The child asks a series of pertinent questions about marriage and opera, such as "Mother, why / would a Japanese and an American / sing Italian at each other? / Why would he get married and not stay? / And have a child he'd leave." The eight-year-old instinctively perceives the clash of two cultures, but, more importantly, Puccini's plot echoes the speaker's situation, the contrast between two cultures. Although the opera exposes the American Pinkerton, who abandons his prepubescent Japanese bride and then returns married to an American woman, the child's questions emphasize the hybridity of language. The Puccini characters sing in Italian, and the mother and daughter practice Italian. The stanza ends with, "But

I'm not asking her." However, the words "*That's men //* is her silent, bitter answer; was always half / her lesson plan."

More importantly, the child begins to understand the relationships of men and women, husbands and wives. With a painterly touch, the mother teaches her daughter Italian and the meaning of absence because men leave. In the fourth stanza, Salter introduces the Star-Spangled Banner and later writes, "*O say can you see*," and the child acknowledges that "yes, now I can . . . I see you meant / like Butterfly to tie a blindfold over / a loved child's eyes." Salter writes "Libretto" from a child's point of view but occasionally inserts an adult's perspective, too. Therefore, the mother, like Butterfly, shields her daughter as Butterfly did her son. For the speaker, this act represents "the saving veil of Art" as the mother "brushed them [Daddy and her brothers] from the shot." Although Salter sets "Libretto" in the living room filled with household items such as a turntable, drapes, and sewing machine, the intellectual sparring between the daughter and the mother transcends the domestic space.

When she completes the text, the child recognizes that "it is only a story." However, the adult poet writing from an eight-year-old self knows that "what's in store / for you [the mother], divorce and lonely death, / is still distant" in 1962. Mother figures appear in several of Salter's poems throughout her career. She eulogizes her mother in "Dead Letters." In the future, the mother and daughter share "nights to come / of operas to dress up for," "silly jokes," "shopping," and "days at home / when nothing is very wrong." The adult narrator reflects on when her "poor, dear parents" made her press her "ear against the wall / for stories that kept" her "near and far, / and because the hurt was beautiful." Thus, through metonymy, the discord between the parents' dissonance symbolizes the cultural clash in the opera.

In constructing this *Madame Butterfly*–type tale, the narrator asks, "Forgive whatever artifice lies / in my turning you into characters / in my own libretto—one sorry hand / hovering above the quicksand / of a turn-table in a house in Detroit / I can't go back to otherwise." Salter's poem is an unremitting negotiation of identity. Puccini's opera, sung in Italian, contributes to the child's identity formation process. The migrant position of the mother inscribes a sort of agency for the daughter who asks for forgiveness, turning her parents into personae. Ultimately, the narrator confesses that she "can't go back" to that house in Detroit even though, by artifice learned by her artistic mother, Salter transports the reader to that moment.

In an earlier collection, *Unfinished Painting*, Salter eulogizes her mother in "Dead Letters." She even dedicates the book to the memory of Lormina

Paradise Salter (1924–1983). Additionally, the jacket cover art is an unfinished painting by Salter's mother, which depicts a child with short brown hair and a burnt red garment, but the rest remains incomplete. The child's right hand rests on the back of a chair. The background includes a brown wall and beige drapes. In my interview, Salter explained that her mother took art classes in New York, and "by that time [Christmas Day, 1947], she had already done her work sketching wounded soldiers in hospitals for the USO. She had also done some fashion sketching for ads for Bonwit Teller . . . and some of those drawings got into the *NY Times.*" In discussing the frame poems of *Unfinished Painting*, "The Rebirth of Venus" and "Unfinished Painting," Post explains, "if a wide-angle survey of ekphrasis in Salter points to the subject's ubiquity as a sign of our visually saturated times and selves—ekphrasis might not be imperially ambitious, just everywhere possible—only a close-up view can reveal the special, nuanced hold the topic has in her poetry" (2009, 168). As an artist/poet, Salter understands the connection between her mother's artistic talents and her own. In a sense, *Unfinished Painting* represents the mother who, like the fictional one in "Dead Letters," remains in her works and various other things. Indeed, the poet-narrator emphasizes this relationship through artwork, dedication, and poems. Like "Libretto," "Dead Letters" includes *Italianità* and memory that connects three generations of women: grandmother, mother, and daughter.

The poem "Dead Letters" is the title of the fourth and final section of the collection and is the longest, broken into five sections. The narrator starts, "*Dear Mrs. Salter: Congratulations! You* / (*no need to read on—yet I always do*) / *may have won the sweepstakes, if you'll send*" (61). Junk mail addressed to the deceased mother functions as the device that moves the narrative forward because of all Americans' commonplace experience of receiving unwanted mail, especially in the 1980s. Additionally, the daughter and mother share the salutation: "*Mrs. Salter.*" The poet struggles with the fact that "I never saw you dead—you simply vanished, / your body gone to Science, as you wished" (61). Since the mother requested a whole-body donation, the family and, in this case, the daughter do not have the opportunity to mourn the loss. There are three parts to a traditional Catholic funeral: 1) the reception of the body, 2) the Church funeral, and 3) the committal at the cemetery. Since the narrator never saw her mother's dead body, she has no closure. The speaker confesses, "I was the one to send you there" (61). However, the daughter-poet will only receive the mother's cremated remains several months later. Salter intersperses excerpts from several letters addressed to her mother: "*Dear Patient: It's been three years since your eyes* / *were checked*" (61). The narrator, who did not *see* the mother's body, highlights the importance of vision. The eye exam reminder notice reinforces the mother's deteriorating health and the effect of time and memory because she "couldn't bear to see" her mother's "cherished face with more / death in it than was there five days before" (61). The stanza closes with a daydream of a "forwarding text / *Dear Mrs. Salter's Daughter: You are next*" (61). The speaker begins and ends with her connection to the mother and the cyclical nature of life because the narrator will soon follow her mother to the grave.

In section II, the narrator continues struggling with the residue of memory: "When I try to concentrate / on who you were, / images of you blur / and pulsate" (62). This line connects with section I, where the optometrist sends a notice to Lormina informing her that three years have passed since her last exam. However, in this section, the poet experiences blurry vision. Perhaps this pulsating blurriness springs from the daughter squeezing her eyes so tight while concentrating on recollections from the past that when she opens them, she blurs her vision. The reader learns that the mother varied from "four to fourteen, / not progressively, / but back and forth again: / testaments to Treatment / after Treatment" (62). Even though the mother taught herself "to live / with less and less," the narrator acknowledges, "I've / turned up happy photographs—// of the ruby-lipsticked girl / (in black-and-white, but I can tell) / on your wedding day" (62–63). In the personal interview, Salter informed me that her mother married on Christmas Day, 1947. The black-and-white picture represents happier times for the mother (especially when considering the narrative of "Libretto") and the daughter rummaging through old stuff. The ruby lips full of life contrast sharply with the dead mother whose body "vanished." One picture of her mother in the hallway has a "gilt barometer." That piece of *Italianità* from the narrator's childhood resonates with many other Italian families with wood or antique gold barometers hung in a prominent position in the house. For the narrator, in-betweenness lurks everywhere: life and death, ruby red and black and white, old and new, happy and sad.

Once again, in section III, the daughter bridges the photographs' happier times with family meals. The poet muses, "Memory drifts / back to well-set tables shared at home—/ those animated dinners you would chair" (64). In both poems, the narrator depicts the mother as vital, presiding over the dining table. During the mother's "Salter Seminars," the daughter admits, "you liked to shock / us with the heedless, vocal sweep / of your opinions: on the Catholic Church" (64). Again, the poet, knowingly or not, sprinkles elements of *Italianità* throughout these two poems. At this moment, the narrator names the Catholic Church and adds a parenthetical aside: "(you hate it, so you think—hate it so much / you'll find a slow way back)." Thus, her mother returns to Catholicism, reinforcing the traumatic moment the daughter learns that the mother's body has disappeared. Friends and family cannot partake in the reception of the body, which typically occurs on the eve of the funeral.

Most importantly, in section III, the daughter introduces another woman, Maria Giuseppe Cazzato. Salter's maternal grandparents are Francesco Paolo Paradiso (anglicized to Paradise) and Maria Giuseppe Cazzato, born in Puglia in a tiny village named Castellaneta. Lormina Paradise is their daughter, and Salter is Lormina's. In a remembered conversation between Mary Jo and Lormina, the mother asks, " 'Can you remember Grandma's laugh?' " The daughter interrupts, " 'I can't.' " However, in a matter of moments, the poet writes, "having voiced the fear, / immediately am able: / it sounded like a baby xylophone, / thrown down a flight of stairs" (66). In the next stanza, the mother reaches into her "magic purse" for a snapshot of her mother and replies, "Here, it's yours" (66). Thus, the grandmother and mother reappear ten years later in Salter's *A Kiss of Space* (1999). In "Libretto," Lormina sews drapes and curses at "her own / mother's machine" (22). Three generations of Cazzato/Paradise women demonstrate how language and memory connect all three.

The mother is dying from cancer by section IV: "your own forever- / unrecorded voice cut short by cancer" (66). In the hospital with family, the daughter writes, "Shrunken and old, collapsible, / head in my lap, you start up in alarm: / 'Mary Jo—I think I'm ill' " (67). Salter renders this traumatic biographical memory to the page where the narrator experiences this confessional moment. The daughter wonders if "it's too late to apologize; / but that you could find it in you still / to register surprise—/ that *you'd* hope to be well . . . / It kept you alive, of course" (67). Thus, these fragments of the departed mother embody all the daughter has left.

Section V reveals that the daughter possesses more than just memories; she retains some physical items of her mother's, such as the philodendron. The narrator returns with repeating lines of seeing: "If you could see your daughter, no green thumbs . . . If you could see your daughter: that refrain / twists like a crimpling weed, a vine of pain" (68). However, the poet realizes that "a crimpling weed" "intertwines forever" (68). The daughter removes plants from her mother's room: "nearly a year ago now, poinsettias / of that wizened, stricken Christmas / you floated through five days before the end" (68). Lormina Paradise Salter dies on Friday, December 30, 1983, thirty-six years and five days after her marriage on Christmas Day, 1947. In the last five lines, the narrator writes, "But I can't let them [philodendrons] go, /

not yet; and granted more time to tend / a growing tenderness, I send //
more letters, Mother—these despite / the answers you can't write" (68).
Henry Taylor Faith acknowledges that "one of the powers that keeps these
poems ["Dead Letters"] afloat is the tone of acceptance that accompanies
grief" (8). Indeed, in the last four lines, Salter employs full end rhyme,
perhaps to signify the permanence of her mother's death. The daughter-poet
celebrates an artist's life, one who cannot reply to letters she still receives
even in death. As an artist/poet, the daughter can "recapture // moments
before they're over" (65). Her mother's memory endures in the mail, doctor
appointment reminders, and the philodendron.

In a later collection, *Sunday Skaters*, dedicated to her father and
brothers, Salter again meditates on her mother. In "Poppies," the narrator
reflects on Pierre Auguste Renoir's *Path Rising through Tall Grass, circa 1875*
(see fig. 3.1), "hung / as a shimmering emblem of home" (39). The speaker

Figure 3.1. Painting by Pierre Auguste Renoir, *Path Rising through Tall Grass,
circa 1875* (*Chemin montant dans les hautes herbes, vers 1875*) (RF 2581). *Source*:
Reproduced by permission of the Musée d'Orsay, Paris. https://www.photo.rmn.fr/
archive/18-502020-2C6NU0AKQZGDX.html).

describes "the child who led the way . . . home // through a heedless field of green and yellow" (39). A few lines later, "just steps behind the child was a woman . . . the red / parasol behind her head / a medal of motherhood, a halo," and the narrator surmises, "the two black-clad / figures descending from the crest / of the hill. Grandparents" (39–40). Thus, the Renoir painting scene merges with the child's imagination, her mother and father, and possibly her grandparents.[7]

In section II, the narrator employs the painting as a "postcard" that "leads [her] back / to a television screen" (40). The speaker acknowledges that "I would have been six or seven, / now old enough that a cold // meant no school, and I lay / in my parents' bed like a queen. / Mother was out in the garden" (40). Thunder sounded, and her "mother / in a long, old-fashioned dress" hurried "out [of] the gate, // a mammoth black umbrella / above her averted face" (41). Her mother's image connects with the "that dot was her big black parasol" (40). Interestingly, the previous line mentions grandparents, but in the following line, the child narrator associates the black parasol with "her." Again, based on the close reading of "Dead Letters," the child might imagine her grandmother, Maria Giuseppe Cazzato, and her grandfather, Francesco Paolo Paradiso (later anglicized to Paradise). Thus, the speaker combined the painting, the unknown film, and the mother "into a dream, // and played it over and over / until it became one seamless / parable that arched / from parasol to umbrella" (42). In the in-between state of sleep and wakefulness, the narrator moves between the artist's rendering of a landscape contrasted with the mother's actual garden. Even the juxtaposition between the parasol and the mother's substantial black umbrella blurs the memories.

The dreamlike quality stresses the importance of vision for the poet. The ekphrastic elements continue with an extended meditation on the situation juxtaposed with the work of art. Salter incorporates narrative descriptions of Renoir's painting and connects the natural scene to a postcard, a television screen, and her mother's garden. In the last twelve lines, Salter joins the moment of spreading her mother's ashes with Renoir's *Path Leading through Tall Grass*:

> You—you've now been gone
> ten years; been dead longer
> than I'd lived when I learned
> you'd leave forever.
> Ten years ago, beneath

> the shelter of some tree
> or other, as you'd asked,
> your child stood with an urn
> of the ashes, and scattered them
> to the breeze, as if a random
> handful might crop up
> in the field as poppies. (42)

Salter will eulogize her mother again ten years later. In other poems, the reader learns that the mother's last wish was to be cremated when she dies, and here the child obeys her mother's wish. The narrator revisits the traumatic experience of the mother's death (December 30, 1983) in "Dead Letters" (1989) and "Poppies" (1994).

In her first collection, *Henry Purcell in Japan*, Salter opens with "For an Italian Cousin" and the words "*Mia cugina.*" But, more importantly, she includes a meditation on her grandmother, Maria Giuseppe Cazzato, with "Mary Cazzato, 1921." The narrator exclaims, "She's lovely—though the photograph / I've kept of her is not / of anyone I knew. Eighteen / back then, in nineteen twenty-one, / and in her rickrack headband, half- / flapper, maybe" (8). As she did in "Dead Letters," the ekphrastic focus on photographs started in 1985. In the second stanza, the poet places confidential material in parentheses: "(She'd had no thought of us at all; / and yet would make us feel // *we* were the reason *she* was here—/ as if, engendered, love's / the engenderer)" (8). The artist plays on the meaning of engender; yes, the grandmother begets children and grandchildren, but the granddaughter's love produces this ekphrastic poem.

Based on the poem's logic, the picture dates from 1921, but the grandmother was eighteen at the time; however, for the narrator, "she was born, for me, / sometime around nineteen sixty." As the mother/daughter pair in "Libretto," this granddaughter remembers Mary Cazzato playing "My Bonnie Lies Over the Ocean" on the piano. The melancholic exile of Charles Edward Stewart lingers in section II where the poet muses, "Pregnant with our deaths (a germ / within the mind suspects), / we carry their date and kind with us / like the embryo's blind sex, / regardless of our ignorance, / for a life's full term" (9). Rather than begin with life, the narrator assigns death with pregnancy because Mary Cazzato carries an embryo "for a life's full term." The implication is that the poet's lineage germinates with the grandmother and continues with the mother to the daughter-poet.

The second stanza presents the opposite; the narrator contemplates, "Still blooming, the bouquet that winds / and spills over her tiny hands / seems then to tumble out // of the frame wherein, expressionless, / she evenly can face / everything she's yet to lose" (9). The poet cultivates gardening imagery developed from the blooming bouquet, a synecdoche symbolizing "everything she's yet to lose." The granddaughter interjects family memories: "the suicide of the brother . . . the freak / event that turned a shock // of her hair, at thirty-two, all white" (9). Then "the skidding truck that killed . . . Angela Paradise, her child" (9). The recollections of her brother's suicide and her daughter's death scatter in the wind of memory. Still, the narrator uses the picture frame to eulogize the grandmother and her loved ones. However, the poem turns in the last two lines; the poet acknowledges that "She lost two in her grief: Grandmother / had been carrying another," which is Mary Jo Salter's mother: Lormina Paradise Salter. Section II ends with the revelation that although two have died, another life grows inside her. Thus, the poet finds partial consolation in the possibility of renewal. Like the garden metaphor in "Poppies," Salter places hope in the case of regeneration found in a germ or blooming bouquet.

In section III, the narrator ponders, "I was barely older, when she died, / than the girl whose portrait clicks / shut like a coffin in my palm. / Black velvet's on the other side" (10). Again, the poet uses a photograph to root the scene in a specific moment. The portrait allows for "a recurrent dream" where Lormina "winks" at the narrator, and together they "climb long stairs . . . to a sunny room I'd / swear I knew—those olive chairs; / dropped in a crystal vase, a rose. / I'd forgotten that she's dead" (10). The poet again repeats the use of flower imagery to connect sections II and III. The bouquet becomes a rose. The grandmother's portrait that "clicks shut" lined with black velvet symbolizes death, yet she returns to her granddaughter in "a recurrent dream."

In the third stanza, the poet acknowledges, "vacantly her eyes / hold nothing of my own surprise. / Shrugging ('What did you suppose?'), / she's gone—and leaves behind a locket / enfolding one last secret" (10). The locket represents another type of womb-like image, the grandmother "pregnant with our deaths"; the pendant aids in the poet's creation of this poem. Salter uses enjambment to conclude the poem. The eighteenth line has no period and propels the reader to the climax: "between two views the living can't / connect: the thoughtless stare / of the girl, and the perpetual black / unblinking regarding, her. / There's never time to call her back—/

to ask her what she meant" (10). The black velvet becomes "the perpetual black / unblinking." Although Mary Cazzato enters the narrator's dreams, the poet-narrator cannot "ask her what she meant." The grandmother remains silent, and yet Salter's eulogy gives her voice. The narrative descriptions of the photograph, the embryo, the bouquet, and the locket give life to the narrator's *nonna* on the page, but each item, or memory of each thing, cannot speak. Like "Dead Letters" or "Poppies," the poet unearths remembrances of the mother and grandmother as if she can replant and cultivate those recollections. Still, like the philodendrons or roses, they will bloom and eventually die.

Diaspora, exile, and migrancy are changing the idea of literary productions such as Salter's "Libretto," "Dead Letters," "Poppies," and "Mary Cazzato, 1921." Indeed, Salter's maternal grandparents emigrated from southern Italy, specifically Castellaneta, Puglia. Her mother, Lormina Paradise, a second-generation Italian American, was born in Lansing, Michigan. However, the artist (Lormina) and the poet (Mary Jo) form new identities through their art/poetry. In the poems, the daughter narrator attempts to reconcile the different parts of her identity represented by her mother and, to a certain degree, the grandmother. Salter cultivates poetic personas of her *mamma* and *nonna* and works *Italianità* such as Puccini into the narratives. Additionally, the motherly figures reappear throughout the poet's oeuvre. She eulogizes them, sometimes using the ekphrastic tradition to concentrate on a picture or painting (Renoir's *Path Rising through Tall Grass*), meditating on the mother or grandmother's life. Identity is liminal, a negotiation of both. A hybrid identity has to translate differing cultures to survive. Thus, the third-generation Salter, as the narrator of "Libretto," "Dead Letters," "Poppies," and "Mary Cazzato, 1921," contends with a strong maternal presence that continues long after death.

Notes

1. "Her second book, *Unfinished Painting* (1989), was a Lamont Selection for the most distinguished second volume of poetry published that year, *Sunday Skaters* (1994) was nominated for a National Book Critics Circle Award, and *Open Shutters* was a *New York Times* Notable Book of the Year." Mary Jo Salter. n.d. https://www.poetryfoundation.org/poets/mary-jo-salter.

2. Mary Jo Salter. n.d. https://poets.org/poet/mary-jo-salter.

3. In "A Poem of One's Own," Salter also lists Shakespeare, Auden, and Frost (30).

4. Some articles published on Salter include Henry Taylor's "Faith and Practice: The Poems of Mary Jo Salter" (2000), Jonathan F. S. Post's "Ekphrasis and the Fabric of the Familiar in Mary Jo Salter's Poetry" (2009), and Jay Rogoff's "The Aesthetics of Contemporary Sonnet Sequences: The Examples of Salter and Muldoon" (2010).

5. See Gay Talese, "Where Are the Italian-American Novelists?," *New York Times*, March 14, 1993.

6. See Dana Gioia et al., "Where Are the Italian American Novelists?," *Italian Americana* 12, no. 1 (1993): 7–37.

7. Jonathan Post, "Ekphrasis and the Fabric of Familiar in Mary Jo Salter's Poetry" (2009), 164–79.

Works Cited

Albright, Carol Bonomo, and Joanna Clapps Herman. 2008. *Wild Dreams: The Best of Italian Americana*. New York: Fordham University Press.

Bacigalupo, Massimo. 2004. "A Note on Mary Jo Salter's America." *RSA Journal: Rivista Di Studi Nord-Americani* 15–16: 145–48.

Barolini, Helen. 1985. *The Dream Book: An Anthology of Writings by Italian American Women*. New York: Schocken Books.

Corn, Alfred. 1985. "The Poet as Private Eye." *New Republic* 192 (15): 40–41.

DePietro, Thomas. 1993. "Where Are the Italian American Novelists?" *Italian Americana* 12 (1): 22–27.

Durante, Francesco, Robert Viscusi, and James J. Periconi. 2014. *Italoamericana: The Literature of the Great Migration, 1880–1943*. New York: Fordham University Press.

Gabaccia, Donna R. 2000. *Italy's Many Diasporas*. Seattle: University of Washington Press.

Gambino, Richard. 1993. "The Need to Reframe Talese's Question." *Italian Americana* 12 (1): 30–37.

Gillan, Maria Mazziotti, and Jennifer Gillan. 1994. *Unsettling America: An Anthology of Contemporary Multicultural Poetry*. New York: Penguin.

Gioia, Dana. 1993. "Low Visibility: Thoughts on Italian American Writers." *Italian Americana* 12 (1): 7–15.

———, Eugene Mirabelli, Albert DiBartolomeo, Rita Ciresi, Thomas DePietro, and Daniela Gioseffi. 1993. "Where Are the Italian American Novelists?" *Italian Americana* 12 (1): 7–37.

———. 1997. "What Is Italian American Poetry?" In *Beyond The Godfather: Italian American Writers on the Real Italian American Experience*, edited by A. Kenneth Ciongoli, Jay Parini, and Ferdinando Salleo, 167–74. Hanover, NH: University Press of New England.

Guida, George. 2007. "Ink in the Streets: Dana Gioia, the New Poetry Wars, and Italian American Poetry." *Italian Americana* 25 (2): 222–27.

Hammer, Langdon. 2017. "Sound and Sense." *American Scholar* 86 (3): 54.

Kaufman, Ellen. 2008. "A Phone Call to the Future: New and Selected Poems." *Library Journal* 133 (7): 89.

Knight, Brenda. 1996. *Women of the Beat Generation: The Writers, Artists and Muses at the Heart of a Revolution.* Berkeley, CA: Conan.

Lehman, David. 1990. "The Not-So-New Formalism." *Michigan Quarterly Review* 29 (1): 140–44.

Mary Jo Salter. n.d. https://www.poetryfoundation.org/poets/mary-jo-salter.

Mary Jo Salter. n.d. https://poets.org/poet/mary-jo-salter.

Miller, Christanne. 1989. "Unfinished Painting (Book)." *Library Journal* 114 (5): 73.

Post, Jonathan F. S. 2009. "Ekphrasis and the Fabric of Familiar in Mary Jo Salter's Poetry." In *In the Frame: Women's Ekphrastic Poetry from Marianne Moore to Susan Wheeler*, edited by Jane Hedley et al., pp. 164–79. Newark: University of Delaware Press.

Preminger, Alex, and Terry V. F. Brogan. 1993. *The New Princeton Encyclopedia of Poetry and Poetics.* Edited by Alex Preminger and T. V. F. Brogan. Princeton, NJ: Princeton University Press.

Pucelli, Rodolfo. 1955. *Anthology of Italian and Italo-American Poetry.* Boston: Bruce Humphries.

Renoir, Pierre Auguste. *Path Rising through Tall Grass, circa 1875 (Chemin montant dans les hautes herbes, vers 1875)* (RF 2581). Painting. Musée d'Orsay, Paris. https://www.photo.rmn.fr/archive/18-502020-2C6NU0AKQZGDX.html.

Rogoff, Jay. 2010. "The Aesthetics of Contemporary Sonnet Sequences: The Examples of Salter and Muldoon." *Literary Imagination: The Review of the Association of Literary Scholars and Critics* 12 (3): 335–43.

Salter, Mary Jo. 1999. *A Kiss in Space: Poems.* New York: Knopf.

———. 2008. *A Phone Call to the Future: New and Selected Poems.* New York: Knopf.

———. 1991. "A Poem of One's Own." *New Republic* 204 (9): 30–34.

———. 1985. *Henry Purcell in Japan.* New York: Knopf.

———. 2013. *Nothing by Design: Poems.* New York: Knopf.

———. *Open Shutters: Poems.* New York, Knopf.

———. 2019. Personal interview. 3 March.

———. 1994. *Sunday Skaters: Poems.* New York: Knopf.

———. 2017. *The Surveyors: Poems.* New York: Knopf.

———. 1989. *Unfinished Painting: Poems.* New York: Knopf.

Talese, Gay. 1993. *Where Are the Italian-American Novelists? New York Times*, March 14, 1993.

Tamburri, Anthony Julian, Paolo Giordano, and Fred L. Gardaphé. 2000. *From the Margin: Writings in Italian Americana.* West Lafayette, IN: Purdue University Press.

Taylor, Henry. 2000. "Faith and Practice: The Poems of Mary Jo Salter." *Hollins Critic* 37 (1): 1–18.
Viscusi, Robert, and Dana Gioia. 1994. "Where to Find Italian American Literature." *Italian Americana* 12 (2): 267–77.

4

Queering Italian American Poetry

Peter Covino's *Cut Off the Ears of Winter*: Psychoanalysis, Performativity, Language

RYAN CALABRETTA-SAJDER

Boasting a long evolution with a rich poetic history, Italian American studies traces its roots in the lyric as far back as 1805.[1] Even though this celebrated history extends to the beginning of the nineteenth century, the scholarly corpus analyzing the genre has yet to receive critical acclaim. This is not solely because of a lack of creative voices within the genre, rather, the field celebrates a plethora of talented poets, many have yet to be truly discovered. As I will demonstrate, a more thorough examination of Italian American poetry is important because the opus is rich and vast, while the scholarship, particularly in quantity, is lacking. In this vein, this contribution aims first and foremost to be a position piece that considers the current state of gendered Italian American poetic voices. Consequently, through analyzing the contribution of noted poet Peter Covino, one of the numerous Italian American lyric voices worth serious critical attention from scholars not only within the realm of Italian American studies but also beyond, this chapter both illustrates the significance of considering these "other" poetic voices and demonstrates the foundational role Covino's opus assumes within the field through applying psychoanalytic and queer theory.

This chapter aims to consider the significance of Italian American queer authors. Initially, it recognizes the long-standing importance Italian

American poetry has within Italian American studies. Next, I explore the volumes dedicated to studying Italian American LGBTQ authors and their influence on the field at large. The majority of this contribution, however, examines the poetry of one homosexual Italian American poet, Peter Covino, and his collection *Cut Off the Ears of Winter* (2005). By exploring Covino's poetry through a Lacanian lens, I argue that the narrator never fully develops sexually from a psychoanalytic reading, blocking any acceptance of his true homosexuality. Moreover, by applying queer theory, I demonstrate how Covino's poetry breaks from the traditional Italian American poetic genre, exploring the unique experiences that have shaped his literary voice.

Queer Italian American Poetry?

Noted in his astute piece "What is Italian-American Poetry?," Italian American poet and scholar Dana Gioia argues that the first evidence of Italian American poetry surfaced through Mozart's librettist, the Venetian author Lorenzo da Ponte (1805),[2] yet "it took another century and a half for enough significant authors to appear to claim the attention of the English-speaking public."[3] His piece delineates noteworthy moments in the early evolution of what can be coined Italian American poetry, underscoring, for example, the contributions of Emanuel Carnevali (1897–1942).[4] Considering a starting date of 1805, one assumes that Italian American poetry would be a field saturated with rich research; unfortunately, this is not the case.

Ironically, one of the earliest works devoted to Italian American poetry, *La parola transfuga: scrittori italiani in America*, was published in Italian in 2003 by Luigi Fontanella (Cadmo) and republished in English as *Migrating Words: Italian Writers in the United States* (Bordighera Press, 2012). Dedicated to Italian American poet Pascal D'Angelo, Fontanella explores the early poetic voice of the genre, focusing on Arturo Giovannitti (1884–1959), Carnevali (1897–1942), and D'Angelo (1894–1932); and more contemporary poets such as Joseph Tusiani (1924–2020) and Giose Rimanelli (1925–2018). His study concludes with Alfredo de Palchi (1926–2020).[5] His manuscript remains fundamental in examining Italian American poetry, exploring the relationship these poets maintained in the United States and Italy, yet 2003 remains rather late for Italian American studies to celebrate its poets. Fontanella's publication remains one of the only scholarly works dedicated to Italian American poetry.

In the controversial article "Where Are the Italian American Novelists?," Gay Talese probes the status of the Italian American novel by challenging how active, or rather lacking, the genre is. Although disputed by many scholars after its publication, Dana Gioia included, I suggest that poetry has not seen the same situation; there are plenty of Italian American poets, even LGBTQ poets.[6] The void within the field is the critical reception to these talented authors yearning to be heard and explored critically.

The first volume dedicated to the study of lesbian and homosexual male Italian American authors is *FUORI: Essays by Italian/American Lesbians and Gays* (1996).[7] Indeed, as early as 1996, Mary Jo Bona's contribution, a scholarly introduction of sorts, "Gorgeous Identities: Gay and Lesbian Italian/American Writers," remains a foundational text of gender studies criticism within Italian American studies. In her piece, Bona explores the similarities between cultural and gender studies, claiming that both "resist a unitary definition" (1). The essays within the volume, she argues, "suggest the writers' continual renegotiation with their ethnic and sexual identities, less out of a sense of frustration or confusion, and more out of an appreciation of the possibilities of richness within their Italian/American and lesbian/gay cultures" (1). She additionally highlights that "the writers in this volume are insistently aware of the intersection between ethnicity and class, ethnicity and community, and ethnicity and Catholicism," illustrating the importance of intersectionality when analyzing aspects of gender and cultural studies (1–2). Bona also refers to the theories of Eve Sedgewick and Judith Butler while examining the autobiographical essays' *bildungsroman*-esque narratives. Indirectly, Bona also calls attention to the significance of writing as a means of dealing with one's *Italianità* while being gay in a family and/or community that finds difficulty in understanding—much less accepting—this kind of difference.

Jumping ahead many years, the chronologically third volume dedicated entirely to gay Italian Americans is *Our Naked Lives: Essays from Gay Italian-American Men* (2013).[8] In 1999, however, three Italian American authors organized a robust anthology titled *Hey Paesan! Writing by Lesbians and Gay Men of Italian Descent*. In the introduction, Giovanna (Janet) Capone, Denise Nico Leto, and Tommi Avicolli Mecca argue that queer Italian American authors face more difficulties than their heterosexual counterparts: "if our [Italian/Sicilian-descended lesbians and gay men] writing has explicit queer content and explicit ethnic content, we face an additional layer of invisibility and prejudice in the publishing world. Consequently, few images of us exist in literature" (1). Not only have Italian Americans at large found challenges in fitting into society, but the prejudice against the community additionally infiltrates the publishing world.

As noted, queer Italian Americans face further hardship. Their struggle is heightened, but the lack of comfort found within the queer community and family life also produces little encouragement or ease: The collection is rich, with more than forty creative contributions from about thirty-five gay or lesbian Italian American authors. There are roughly seventeen poems by ten poets. The poems address three main themes: reclaiming cultural identity, coming out, and mixed identities. These three main sections, which also serve as organizational themes, focus on various moments of self-development and realization of the individual. These authors' experiences stand out for the numerous obstacles placed in their paths and their abilities to overcome them and feel united. One of the most noteworthy poets from the collection, Vittoria repetto, recently passed away in April 2020 from complications of Covid-19. Having no living family in the United States, when she was found dead, her body went to the morgue, where it remained at length until it could finally be identified. Fellow poet and scholar George Guida learned of her passing and initiated a collection for a scholarship to be offered in her name in collaboration with IAWA and IASA. These are the real tales of many LGBTQIAA+ folx.[9]

Considering the publication date of *Hey Paesan!* and with no updated version of the anthology in sight, the representation of queer Italian American poets is truly lacking within the field of Italian American studies. Even within the worlds of academia and pedagogy, where many of these queer folx reside, no one has discussed an entire course dedicated to Queer Italian Americana.[10] The wealth of literary production exists in both formal and informal publications. Many Italian American poets who are now in their sixties and seventies have received little to no critical attention. Moreover, another generation of poetry has been born, including Annie Lanzillotto's *Schistsong* (2013) and *Hard Candy: Caregiving, Mourning, and Stage Light* and *Pitch Roll Yaw* (2018) and Nicole Santalucia and her three collections: *Because I Did Not Die* (2015), *Spoiled Meat* (2018), and *The Book of Dirt* (2020). Thus, it befalls the next generation of scholars to bring into light the contemporary queer Italian American poets. Recently, Italian Canadian author Licia Canton edited *Here & Now: An Anthology of Queer Italian-Canadian Writing* (2021). To date, *Here & Now* is the most inclusive and extensive representation of LGBTQ+ writings of Italian Canadians, with more than thirty creative contributions accompanied by a scholarly introduction by Domenic Beneventi, Michela Baldo, and Paolo Frascà. Volume 2 of this anthology was just released in 2024. This team is also finalizing a documentary film on Queer Italian Canadian authors and has already begun work on another revised anthology.

To return to the rhetorical questions of both Gioia and Talese, Italian American poets have been present for more than two hundred years. Although we may be slow at appreciation, Italian American poetry is expansive and rich, intertwined with diverse literary traditions. Exploring Covino's *Cut Off the Ears of Winter* is just the beginning of a pertinent scholarly inquiry.

The Case of Peter Covino

Although Gioia's article rather systemically summarizes the "state-of-affairs" for much Italian American poetry, his observations fall short when discussing queer Italian American poetry. In fact, Covino's poetic opus distinctly stands out from most of his predecessors' lyric voices, particularly in theme, but also in structure, as each poem intertwines reality with a personal discovery. Moreover, Covino's poetry places his reader into a traumatic world of familial abuse, both physical and emotional, present in many Italian American households for homosexual and heterosexual youth but rarely discussed or presented to the public. The poet's courage in confronting some of these themes is expressed with a gentleness of emotion only an empathetic professional can evoke. As Diana Fuss has argued, "Sexual identity may be less a function of knowledge than performance, or, in Foucauldian terms, less a matter of final discovery than perpetual reinvention," which rings true for Covino's poetry as we observe a cycle of sacrifice in pursuit of the *bildung* of the poet (Fuss in Bona 1996, 6–7). Particularly in *Cut off the Ears of Winter*, Covino's narrator cycles through moments of revelation, sacrifice, and rebirth.

Before entering Peter Covino's poetic production, it is necessary to provide background information to contextualize his voice more accurately. Covino was born in Sturno, Italy (Province of Avellino, Campania Region) and lived there as a young boy. He completed a bachelor of arts degree at Amherst College and continued his studies at Columbia University's School of Social Work, finishing a master of science degree. Then Covino dedicated more than a decade of his life to work in foster care, AIDS services, and youth and family services in New York City. While serving his community, he returned to school to complete a master's degree in creative writing from City College of New York. He later pursued a PhD in creative writing and English literature at the University of Utah, where he was a Steffensen Cannon Fellow. His unorthodox formation enhances his poetic voice thematically, touching on a wide range of topics in a manner diverse from most Italian American poets.

Currently, he is an associate professor at the University of Rhode Island, where he works in poetry, translation, and literary studies. He is the author of *Straight Boyfriend* (2001), which won the 2001 Frank O'Hare Chapbook Prize. He has published two collections of poetry, *Cut Off the Ears of Winter* (2005) and *The Right Place to Jump* (2012). *Cut Off the Ears of Winter* was a finalist for three literary awards: the 2007 Paterson Poetry Prize, the 2006 Publishing Triangle's Thom Gunn Award, and the 2005 W. S. Di Piero Bordighera Prize. It was also awarded the prestigious 2007 PEN/Joyce Osterweil Award, which celebrates the work of an emerging American poet. He is one of the founding editors of Barrow Street Press. He has published his translations, poetry, and scholarly articles in more than thirty journals and just published a bilingual translation of work by the acclaimed Italian poet Dario Bellezza, published in 2025 with the University of Wisconsin Press. Covino recently received the 2019 National Endowment for the Arts Translation Fellowship; he has also received fellowship grants and residencies from the Richmond American International University of London, the Nida Translation Institute, and the American Academy in Rome. Covino is an established poet; he is listed in the Encyclopedia of Contemporary LGBTA Literature of the United States. Practically no scholarly attention has been granted to his opus, including, surprisingly enough, the most recent and noteworthy anthology of Italian diasporic poetry, *Poets of the Italian Diaspora*: *A Bilingual Anthology*.

Poets of the Italian Diaspora is a foundational work for Italian American studies. Even though Covino's poetry touches on the concept of "in-betweenness," it is no surprise that Covino's work is not present. In his "Italian Roots in Global Soil" in *Poets of the Italian Diaspora*, Sante Matteo underscores a thematic vein that unifies most of the genre: "This anthology of poetry of the Italian diaspora reflects the tension between the centrifugal impulse to leave one's home and seek other lands of opportunity and the countervailing centripetal impulse to remain home-bound or to return homeward" (2014, xvi). As one of the most delicate and noted motifs, the sense of in-betweenness has also been an inherent theme throughout the Italian American canon. Poets of Italian descent have been struggling at length with the relationship between the *patria* and the adoption of the new homeland, and in the twenty-first century, this theme is no longer a novelty (Calabretta-Sajderer 2016, 358–69; Calabretta-Sajder 2021,165–98).

Although verified by numerous Italian American poets, the place and/or the concept of place for Covino does not function in the same manner as with his predecessors, opening the field up to a new generation of Italian diasporic or Italian American poets. Even if Covino was born and spent his early years in southern Italy, this concept of in-betweenness, at least in the sense of Italy versus the United States, is not dominant in this lyric voice from a traditional standpoint.[11] In fact, Covino's relationship with the *patria* is much more complex than that of other Italian American poets. In certain poems, Italy is perceived as the cause of family pain and grief; the narrator's father feels indebted to assist his family in Italy, only to be consistently swindled in the end.

Instead, in "Gorgeous Identities: Gay and Lesbian Italian/American Writers," Mary Jo Bona suggests that the in-betweenness most present in gay and lesbian Italian American literature stems from the fact that "the intersection between ethnicity and sexuality reinforces their ongoing negotiation and recreation that naming and identifying requires" (1996, 4). Bona's observation is particularly true of Peter Covino's journey to adulthood within the United States, which differs from that of most of his contemporaries for multiple reasons: in the familial abuse he experienced from his father and growing up homosexual in a migrant household, his first career in social work fighting to save youth, and his aiding those living with AIDS complications. Thus, the concept of Italian masculinity penetrates his collection, as the narrator's father asserts this emotional baggage on the narrator. Of course, the narrator accepts and pressures himself to adopt this toxic lifestyle in his own youth. To justly explore the themes present in *Cut Off the Ears of Winter,* this analysis includes a philological reading at times, as well as an interpretation from a psychoanalytic and queer theoretical approach.

Cut Off the Ears of Winter: Sacrifice, Reflection, Forgiveness?

The title of Covino's first collection refers to the artist Vincent van Gogh's "attempt to deflect the negativity he felt overwhelming," as Tamburri has already suggested (2009, 158). Yet the reference goes beyond the allusion to the complicated artist. The volume opens with an epigraph: "Then said Jesus unto Peter, Put up thy sword . . ." (John 18:11). Through this allusion, the poet offers a reference to the Passion of Christ, the moments right before Jesus is arrested and put on trial. According to the "Pulpit Commentary," this biblical moment narrates the agony felt throughout the New Testament.[12] The narrative of the final days of Jesus's life, as presented by the Catholic Church at least, invites believers to participate as much as possible in the journey Christ assumed as the savior of humanity; there exists a sense of sacrifice implicit within the Passion. A parallel situation simultaneously prevails in this collection, highlighted by the penultimate poem, "Tonight, the Survivor." The collection, divided into three sections, charts a movement toward self-realization and understanding, which attempts to make the narrator whole.

Additionally, a connection exists: Peter Covino and Peter the Apostle share their common first name and as such a metaphorical role as activist, but also survivor. Within the biblical narrative, we are reminded that in the Garden of Gethsemane, Peter the Apostle strikes the right ear of Malchus, a high priest's servant (John 18:10), and the missing piece of the biblical citation from the epigraph, which is Jesus's response, "the cup which my Father hath given me, shall I not drink it?" (John 18:11). This second half of the citation underscores the father-son connection within the trinity. This strained, yet crucial relationship between father and son is clearly present throughout the collection through the voice of the narrator and his father. Connecting back with the agony that van Gogh felt when cutting his own ear off, I argue that this collection's overall tone is that of anguish and torment. This feeling manifests itself through various themes directly related to the narrator's life and others more metaphoric in nature. In fact, this sense of hopelessness is manifested through the narrator's voice and the subjects within the opus. Thus, Covino is not afraid to honestly explore the narrator's emotional facets in a very raw sense. Psychoanalysis provides a compelling entry into Covino's work. Noted French psychoanalyst and psychiatrist Jacques Lacan studied various aspects and moments of child development. At the Fourteenth International Psychoanalytical Congress hosted at Marienbad in 1936, Lacan pitched his concept of the mirror stage, critical for the child developing into adulthood. Lacan argued: "The mirror stage is a phenomenon to which I assign a twofold value. In the first place, it has historical value as it marks a decisive turning point in the child's mental development. In the second place, it typifies an essential libidinal relationship with the body image" (*Some Reflections on the Ego*, 1953). Lacan's use of the term "historical value" refers to the development process of the mind within the child's confines, while structural value deals with the libido and its expression of body politics. Later in his career, Lacan tries to clarify the process of the mirror stage, claiming that the reflection in the mirror marks the moment when the individual can differentiate the "imaginary," a moment of narcissism that sets the stage for the fantasies of desire, from the "real," a "state of nature as a time of fullness or completeness that is subsequently lost through the entrance into language (Felluga 2011); self-identification of the Ego, thus, occurs in this stage of development. The Ego identity stage is when the child can experience his/her/their sense of who they are and act on that sense in a manner that offers continuity and sameness.

In this light, "Cut Off the Ears of Winter," the first poem of the collection, assumes the title of the collection. Through the narrator's use of negative images and a desperate tone, this opening poem sets the mood for the collection. The plethora of references to literary modernism, particularly the allusion to Italo Svevo's *La coscienza di Zeno* (1923),[13] requires the adoption of a Lacanian lens. The reference to Zeno, "This is my last dollar, / last cigarette, last match" (Covino 2007, 20–21), reminds the reader why and how Zeno contemplates his last cigarette before quitting. As Zeno discusses his life with his therapist, the doctor suggests he write as a means of psychoanalytic therapy, which the doctor apologies for in the preface. In this vein, the book assumes autobiographical characteristics, as it becomes a memoir presented as a stream-of-consciousness narrative. *Cut Off the Ears of Winter* also acts as a sort of autobiography of the author, as previously suggested. Of course, the irony with Zeno is his immediate belief in being cured, as he continually has another "last cigarette"; a similar sentiment exists with "our" Zeno-esque narrator.

The repetition of the word "last," which occurs a total of four times in the opening poem, three in the final two lines, draws the reader's attention to a finality as alluded to within the poem's title, as Christ's final days on earth. The attention paid to the adjective "last" therefore attempts to bring closure to the poem, which is full of chaos as experienced by Peter the Apostle when he denies Christ three times before the cock crows. Peter the Apostle knew of the prophecy and insisted that Christ would be wrong, yet he could not defeat his own psyche and failed both himself and his appreciation for the Savior; pride cometh before the fall. Yet, in this early poem, our narrator is much less confident; he accepts his fate as is and does not yet long for the Lacanian *I* in the process of development. At this stage, he does not separate from the mirror, as he has not formed his own language.

The chaos presented in the poem is external to the narrator. The narrator describes the difficulty of life outside in the neighborhood: "where rubble-strewn streets / are covered in dust from remodeling," or "a chain gang of transvestite prostitutes / litters the front yard—the Police Station / next door also on fire, burning," (Covino 2007, 4–5, 14–16). These peripheral situations have poisoned the narrator's ears and tainted his life. The confusion of the external world tries to cloud the internal situation of the narrator. Yet his focus remains on him—and the simple things: "my last dollar, / last cigarette, last match" (Covino 2007, 20–21), small possessions will ensure his survival from day to day or even block out the world that his ears absorb. Even without hearing, the reader experiences the private thoughts of the narrator.

The poem's organization—beginning with the narrator's personal life, moving to the societal life within the neighborhood, and finally ending on the personal—creates a microcosm. Or rather, the narrator attempts to draw a larger concept from a smaller one, closer to the narrator's own residence. The reference to "transvestite prostitutes" recalls a contemporary, "queer" allusion to Christ and Mary Magdalene as they convene in front of the burning police station, representing the collapse of equality and justice for all, another allusion to when Pontius Pilate allows the crowd to choose who should be let free, Jesus or Barabbas.

As already noted in the opening poem, suffering is at the heart of each section of *Cut Off the Ears of Winter*. One subtheme to which the author pays particular attention is the complications faced by victims of the AIDS epidemic. Of particular interest is "April 18th—Thinking About Lionel, Recently Dead of AIDS," which addresses the concept of surviving, as the narrator considers various people who almost made it, starting with Brook Berringer, a quarterback from Nebraska who was about to be selected in the NFL draft but suddenly died two days prior:

> And one day, toward the end, Lionel called me into his office,
>   which made me nervous
> because he never did that, and he said not to live in fear like
>   he has his whole life,
> *because sometimes when you take chances, you win.*
> And I can't help thinking what a fine name Brook Berringer
>   is—(Covino 2007, 28–33)

Suffering abounds in the poem, yet the concept is layered, beginning with Brook Berringer and his tragic story, which connects the narrator back to the narrator's childhood, "which is unusual since I love the white noise of football / reminds me of childhood. / and he almost made it to the pros.

I'm thinking about almost / making it" (7–9). The poet continues by discussing three specific situations in which one almost makes it: 1) the drug addict who breaks before a drug test, 2) the alcoholic who abandons his sobriety the night before his anniversary, and 3) Kate's dad, a drunk who left the family. These three examples of "almost" build the poem's tension as they demonstrate people who are in control of their destiny, at least to a certain extent. The poem both opens and closes on Berringer, who had no control over illness and death, not Lionel, who died of AIDS complications.

As a whole, Lionel has a spatially minimal role within the poem with only four lines, yet he holds a critical position in the title and a foundational role for the poem's overall meaning. The four-line stanza is composed of seven short clauses, along with clear use of enjambment, which creates a sense of anticipation for the reader:

> And one day, toward the end, Lionel called me into his office,
>   which made me nervous
> because he never did that, and he said not to live in fear like
>   he has his whole life,
> *because sometimes when you take chances, you win.*
> And I can't help thinking what a fine name Brook Berringer
>   is—(Covino 2007, 28–33)

Although the narrator never directly addresses the concept of AIDS, it is a motif often used during the AIDS epidemic within the subgenre of AIDS literature.[14] It is clear Lionel has "It."[15] He shares the universal advice not to live in fear, which an entire generation of gay men was forced to do.

These three critical lines underscore a queer reading of time, particularly because they are the only three in the poem relating to Lionel, one that few heteronormative folx could equally grasp. Regarding time, Elizabeth Freeman argues "that naked flesh is bound into socially meaningful embodiment through temporal regulation: binding is what turns mere existence into a form of mastery in a process I'll refer to as *chrononormativity*, or the use of time to organize individual human bodies toward maximum productivity" (3). In this citation and throughout *Time Binds: Queer Temporalities, Queer Histories*, Freeman demonstrates how chronological time, *chrononormativity*, and other aspects like gender performance consciously or unconsciously create repetition that endangers gender identity (4). The narrator breaks the typical chronological timeframe as he interweaves tales of one heterosexual man among the stories of various queer characters, one being Lionel, who is dying from complications of HIV. Moreover, the reader understands that once being infected with HIV during the eighties and early nineties, death became only a matter of time; time itself becomes a certain protagonist.

The ironic ending suggested as advice with the possibility of triumphing ends dismally with the reminder that Lionel, who died of AIDS complications, passed after Berringer reached his height. In this sense, the poem reminds the reader that sometimes fate just happens, and no matter how prepared or "good" we are, some things remain out of the individual's control. In fact, the reference to St. Agatha, patron saint of rape victims, breast cancer patients, and martyrs, among other groups, illustrates the sacrificial position Lionel assumes in the poem. Yet Lionel's character offers advice to the narrator, which he did not follow: "not to live in fear," demonstrating a Lionel who never fully developed in the Lacanian sense. Additionally, it proves how queer time cannot function in a heteronormative world. As Freeman has argued, "Zerubvael's 'hidden rhythms,' Bourdieu's 'habitus,' and Butler's 'gender performativity' all describe how repetition endangers identity, situating the body's supposed truth in what Nietzsche calls 'monumental time,' or static existence outside of the historical movement" (Freeman 2010, 4). Lionel's character is thus caught within "monumental time." Last, this advice serves the narrator on his journey, both through life and through the collection.

By setting up this series of examples, the reader is invited to reconsider the individuals' perspectives, especially because of the opening example, an athlete's death in a plane crash. Using an athlete, the poet creates a sense of homage, as people admire and are often inspired by famous personalities. Yet the poet initiates the poem with a somber tone about a tragic situation hitting national news, and he grabs our attention as he proceeds to offer other examples that are more mundane and personal. In mentioning Lionel suffering from AIDS complications, one would expect a much more noteworthy response, yet the focus largely remains on Berringer, forcing the queer character into a secondary position. Such examples ask the reader to create emotional bonds with the individuals and introduce situations that are unorthodox to the average reader. At first read, one may not be sympathetic to these characters within the lyric, yet the tone switch presented by "I'm thinking about almost / making it: / why" aligns the reader with the narrator to assume a more understanding or empathetic perspective.

Another theme that highlights Covino's unique poetic voice is his treatment of sexuality and the many manifestations it encompasses in both his life and work. In "At the Triple Treat Theatre," for example, we experience the thrill of visiting an adult bookstore, a place that does not respect typical definitions of time and space. The alliteration present in the title prepares us for what is to come. In fact, it is here that the poem offers a *bildung* for the narrator:

> I used to pretend I stumbled into the place
> casually, after a long day of shopping or
> I'd pretend I was drunk
> trying not to act drunk. (1–4)

In the opening stanza, the narrator demonstrates the embarrassment attached to his sexual identity. As the verb "pretend" underscores, the narrator shares signs of being closeted and, more so, hiding his homosexuality. This poem demonstrates the narrator's process of understanding his gayness in the only place he feels comfortable at this point in his development, maintaining his closetedness. In *Disidentifcations: Queers of Color and the Performance of Politics*, José Esteban Muñoz explains, "The cultural performers I am considering in this book must negotiate between a fixed identity disposition and the socially encoded roles that are available for such subjects" (1999, 6). In reality, this physical space is enticing because the narrator eventually feels somewhat able to express his sexual urges there.

In this initial stanza, the narrator demonstrates the difficulty of performing his homosexuality. Additionally, the poem illustrates the challenges of being homosexual and the shame that accompanies this reality within the private space of the bookstore. Our narrator is forced to perform his sexual interests within the confines of the closet. Considering the concept of "disidentification," the narrator lies to both himself and the reader, "I used to pretend I stumbled into this place / casually" (1–2), and we experience a moment of disidentification for the narrator, highlighted by his use of enjambment. The term "casually," broken by the line, highlights the level to which the narrator attempts to disassociate himself from the place. As noted by Jean Laplanche and Jean-Betrand Pontails in the following passage, the narrator attempts to adhere to a strict definition of "identification": "[A] psychological process whereby the subject assimilates an aspect, property or attribute of the other and is transformed, wholly or partially, after the model the other provides. It is by means of a series of identifications that the personality is constituted and specified."[16] Yet as much as the narrator attempts to assimilate into his homosexual self, he is blocked in the identification process, which Sedgewick claims "always includes multiple processes of identifying with. It also involves identification as against; but even did it not, the relations implicit in identifying with are, as psychoanalysis suggests, in themselves quite sufficiently fraught with intensities of incorporation, diminishment, inflation, threat, loss, reparation, and disavowal."[17] In this manner, Sedgewick calls for a reconsideration of the dynamics engaged with his identification. Muñoz, in agreeing with Sedgewick, brings the discourse to a higher level—disidentification. The reader is forced to analyze this process, which in Sedgewick's terminology would be treated as another type of closet, as evidenced in more detail later in the poem to blur the lines even more, as we consider the space of the theater.

As the poem continues, the narrator is so uncomfortable that he must calm himself down before fully entering and enjoying himself at the bookstore as noted: "catch my breath" and "waiting / for myself to stop teetering" (5–7). The sex-craved boy is so nervous that he must prop himself against the door and gather himself before he continues to pleasure himself in another way, rummaging "through the porno magazines, / in quick impulsive start-and-stop motions" (8–9), creating the visual representation of the young boy masturbating. His horny character additionally illustrates his closeted state as he withholds the ability of self-pleasure in home-life environments. Ironically, the narrator uses an interesting image through the simile, "as if someone were ready to fight me / for the only item of its kind / still on sale." (10–12). The simile here brings masturbation to the economic level, a rather untypical comparison, as the youth must pounce at the possibility as it presents itself.

The poem changes tone and time in the brief, three-line third stanza, beginning with the clause "But now," taking the reader to the present, full of sexual confidence and prowess:

> I strut into the place,
> with my head up (as if I owned it)
> and I do a beeline straight to the video booths. (13–15)

Stanza 3 introduces the narrator after he has embarked on his journey toward self-awareness as he moves from barely able to rustle through the pornography section while masturbating to knowing exactly what he wants and "beelining" to the video booths where he can privately enjoy himself.

In many regards, the fourth stanza represents the heart of the poem, as it offers a sort of reflection, punning on the concept of sleep. In this part of the poem, the narrator realizes his "growth," or lack thereof, and ponders it, as he notes that now he has become one of the people he used to encounter as a youth: "I have become that foul smelling / cubicle with the red light on" (17–18). The red light carries various connotations for the reader from the red light districts, otherwise known as "pleasure districts," which are neighborhoods or pieces of neighborhoods in an urban area with a large concentration of prostitution or sex-oriented business, including sex shops, strip clubs, and adult theatres.[18] When exploring the color red as "occupied space," the narrator becomes just a "foul smelling cubicle," underscoring a loss of personhood and respect for himself. He has become the incarnation of animalistic or prostitution sex, another image implicit by the "red light" of line 18.

The conceptualization of sexual mastery is enhanced within the stanza. In fact, we are introduced to the narrator's dreams, with its repetition three times, twice in the shape of an anaphora:

> And I dream I can hump as well
> as anyone; and I dream
> I can enjoy all that exciting humping.
> And I dream that I hump for twenty-four hours,
> (and it only costs 25 cents a minute).
> I'm always humping, in the bed,
> in the shower, in the jungle,
> on the grass, on the floor. (19–26)

In this latter part of the fourth stanza, the poet's sexual desires become clear. In the first mention of dreaming, the poet aims to be able to "last," to "make it" from a quantity perspective underscored by the "25 cents a minute," and initiates a type of mental competition throughout the stanza. In addition to being able to compete with other lovers, he hopes to enjoy it, which underscores a sense of doubt expressed within his dreams/actions/ desires. In the third repetition of the dream, the narrator yearns for longevity and stamina to continue in his private booth, as it not only is a good financial bargain, as suggested by the twenty-five cents a minute, but also adds to his manhood.

Lines 24–26 work together, intensifying the dream that has already been explored. These lines draw a parallel between the dream and the places/ spaces themselves. The locations where the narrator humps are noteworthy: He begins at home, in rather common spaces, and moves to much more exotic ones, such as the jungle or on the grass. These two places remove the narrator from his private booth and place him, metaphorically, in an erotic public space. However, because it is only a dream, the narrator's pleasure remains in the metaphorical closet; he expresses himself in a queer space that remains intangible to him. He concludes with humping on the floor, a space connotated as dirty and cheap. As the poem progresses with the various places mentioned, a sense of excitement, alluding back to line 21, becomes evident. In fact, in lines 24–26, the poet's use of rhythm, paired with the multiple commas, evokes the idea of ejaculation.

Yet the poem plays with the concept of sleep: "And you know, I'm really starting to get tired" (27). The poem's conclusion can be read through a funny or lighthearted tone; however, there seems to be a darker side embedded. How does this discomfort of "being tired" work for the narrator, for the reader? Should the reader laugh and move on to the next poem, or feel a sense of compassion for the narrator, *il sentimento del contrario,* as Luigi Pirandello argues? In *L'umorismo,* Pirandello differentiates between the comic and humor when describing the process of reflection. According to Pirandello, reflection creates "the feeling of the opposite/*il sentimento del contrario*" (Pirandello 1960, 113). Pirandello exemplifies his theory with the image of an old woman with dyed hair, made up with oils and too much makeup, attempting to seem young. Pirandello laughs at the older woman trying to preserve or even re-create her youth and defines this as a comic reaction. However, if one goes beyond that basic observation and considers the situation more fully, considering that the woman dresses in this manner to impress her husband or fit society's definition of what a woman must look like, or to conceal wrinkles, he says: "if reflection comes to suggest all this, then I can no longer laugh at her as I did at first, exactly because the inner working of reflection has made me go beyond, or rather enter deeper into, the initial stage of awareness: from the beginning *perception of the opposite,* reflection has made me shift to a *feeling of the opposite*" (Pirandello 1960, 113). Thus, how do one view the narrator? Is this just another example of the narrator sacrificing his own beliefs to be accepted, or does he want to hump on the floor? Is this another moment in which the poet is queering time, even though only in his dreams?

This stanza reminds the reader of the red-lit room where the narrator continues to watch porn, and yet "When I try to change the channel / nothing comes on the screen clearly" (28–29). His own ability to focus on the images is poor because his dreams cloud them. Or the quality of the video and its static hinder both the physical and emotional response that present themselves later in the stanza. The narrator's blurring of time and reality obscures a true sense of identity and adds to the feeling of *bildung.* Yet he continues to create his porn-star persona believing not only in himself but also attempting to "watch and learn" from "this dirty / twelve-inch screen has lines through him [porno star]" (32–33). Although the narrator attempts to give himself over to his sexual urges completely, he is blocked; he cannot focus on the porn in front of him, "instead of that familiar grunting / and gasping, I hear static. / Everything is static" (35–37). Consequently, his inability to fully enjoy the experience illustrates how consumed the narrator is, so much so that he feels he has lost himself in this process as the poem concludes:

> And the twelve-inch video monitor,
> in that dark booth, threatens to swallow
> me whole, I am swallowed whole. (38–40)

As the poem closes, we are reminded of the closet-like image introduced at the beginning of the piece. Even though the narrator believes he has grown into a new person, has he? Is he still the young, embarrassed youth from the beginning two stanzas? Even if he tries to be more comfortable with his sexuality, he remains shut up in the closet, masturbating to pornography for a quarter of a minute. He hoped to grow, yet with the enjambment of line 39, the repetition of the verb "swallow," and the fact that he has lost all control by the final line of the poem, the narrator seems even more lost at the end of the poem because he has become delusional, as implied by the dreamlike state throughout. In the last two lines of the poem, we see how the narrator is "swallowed whole": first, psychoanalytically, the narrator is blocked from development and, as such, sexual pleasure. Second, the narrator is consumed by the closet as he is prevented from living freely as a homosexual male. In the end, he can only pretend to be gay, which returns to the opening of the poem; arriving at being gay, as a verb, is never achieved.

Moreover, he describes a false sense of growth thus, in the end, he is like Pirandello's old woman, making decisions only to gain the attention of others and lose oneself in the process. In this regard, the narrator once again sacrifices himself. Looking at the lyric through a psychoanalytic lens, we note the young narrator's attempts to feel comfortable, arriving at the stage of development in which he recognizes himself in the mirror. But does the narrator ever truly arrive at this stage? His attempts are unsuccessful. As he sees his own reflection in the TV within his private booth, he cannot see the porn stars because of the lines on the TV, nor can he hear them grunting. Rather, he focuses only on seeing and hearing the constant static from the TV, blocking any possibility of growing into that porn star he once dreamed about becoming. From a Lacanian perspective, even though the narrator attempts to see himself through the reflection of the dirty twelve-inch screen, an allusion to the mirror stage, he is incapable, demonstrating a block in his sexual development. He cannot surpass the mirror stage and, as such, cannot distinguish himself as "other."

Last, it is important to consider the performative role our narrator assumes in this selection. Muñoz explains, "The cultural performers . . . must negotiate between a fixed identity disposition and the socially encoded roles that are available for such subjects." As he attempts to come out, the Italian American narrator mimics the cultural performers of Muñoz as he follows queer examples from the community by spending time in the adult bookstore closeted (1999, 6). The narrator is forced to confront his own gender bias by maintaining a heteronormative front, denying himself pleasure, and not accepting and exploring his sexual identity.

Moreover, in "Feeling Brown, Feeling Down: Latina Affect, the Performativity of Race, and the Depressive Position," Muñoz argues, "Feeling brown in my analysis is descriptive of the way in which minoritarian affect is always, no matter what its register, partially illegible in relation to the normative affect performed by normative citizen subjects" (2003, 415). This is evidenced through the narrator's performative nature of entering the adult bookstore early on and then later. One cannot ignore his performative nature as he consciously enacts his sexuality in a private booth watching porn. In this sense, then, the narrator performs his sexual prowess in the silence of the closet. As Sedgewick suggests, " 'Closetedness' itself is a performance initiated as such by the speech act of a silence—not a particular silence, but a silence that accrues particularity by fits and starts, in relation to the discourse that surrounds and differentially constitutes it" (2008, 3). Therefore, the narrator has yet to arrive at a moment of full awareness of his identity.

Section II reveals a heightened theme of sacrifice. The first poem of section II, titled "The Rising," alludes to sexual violence within the narrator's family. The poem, which consists of three simple sentences, is cut decisively with enjambment, bringing all three simple sentences together in a smooth yet intricate manner:

> Occasionally
> he washes up,
> covered in seaweed.
> And mother
> wraps herself in

the shower curtain.
I'm in bed
with my sister,
comforting her.

The poem's pace intensifies while creating suspense for the reader by using very short verses paired with purposeful enjambment noted in the first two lines: "Occasionally / he washes up." "He washes up" continues with "covered in seaweed," which at first seems odd, but, according to the urban dictionary, "seaweed" is the "name for sweaty pubic hair popping out."[19] This definition seems most appropriate in this reading, as it creates a gross, almost bestial image of the father's character preparing to abuse his children sexually. Although not explicit, the narrator describes a scene of incest from his/her/their childhood. The pronoun "he," which alludes to the father, has just finished molesting the narrator's sister, and in the final line of the poem the narrator comforts the sister after the act. The reference to washing thus recalls an event that would occur "occasionally" after the sexual act. Additionally, the adverb "occasionally" underscores a sense of time, paired with the pace of the line, that illustrates another level of crudeness forced on his children. Moreover, "occasionally" indicates when "he washes up" (2), not the frequency with which he would molest his daughter (and later the narrator).

The narrator's mother also showers, as the enjambment of her three lines pushes through the reading quickly until we arrive at the period, which forces a pause in the rhythm. As the poem continues its rhythm, the narrator calls his mother out for not only being aware of the molestation, but also for hiding it, as she covers herself in the shower curtain as a sign of either embarrassment or shame. The final three lines bring the poem together and explain the previous two sentences. The enjambment again in lines 7 and 8 creates a sense of unity with the narrator and his sister; however, the comma that separates lines 8 and 9 underscores the poem's focus: the narrator comforting his sister after being violated by their father. Although the father "washes up" only occasionally, there is no true cleansing in the poem. Both parents attempt to cleanse themselves from the situation, but the narrator and his sister remain "dirty" to it, as there are no references to them showering. Therefore, the narrator is stuck balancing the familial situation of the parents and his sibling, in this situation emotionally.

In the subsequent poem, "Box of Broken Things," the reader is faced with the consequences of the father's mistreatment of his children. The poem's epigraph is Dante's *Inferno* XXX111: 61, 62, ". . . *tu ne vestisti queste misere carni, e tu le spoglia.*" To understand the poem and the allusion to Dante, it is critical to quickly explore the entire *terzina*:

> immediately rose and told me: "Father,
> it would be far less painful for us if
> you ate of us; for you clothed us in this
> sad—flesh It is for you to strip it off." (60–63)[20]

As Robert Hollander claims, the treatment of Ugolino's sin against God and his children has two possible interpretations. Traditionally, Dante scholars have accepted and celebrated Italian literary critic Francesco De Santis's interpretation of "the drama of paternity" (De Santis in Hollander 2008, 334).[21] On the other hand, John Freccero challenges De Santis's "sympathetic" reading, arguing that Ugolino's "tragedy is a failure of interpretation, as well as an inability to accept the suffering of his own children" (Freccero in Hollander 2008, 335).[22] According to Freccero, Ugolino "is condemned by Dante not only as a traitor but also for the inability to grasp the spiritual meaning in the letter of his children's words" (Freccero in Hollander 2008, 335; original on 58). All this to state that the epitaph prepares the learned reader for a tale in which a father commits treason against his own family.

The poem, structured into four stanzas, two beginning with "Place into it" and two with "Place yourself in your," explores the numerous errors the father makes with this family. "Place into it" refers to the title's "Box of Broken Things," while the second half of the poem calls on the father to consider his life through other people's perspectives. The poem challenges the father to completely reconsider the series of decisions he made to destroy his family. The first stanza introduces the father's anxiety about migrating—attempting to become a successful migrant yet never returning to Italy for retirement or burial. The second example of the poem cites the father's physical abuse of his children and his sexual infidelity against his wife. The colon after "fucking behind mother's back" opens a significant parenthesis in the husband and wife's relationship, noting not only his infidelity for "forty-seven husbandless years" (7), but also his "inability to act on your love / for other men" (8–9).[23] The enjambment here creates a surprise for the reader, as we do not expect the narrator's father to be a closeted homosexual. The final example provided in the first stanza connotes the father's pedophilia and how he financially buys his children's silence.

The father's image as a pedophile continues into the second stanza as he uses the TV to view himself having sex with his children, assumingly as a reflective means.[24] The expression "place into it" evolves to "place yourself in" midway through the second stanza, with the line

Place yourself in
our shoes and forgive yourself
for eating from us a lifetime
of pleasures. (18–21)

The change in the repetitious phrase makes a shift in tone and point of view critical for the poem. With "place yourself in," the narrator deconstructs the box, as things are no longer being "put inside" or "hidden," but rather the narrator deflects the sins of the sinner, similarly to Dante. Moreover, the phrase "for eating from us a lifetime" is an additional allusion to Dante's Ugolino, stuck in the ninth circle of Hell with all the traitors.

The narrator enhances the eating metaphor in the following anaphora:

Place yourself
at the dinner table like a place
setting that you tinkle against
your teeth; I'm the fork,
I'm the fork, my sister's a spoon. (21–25)

The very rich metaphor again relies on enjambment for the flow of lines 21–23, pushing the reader until the semicolon, when we are presented another important piece of the pie—the fork and spoon—which provide another level of meaning. The fork and spoon serve as visual sexual representations of the psychoanalytic positions the children were forced into sexually. On a first reading, the father sits at the table "using" the silverware to feed his appetites. Moreover, the act of "tinkling" the silverware against his teeth incites a sense of gluttonous desire and simultaneously creates a feeling of crass behavior. Additionally, for those at the table being subjected to the "tinkle," the sound and motion generate an uneasy tension about which child will be eaten tonight. The figurative image is so grotesque that the reader would prefer not to move further with the reference. The image of the fork, however, also recalls the phallus and the father's desire to have it. In a psychoanalytic reading, the tinkling of the fork against the father's teeth alludes to both oral and anal sexual relations, particularly with the repetition of the line "I'm the fork, / I'm the fork" (24–25). Furthermore, the father also desires the sister, "my sister's the spoon," suggesting that he is penetrating her through the act of spooning, which is a sexual position in which the larger person embraces the smaller person in front of him/her/them. The "little spoon" lies against the chest and genitals of the "big spoon." There is also a sense of power in these positions, as the "big spoon's" position is from behind the "little spoon" and the big spoon has "pinned" the little spoon down.

The fourth and fifth stanzas deal with placing the father in his daughter's shoes, "the stilettos that pierce / the back of her children's heads" (27–28) and grandchildren's place "and feel what it's like to be / split up." (29–30). The first reference again demonstrates how the father's, now grandfather's, physical abuse ruins others' lives, either physically or figuratively. The second reference evokes the division the actions of the father, who is also the grandfather, caused others. The final line of the poem is the only one that is not a repetition of "Place into it" or "Place yourself" and reads:

Quarter yourself and feed
yourself to yourself, on those nights
you are hungry, feed yourself. (30–32)

This final command returns the reader to the incipit of the poem, as it serves to allude to Dante and the *contrapassi* from the *Inferno*. Instead of Ugolino eating his own children, the narrator sends his father to feed himself, attempting to break the cycle of abuse in Dante's world but most importantly within his own household.

In this vibrant verse, we note the reference to Dante and the parallel adoption of a psychoanalytic theoretical lens between Ugolino and the father character. Although Ugolino's children have virtually no lines in the canto, particularly because the story is told from his perspective and not the children's, similar strains of theory persist in both tales. In "Box of Broken Things," the narrative explores the relationships between the father and his progeny. The poem highlights the father's own loveless relationship with his wife, the narrator's mother, and how he remained a closeted homosexual and pedophile, affecting everyone's life negatively. The father's homosexual/pedophilic nature silence "broke" so many of the items that went into the proverbial box. However, it is critical to remember that the inherent reason that all those items were broken stems from the father not accepting his own sexual identity, which can also be reflected in the narrator's own struggle.

The next poem in the sequence addresses the sexual identity of the narrator and explores the power of gender within language. "Poverty of Language" is divided into two sections, a type of interlude and a second section focusing solely on the narrator's name calling. Part 1 begins

> If a mother were to say: "I pray
> to the Virgin you die of AIDS."
> You see I'm doing it again,
> shutting you out.
> "I should have eaten *you* at birth."
> This language is wealth,
> a red dress,
> an injection. (1–8)

The irony of the opening line, a mother praying for her son to die of AIDS, is only heightened by the enjambment that increases the rhythm of the line along with the surprise that comes at the end of the second line. This irony is not unusual for an Italian American Catholic family, as un-Christian as the sentiment truly is. Yet the bond between an Italian American mother and son is stereotypically celebrated, especially in a home in which the father-son relationship is challenged.[25]

Here, the narrator unveils the only way he can survive, shutting out his own mother from his life. And even as he does so, we hear the mother's response, "I should have eaten *you* at birth," which reminds the reader again of Dante's *Inferno* 33 and the abuse of familiar relationships. Moreover, the observation "this language is wealth" illustrates the powerful words encountered in daily life and how they can either create or destroy.

Language plays the most critical role in the second half of the poem; the narrator incorporates various Italian phrases used at home, underscoring the migrant aspect of integration and expressions used in ridicule and scorn:

> Father spoke to us
> in erudite Italian:
> *pederasta*—pederast,
> *infangare*—to muddy,
> to soil
> as in ruining one's name.

In the first segment, the father communicates in learned Italian, probably referring to standard Italian. The vocabulary that defines him is *pederasta*, which has been previously evidenced in the collection, and *infangare*, which does refer to muddying, yet a stronger, more pertinent synonym would be to tarnish or to dishonor. Compared to the mother, who communicates in dialect, a class structure is drawn by the narrator:

> On the other hand,
> Mother spoke
> in a strange combination
> of denial
> and Southern Italian dialects
> *femminiello,*
> she'd call me
> *femminiello,*
> she'd call my sister
> *femminiello,*
> my father
> *femminiello*—one-half little girl,
> one-half little faggot.

The poem concludes as it began, from the perspective of the mother, in a circular manner suggesting a return to the womb. However, it is notewothy that the mother would call her children "femminiello," but not her husband, who by nature seems to be suggesting he is one. This poem connects the "silence of the closet" of the narrator's father, already seen in "Box of Broken Things," and bastardizes it twice over: thematically and linguistically, overtly questioning the father's sexual identity.

Although much of the "dialogue" comes from the narrator's mother, the poem is hardly feminist. Indeed, we are presented with the view of the family from her perspective. The mother calls each family member *femminiello*, a term typically used to refer to homosexual men with ambiguous gender features, often feminine (some refer to them as the third gender), within Neapolitan culture. Though said to bring luck, much ambiguity revolves around the true culture of the *femminielli*. For example, *femminielli* are often invited to perform at ceremonies, including weddings and christenings. At the same time, however, they are often ridiculed and live in a separate community, ostracized from the general populous. The final line of the poem, "one-half little girl, / one-half little faggot," sums up the emotional sentiment of the narrator's mother; to be called this by your own mother is like having your mother say, "I pray to the Virgin you die of AIDS." The poem exposes the homophobic mother through her hateful tone, ridiculing nature, and complete lack of compassion, the opposite stereotype of Italian mothers.

In fact, the mother presented within these two poems breaks the stereotype of the *mammone* relationship so often cited in the Italian American experience. Many mothers and homosexual sons encounter issues, particularly when the son is either outed or outs himself. In many various representations in literature and media studies, mothers still demonstrate a level of compassion, and often at some point, there is moment of reconciliation, even if it comes late or at the moment of illness and/or death.[26] What is unique in Covino's collection is the direct harshness and raw nature the narrator's mother exudes throughout the collection from both word and action. Her reactions to the narrator underscore the "othered" nature present in the poetry and align with Muñoz's concept of disidentification, as the mother's nastiness creates such a barrier to the narrator that he bonds more closely with his incestuous, pedophile father.

In "His Touch," the reader learns about the lasting psychoanalytic effects the narrator suffered from his father's abuse, if his long-term wounds were not already clear. Playing again with anaphora, three of the four initial stanzas begin with "Today I learned":

> Today I learned the cost of living has not gone up.
> I am not worth a three-percent raise.
> Today I learned I can't live a day without
> coming back to you, back to that point.
> Not ten years of therapy, not an ocean
> between us, a generation gap.
> Today I learned the money I earn
> will never be enough: (1–8)

The narrator sets up the poem through parallelisms. His own understanding of his selflessness is directly connected to another outside source—his lack of a raise—linking his professional and private lives.

In verse 4, the narrator notes the root of all issues, "back to that point," a point that nothing could fix or erase. Even his most important memories of life are still tainted from that point recalled in line 4:

> How I have re-created those nights,
> my first communion, my marriage;
> and how I enjoy these reenactments,
> love-father, father-lover,

> as much seducer as seduced
> as much only child as fatherless son. (11–16)

Looking deeper at the poem, the narrator's happy moments are all laced with thoughts of abuse, which hinder his own identity process.

According to Lacanian psychoanalysis, the narrator experiences both the Imaginary and the Real, and he initiates his quest to reach the *I*, the moment of owning his own language. In Covino's opus, the concept of memory and return, whether physical or solely emotional, is inescapable. The narrator is incapable of separating from the father because of the extensive mental and emotional damage suffered through years of sexual abuse. He has been conditioned, almost animalistically, to transform his pain, suffering, and abuse into celebrated memories, or else he would remain void, "as much only child as fatherless son." Considering the role of the mother as presented within the collection, this comes as little surprise. In fact, the only healthy relationship presented within the collection is that of his sister, which is also compromised because of the father's abuse.

The inescapable sentiment continues, and although the "point" will never be removed, healing and remedy still exist:

> And if I could carve myself
> out of myself,
> if I could bleed
> a thousand baths—
> because even then I'd repair myself
> the way water does after it is entered.
> Oh, the slippery friction of it,
> the slippery fiction. (17–24)

The two hypothetical "if" clauses demonstrate a desire for figurative rebirth, even though it is not literally possible. Yet line 20's hyphen changes the tone, even if briefly, offering a sense of renewal and possibility; the narrator would still "repair" himself as water does. The water reference reinforces the interpretation of cleansing and rebirth. And when the narrator speaks of water entering, as a liquid, water conforms to its container; if it does not have form, it will create its own based on its vessel. Thus, line 22 is very powerful as it suggests that although the process proves challenging and painful, underscored by the "slippery friction" the narrator must endure

(23), he will never be able to forget nor move on completely. However, as much it may seem to be "slippery fiction," it is not. Psychoanalytically, the narrator is forever connected to the horrors and, as such, to his father. In fact, he cannot hate his father; he remains faithful to him.

Preliminary Conclusions

As demonstrated early in this contribution, Italian American literature boasts a rich and developed poetic oeuvre. Dating back to 1805, Italian American poetry is clearly expansive, abundant, and valuable as both a literary genre and a cultural artifact. This expanded presence debunks the myth that Italian migrants were primarily uneducated peasants who could not integrate into new societies, whether linguistic or cultural. Rather, this literary production illustrates a nuanced understanding of the country to emigration and immigration as well as the challenge of reinventing oneself in one's newfound home.

Although this rather short contribution focuses solely on Covino's first publication, *Cut Off the Ears of Winter*, his second, *The Right Place to Jump* (2012), is just as rich. In the latter, the narrator struggles with his sexual identity, growing up homosexual in an Italian American Catholic household where sexual abuse and toxic masculinity emerge regularly. Through psychoanalytic and queer theoretical lenses, I have argued that the narrator strives to become whole, breaking away emotionally and psychologically from the damage both parents have inflicted; however, he is unable to forget his past completely. Through a selection of poems, the reader experiences the trauma the narrator encounters by his parents' abuse, both verbal and sexual. These experiences become part of his identity, and he can never truly break mentally or emotionally from them as seen in the following poem, "Telling My Story." Even here, the narrator recounts his story once again. Unfortunately, space does not allow for a close analysis of the poem, thought is may not be necessary, at least to illustrate my point. In this most intense piece of the collection, we immediately note that our narrator remains loyal to his father:

> And I realize when my father denies everything
> and tells us he's a good father, he's partially right—
> he fed us, he woke us for school
> he sent us to good college, etc.

> And still today in his especially pathetic way,
> he tries to make it up to us
> with money and trips (and we like that,
> and worry about getting written out of his will). (55–62)

Here we experience the narrator's acceptance of his father's behavior again, not because he does not realize nor understand the gravity of the situation, as the poem discusses earlier. Rather, our Italian American queer narrator is stuck with performing his sexual identity in the adult bookstore's closet. His connection with his father remains unhealthy, as his performative gender nature paired with his familial abuse obstructs any positive development. From a psychoanalytic reading, the narrator is blocked in the maturation process and returns to his father instead of being able to move forward to the *I* stage in psychic development. And his Italian American nature of loyalty to family can never be broken.

By investigating Covino's poetry from a queer perspective, we are forced to acknowledge the unique path of self-discovery the narrator embarks upon, one that is rarely represented in Italian American literature, especially this candidly. Moreover, we note that the narrator has an uncommon relationship with both space and time, which becomes evident as he attempts his *bildungsroman*. In the end, the narrator is incapable of fully completing his development, as noted by the return to his father. The collection reads as a series of sacrifices the narrator must endeavor to survive.

Although this piece introduces a small slice of Covino's poetic richness, it is the beginning of a much longer exploration I hope to conduct not only of his poetry, but also in queering Italian American poetry on a grander scale. Covino is just one important name in a list of talented Italian American LGBTQ+ poets and authors in the community. Only through studying these noteworthy artists and inviting them to read/perform their poetry will they be celebrated in a loftier manner.

Notes

1. See Dana Gioia for a more detailed account of the evolution of Italian American poetry, http://danagioia.com/essays/american-poetry/what-is-italian-american-poetry/.

2. Lorenzo da Ponte was the first professor of Italian literature at Columbia College, a position for which he earned no formal faculty salary. He was also the

first Roman Catholic priest to be appointed to the faculty, and the first to have been raised Jewish. Da Ponte was compensated per student for his work. According to Paul Cohen in "Columbia II: The Legacy of Da Ponte," the librettist was only compensated for his first year and never had other students, even though he remained "faculty." Moreover, to sustain himself, he offered the college his books to be purchased. They did, in two installments, and these funds have been turned into the Lorenzo da Ponte Professorship in the Italian Department (Cohen 1986, 16).

3. See http://danagioia.com/essays/american-poetry/what-is-italian-american-poetry/.

4. See also Buonomo and Russo 2010–2011, 21–22, 90–94.

5. For the latest work dedicated to de Palchi, see Linguaglossa 2020.

6. Peter Covino is just one example in a long line of noteworthy Italian American poets. Other examples include Vittorio epetto (she used the small "r" against the patriarchy), Annie Lanzillotto, Mary Jo Bona, Giovanna Capone, and Nicole Santaluccia, among many others. See *Hey Paesan!* for a more robust list.

7. The collection, which houses essays by Tommi Avicolli Mecca, Giovanna Capone, Theresa Carilli, Philip Gambone, Rachel Guido DeVries, and Mary Cappello, provides the reader with an insight into the difficulties of being gay and Italian American. It reflects on the difficulties faced by those who come to the realization of who they are and often struggle to "fit in" or even "survive" in certain households. All the pieces are personal in nature, reflective, and touch upon hardships faced during their upbringing within an Italian American family. Varying in tone, each still pinpoints how unaccepting Italian American culture can be in relation to the homosexual community.

8. The volume consists of fifteen articles from various generations of gay Italian American men. Even though the autobiographical essays span four generations and includes more prominent Italian American authors, some marking their debut, the stories' general themes remain the same. The volume explores memoir-style essays about growing up, traveling, and living as gay Italian Americans. George DeStefano, whose essay appears in *Our Naked Lives* and who also contributed its foundational chapter, "*Fuori per Sempre*: Gay and Lesbian Italian Americans Come Out," in *The Routledge History of Italian Americans* (2018, 565–80), is a noteworthy addition to the field.

9. For more information about the scholarship fund or to donate, see https://www.italianamericanstudies.net/campaigns.

10. During my Fulbright fellowship at the Università della Calabria (Unical) in spring 2017, I taught a graduate-level course for the *magistrale* on Queering Italian Americana. In fall 2024, I was the Tiro a Segno Fellow at New York University, where I taught a graduate seminar titled "Queering the Italian American *Bildungsroman*."

11. I am not arguing that it is completely void, but rather that it assumes a minor role in his works compared with the more "foundational" Italian American poets like Joseph Tusiani, Paolo Valesio, Giose Rimanelli, etc.

12. See https://biblehub.com/commentaries/pulpit/john/18.htm.

13. *La coscienza di Zeno* (1923) is a modernist novel written in a stream-of-consciousness style. It was Svevo's third novel, but it was the work that introduced him to the international stage, in part because of James Joyce's admiration for the normal along with Italian poet Eugenio Montale. It was translated into English as *Confessions of Zeno* in 1930. The book recounts the fictional memoir of Zeno Cosini, the protagonist of the film, as he follows his psychiatrist's recommendation to journal everything that occurs as a sort of therapy to overcomes his illness. He includes information about his father, business, wife, and use of tobacco. It is narrated in the first person.

14. In the subgenre of AIDS literature, often the narrator/author does not name the disease but rather describes it. Or it is mentioned in the beginning and not throughout the text, even though the reader—particularly one who experienced the pandemic—would clearly understand that the protagonist(s) has it. See Calabretta-Sajder 2021, 25–44.

15. For more information on nomenclature in AIDS literature, see Calabretta-Sajder 2019, 43–59.

16. See Laplanche and Pontails 1973, 206.

17. See Sedgwick, 2008, 61.

18. For the most part, red light districts have been associated with female prostitution, although some cities also affiliate them with male prostitution. See Caves 2005, 559. Red light districts evolved from the red lights historically used in brothels.

19. See the Urban Dictionary, https://www.urbandictionary.com/define.php?term=Seaweed.

20. See Barolini 2018.

21. For the original, see De Santis 1967, 681–704.

22. For the original, see Freccero 1977, 57.

23. The gender identity of the narrator's father is unclear. We understand from the narrator that his father is a pedophile. It is the mother who "outs" him as homosexual, too. It is important to underscore the difference.

24. The line read "the nights / you wandered into the living room / to watch yourself fuck us / on the TV." With the preposition "on," it may be possible that the father recorded his sexual encounters with his children and rewatched them for pleasure later. This reading is even more intense than the original one.

25. It is important to recall the role of the *mammone* in Italian society. The *mammone* is an Italian man who resides with his parents usually until he marries. His mother generally continues to assume all his care: cooking, cleaning, etc. Mothers who do not embrace their male children in this way are often looked down upon within Italian society. Currently, I would argue, this phenomena is evolving, however slowly.

26. Among many examples, see Robert Ferro's *Second Son*, Tommi Avicolli Mecca's "Memoirs of a South Philly Sissy," Philip Gambone's "Learning and Unlearning and Learning Again the Language of *Signori*," Anthony Wilkinson's *My Big Gay Italian Wedding*, and Steve Galluccio's *Mambo Italiano*.

Works Cited

Barolini, Teodolinda. 2018. "*Inferno* 33: The Wolf and the Zombie." *Commento Baroliniano*, Digital Dante. New York, NY: Columbia University Libraries. https://digitaldante.columbia.edu/dante/divine-comedy/inferno/inferno-33/.

Barreca, Regina. 2022. *Don't Tell Mama! The Penguin Book of Italian American Writing*. New York: Penguin.

———. 2022. Introduction to *Don't Tell Mama! The Penguin Book of Italian American Writing*. New York: Penguin.

Barolini, Helen. 1985. *The Dream Book: An Anthology of Writings by Italian American Women*. New York: Schocken Books.

———. 2000. *The Dream Book: An Anthology of Writings by Italian American Women*. 2nd ed. Syracuse: Syracuse University Press.

Bona, Mary Jo. 1996. "Gorgeous Identities: Gay and Lesbian Italian/American Writers." In *FUORI: Essays by Italian/American Lesbians and Gays*, edited by Anthony Julian. West Lafayette, IN: Bordighera Press.

Bonaffini, Luigi, and Joseph Perricone, eds. 2014. *Poets of the Italian Diaspora: A Bilingual Anthology*. New York: Fordham University Press.

Bonomo Albright, Carol. 2000. "Earliest Italian American Novel: *Lorenzo and Oonalaska* by Joseph Rocchietti in Virginia, 1985." *Italian Americana* 18 (2): 129–32.

Buonomo, Leonardo, and Russo, John Paul. 2010–2011. "Introduction to Forum: The Emerging Canon of Italian American Literature." *RSA Journal* 21–22: 90–94.

Calabretta-Sajder, Ryan. 2016. "Rediscovering Joseph Tusiani: From "Return" to *Il ritorno*: A Psychoanalytic Approach." *Italica* 93 (2): 358–69.

———. 2019. "AIDS, Italian Americana, and the Creation of a Genre in the American Canon: Robert Ferro's *Second Son*." In *Representation of AIDS in Literature, Media, and the Arts*, edited by Aimee Pozorski and Christine Cynn, 43–59. Lanham, MD: Lexington Press.

———. 2021. "AIDS in the Italian and Italian American Canon: Death as a Metaphor for a Profession in Peril." In *Diversity in Italian Studies*, edited by Siân Gibby and Anthony Julian Tamburri, 25–44. New York: John D. Calandra Italian American Institute.

————, Luigi Bonaffini, and Joseph Perricone, eds. 2014. *Poets of the Italian Diaspora: A Bilingual Anthology*. New York: Fordham University Press. Reprinted in *Annali D'Italianistica* 36 (2016): 611–13.

Capone, Giovanna (Janet), Denise Nico Leto, and Tommi Avicolli Mecca. 1999. *Hey Paesan! Writing by Lesbians & Gay Men of Italian Descent*. Oakland, CA: Three Guineas Press.

Carnevali, Emanuel. 2006. *Furnished Rooms*. Edited by Dennis Barone. New York: Bordighera Press.

Caves, Roger W. 2005. *Encyclopedia of the City*. London: Routledge.

Cohen, Paul. 1986. "Columbia II: The Legacy of Da Ponte." *Italian Americana* 8 (1): 14–19.

Covino, Peter. 2005. *Cut Off the Ears of Winter*. Kalamazoo: Western Michigan University.

————. 2010. "Innovation, Interdisciplinarity, and Cultural Exchange in Italian American Poetry." In *Teaching Italian American Literature, Film, and Popular Culture*, edited by Edvige Giunta and Kathleen A. McCormick. New York: Modern Language Association.

————. 2012. *The Right Place to Jump*. Kalamazoo: Western Michigan University.

De Santis, Francesco. 1967. "L'Ugolino di Dante." *Opere* 5 (Turin): 681–704. Originally published in 1869.

DeStefano, George. 2018. "*Fuori per Sempre*: Gay and Lesbian Italian Americans Come Out." In *The Routledge History of Italian Americans*, edited by William J. Connell and Stanislao G. Pugliese, 565–80. New York: Routledge.

Durante, Francesco, ed. 2014. *Italoamericana: The Literature of the Great Migration, 1880–1943*. Edited by Robert Viscusi. New York: Fordham University Press.

Felluga, Dino. 2011. "Modules on Lacan: On the Structure of the Psyche." Introductory Guide to Critical Theory. January 31. Purdue University. http://www.purdue.edu/guidetotheory/psychoanalysis/lacanstructure.html.

Fontanella, Luigi. 2012. *Migrating Words: Italian Writers in the United States*. New York: Bordighera Press.

Freccero, John. 1977. "Bestial Sign and Bread of Angels (*Inferno* 32–33)." *Yale Italian Studies* 1: 53–66.

Freeman, Elizabeth, 2010. *Time Binds: Queer Temporalities, Queer Histories*. Durham, NC: Duke University Press.

Fuss, Diana. 1991. "Inside/Out." In *Inside/Out: Lesbian Theories, Gay Theories*, edited by Diana Fuss, 1–10. New York: Routledge.

Gioia, Dana. n.d. "What Is Italian-American Poetry?" http://danagioia.com/essays/american-poetry/what-is-italian-american-poetry/.

Giordano, Paolo. 2016. Introduction to *A Clarion Call. New Poems*, by Joseph Tusiani. New York: Bordighera Press.

Giunta, Edvige, and Kathleen Zamboni McCormick. 2010. *Teaching Italian American Literature, Film, and Popular Culture*. New York: Modern Language Association.

Hollander, Robert. 2008. "*Inferno* XXXIII, 37–74: Ugolino's Importunity." In *Dante Alighieri: Inferno*, translated by Michael Palma, edited by Giuseppe Mazzotta, 334–42. New York: W.W. Norton & Company.

Lacan, Jacques. 1953. "Some Reflections on the Ego." *International Journal of Psychoanalysis* 34: 11–17.

Laplanche, Jean, and Jean-Betrand Pontails. 1973. *The Language of Psychoanalysis*. Translated by Donald Nicholoson-Smith. New York: W.W. Norton.

Linguaglossa, Giorgio. 2020. *Alfredo de Palchi: The Missing Link in the Late Twentieth-Century Italian Poetry*. Translated by Steven Grieco-Rathgeb. Lanham, MD: Fairleigh Dickinson University Press.

Matteo, Sante. 2014. "Italian Roots in Global Soil." In *Poets of the Italian Diaspora: A Bilingual Anthology*, edited by Bonaffini, Luigi and Joseph Perricone. New York: Fordham University Press.

Mazzotta, Giuseppe, ed. 2008. *Dante Alighieri: Inferno*. Translated by Michael Palma. New York: W.W. Norton & Company.

Muñoz, José Esteban. 1999. *Disidentifications: Queers of Color and the Performance of Politics*. Minneapolis: University of Minnesota Press.

Muñoz, José Esteban. 2003. "Feeling Brown, Feeling Down: Latina Affect, the Performativity of Race, and the Depressive Position." In *The Routledge Queer Studies Reader*, edited by Donald E. Hall and Annamarie Jagose. New York: Routledge.

Pirandello, Luigi. 1960. *On Humor*. Edited and translated by Antonio Illiano and Daniel P. Testa. Chapel Hill: University of North Carolina Press.

Pucelli, Rodolfo, ed. 1955. *Anthology of Italian and Italo-American Poetry*. New York: Humphries.

Roof, Judith. 2016. *What Gender Is, What Gender Does*. Minneapolis: University of Minnesota Press.

Sedgewick, Eve Kosofsky. 2008. *The Epistemology of the Closet*. Berkeley: University of California Press.

Svevo, Italo. 1958. *Confessions of Zeno*. Translated by Beryl De Zoete. New York: Vintage Books.

Tamburri, Anthony Julian, ed. 1996. *FUORI: Essays by Italian/American Lesbians and Gays*. West Lafayette, IN: Bordighera Press.

———. 2009. "Peter Covino." In *Encyclopedia of Contemporary LGBTQ Literature of the United States*, edited by Emmanuel S. Newson, 157–59. Santa Barbara, CA: Greenwood Press.

———, Paolo A. Giordano, and Fred L. Gardaphé, eds. 2000. *From the Margin: Writings in Italian Americana*. 2nd ed. West Lafayette, IN: Purdue University Press.

Tonelli, Bill. 2003. *The Italian American Reader*. New York: HarperCollins.

Urban Dictionary. www.urbandictionary.com.

Section 3

Blurring the Past, Redefining the Future

Italian Americans and Memoir

5

Memoir and the Invention of Italian American Experience

A Tribute to Louise DeSalvo

John Champagne

She believed in the fundamental accuracy of memory and she understood that telling what you remembered, and writing down what had happened to you when you were young were radical acts of personal history that would force the rewriting of social history [sic].

—Louise DeSalvo, Virginia Woolf, The Impact of
Childhood Sexual Abuse on Her Life and Work

I use theory and practice here as a shorthand for what I would prefer to call the conceptual categories of lived experience and critical imagination, which might begin to capture something of the different forms of abstraction that constitutes each. This formulation is counter to much contemporary scholarship, which tends to position "experience" as the "ground" against which abstraction is rendered superfluous to social change, which in turn requires that "experience" be consciously and concretely delivered. This flatlining of the complexity of experience requires that we misrecognize the way it functions *as an analytic category* and leads to rather impoverished understandings of the work of memory, narrative, identification, and desire. [italics in the original].

—Robyn Wiegman, Object Lessons

> Theoretical discourse . . . is always subject to its own discursive limit
> of rationalism and abstraction—a limit that translates into a necessary
> distance from the experiences being alluded to—in such a manner as
> to neutralize precisely the very emotional effects of injustice that per-
> sist as the remnants of lived experience. When critics protest against
> (poststructuralist) theory's inadequacy, they are implicitly alluding to
> these remnants of lived experience; consequently, it is also to the rift,
> the incommensurability, between theoretical and nontheoretical writing
> as such that they are unwittingly pointing.
>
> —Rey Chow, *The Protestant Ethnic and The Spirit of Capitalism*

The prolific career of Louise DeSalvo (1942–2018) often straddled that
rift between theoretical and non-theoretical writing to which Chow refers.
DeSalvo's first book, *Virginia Woolf's Voyage Out: A Novel in the Making*, was
a revised version of her dissertation completed to fulfill her PhD from New
York University. It was published in 1980. Seven years later, she published
a novel, *Casting Off*. While she continued to produce literary criticism—a
book on Nathaniel Hawthorn; a study of revenge in the literature of Woolf,
D. H. Lawrence, Djuna Barnes, and Henry Miller; additional books on
Woolf, including a career-changing, iconoclastic study of the sexual abuse
to which Woolf was subject and the effects of that abuse on her life and
work—that scholarship increasingly vied with her commitment to writing
and teaching memoir: Her 1997 *Vertigo*, on her life as a white working-class
Italian American feminist, was published the same year as her *Breathless: An
Asthma Journal*, which was followed three years later by *Adultery: An Intimate
Look at Why People Cheat*, a hybrid work of memoir, literary criticism, and
rumination.[1] Her last book, *The House of Early Sorrows*, which reprinted (in
revised versions) many of her previously published autobiographical essays,
was published in 2018.[2]

Louise was my teacher. But she was more than that. Under her guidance, I spent my senior year of college writing my first book. In the fall of
1985, Louise was teaching a course in novel writing at Hunter College but,
as anyone who knew Louise might suspect, insisted on doing it in her own
very particular way. No workshopping: Workshops were deadly, anathema to
the kind of self-care and nurturing of the spirit all writing required. They
led writers to stop themselves short before they had sufficiently gotten what
they needed to out on the page. Reminding us of the long and arduous
periods of revision Woolf required of herself—periods of revision so taxing

that they aggravated her mental illness—Louise insisted that nothing was more deadly to powerful, convincing, and committed prose than the writer's own tendency to censor her thoughts.

What we did during class time instead was to look at how other writers had handled certain difficult problems or subjects. For example, how to write about sex—one of Louise's favorite topics; the others were food and her Italian heritage—was approached via an analysis of excerpts from Anaïs Nin's *House of Incest*. (A few days after writing this sentence, I recognize that the title of her final book refers intertextually to Nin's.) We would each have a day to present our work to the class and individual time with her during office hours. Believing that the pages I produced could indeed be revised into a novel, Louise helped me to drop all the courses I had planned to take that spring, including an honors independent study on theories of political art, and instead devote myself to finishing my novel.[3] At the time, I was twenty-four.

When I think back on this experience, I wonder what she saw in my work that would lead her to do something I would likely never encourage, never mind assist, one of my own students in doing. When a draft of the novel was finished, Louise gave me the name and phone number of an editor at Viking and a strict set of instructions concerning how to act as my own agent: Never speak to an editorial assistant; go right to the person authorized to decide whether to publish your manuscript. Learn how to speak convincingly about your own work. What makes it unique but familiar, something that might pique an editor's interest but also convince her that the book could accommodate the press's vision and understanding of its own audience? If the editor ultimately passes on the manuscript but offers words of encouragement, convince her to give you the name of an editor at another press. And be prepared to be rejected many, many times. Rejection is just part of the process. Louise's advice was always loving but no-nonsense, pragmatic, and self-assured—the voice she probably wished her own father had used with her when, for example, teaching her to swim. Sometimes, her father's "spectacular tenor" could express parental pride and encouragement; however, it could also be relentlessly disapproving, accusatory, judgmental.

Louise's advice proved invaluable: After being rejected by first Viking and then New American Library, I got ahold of the name of an editor at Lyle Stuart, Mario Sartori. I will never forget the moment when I received the phone call that the book had been accepted. I was standing in the kitchen of my partner at the time in a rent-controlled fourth-floor walk-up on East 73rd, and to try and brighten up this dark sliver of a room, I had painted that kitchen what were then considered "southwest" colors—turquoise and melon—and as my partner's cat, which frequently hissed at me, curled around my legs, and Mario said he wanted to publish the book, I replied, "Are you sure?"

Louise was my teacher. But she was more than that. She was my mentor, my role model, the professor I wanted to be when I grew up—with her long skirts, extravagant shawls, and chunky jewelry. She was a stylish dresser, a presence, someone whose husky voice and frankness—about relationships, she once said to me, "You have to figure out if the fucking you're getting is worth the fucking you're getting"—filled the room, a more generous mother than mine, given her history of mental illness, could ever hope to be. (It was only years later that I learned that we shared this, a mother with a long history of mental illness that included electroshock therapy and whose illness interfered with her ability to take care of her children.) I loved Louise. And we both identified not simply as Italian Americans, but as *southern* Italian Americans.

When I wasn't writing my novel, however, I was passionately pursuing this relatively new, odd animal called literary theory. I distinctly remember one of my male professors at Hunter, a tall, Jesuit-educated, balding, distinguished man with a booming voice, tell those of us in his Modern American Poetry class that there was this thing called poststructuralism that we would not be discussing. So I found two other professors I also loved, John Potter and Elizabeth Beaujour, who ran the Thomas Hunter Honors program, of which I was a member, to do an independent study with me in which we would struggle together through some difficult texts. Every two weeks we met to discuss what was then called semiotics, including works by Barthes, Derrida, Foucault—the only requirement being that I had to produce a piece of writing in response to whatever I had read. In between, I also managed to take independent studies in poetry writing with Eve Leoff and Audre Lorde, two more of Hunter's most generous professors. (When the editor at Viking worried that my novel was too brief, Louise pragmatically advised me to insert into it whatever "unused" writing I possessed, including the poems I had written with Eve and Audre. It worked, and they remained in the book.)

Almost all these people are gone now. Audre and John died in the same year, 1992. Louise and Eve both died in 2018. I just googled "DeSalvo," and up came Louise's Italian Wikipedia page, and I see photos of her, and then follow one of those photos to the fall 2020 issue of *Assay*, which is a tribute to her, and I say to myself, "Don't, don't read these essays. Don't read these essays. You are having a hard enough time figuring out what to say about this woman to whom you owe such an incalculable debt of gratitude."

When Louise discovered that I was interested in poststructuralist theory, her response was along the lines of "John, you're not really a theorist; you're a fiction writer or a memoirist." For Louise was of that generation of feminists "before" the turn to French theory, a generation that understood writing about one's experiences as a woman to be crucial to the struggle for autonomy. Her memoirs were unflinching, as she was fully committed to the belief that memoir was a vehicle for coming to terms with the past, not simply the past of the individual, but the past of that society of which the memoirist was a member. Identifying with Woolf, DeSalvo might (also) have been speaking of herself here: "the memoir was a radical form of history because it so often described pain, sorrow, suffering, humiliation, trauma, and sexual violence, . . . Rewriting history from the point of view of the victim, of the outsider, was a project to which Woolf was personally committed" (DeSalvo 1989, 15).[4] Around the issue of identity, Louise had had some kind of public scrape with Gayatri Spivak that ended with Louise saying, perhaps even in our novel-writing class, "How dare a high caste Brahman woman tell me there are no working-class intellectuals in the US!" Years later, when I repeated this anecdote to another graduate student (I was completing my PhD at the University of Pittsburgh at the time, Spivak was there as a Mellon professor, and we were all both terrified and in awe of her), my colleague replied, "Wow. Ethnicity, class, and gender, all in one anecdote."

My hope is that readers will now return to my epigraphs with a clearer sense of their purpose and a clearer sense of why it is so difficult for me to write this essay. As any of its scholars know, the status of experience in the fields of what Robyn Wiegman calls identity knowledges has always been fraught—as has been my own role in these debates, thanks to a single chapter in my first scholarly monograph (Champagne 1995). Based on that chapter, Ernesto Javier Martínez argued, "White queer scholars like John Champagne . . . cast doubt on and minimize the identity-based knowledge generated by people of color" (2012, 26). Note here the critical slide from my critique of experience to a discussion of identity-based knowledge, as if knowledge and experience were commensurate, as if "being" and "knowing" were identical. Such a position is, de facto, a diligently anti-psychoanalytic one.

This same critic further contends that "these patterns of erasure and misappropriation reflect a racial logic grounded in the supposition that writers of color are less theoretically astute" than their white critics (Martínez

2012, 26–27). Such a critique ignores 1) how my critique of the category of experience has not been limited to the work of writers of color; 2) my scholarship's substantial investments in the insights of two particular writers of color, Kobena Mercer and that sometime antagonist of DeSalvo, Spivak, once falsely accused in print of being my mentor; 3) another writer of color's far more trenchant, pointed, and convincing critique of experience than my own, that of Chow. That Martínez's critique could somehow "overlook" Spivak, Mercer, and Chow as both theoretically astute and writers of color who do not assume that the category of experience is sacrosanct evinces the way that the locution "writers of color" is not simply descriptive but rather constitutive; it is deployed not simply to name a preexisting subject but to constitute a subject whose authority to speak and be heard is confirmed by the appropriate identity credentials.

One of the earliest and most important contributions to the critique of experience was feminist historian Joan W. Scott's "The Evidence of Experience" (also cited negatively by Martínez), which characterized the documenting of subaltern experience as "a highly successful and limiting strategy for historians of difference" (1993, 399). As Scott argues,

> Making visible the experience of a different group exposes the existence of repressive mechanisms, but not their inner workings or logics. . . . For that we need to attend to the historical processes that, through discourse, position subjects and produce their experiences. It is not individuals who have experience, but subjects who are constituted through experience. Experience in this definition then becomes not the origin of our explanation, not the authoritative (because seen or felt) evidence that grounds what is known, but rather that which we seek to explain, that about which knowledge is produced. (401)

Scott adds that the recourse to experience buttresses claims for referentiality: "What could be truer, after all, than a subject's own account of what he or she has lived through?" (399). Chow calls this claim for referentiality the "age-old realist fallacy" (2002, 113).[5] Even champions of experiential knowledge acknowledge its investment in realism when they refer to the critique of experience as antirealism (Martínez 2012, 26).

·To Scott's reference to the seen or felt, we should add the "heard," for the investment in experience frequently grounds its authority in the "voice" of the experiencing subject that has been freed from repression either culturally or even psychically induced—as DeSalvo's reference to Woolf's "telling," cited in my epigraph, demonstrates. This reference to both voice and a model of power as repression reveals that what is at issue here is the claiming or restitution of the subaltern subject's sovereignty, autonomy, and agency.

As my epigraphs from Chow and Wiegman imply, the two projects Scott lays out here—the making visible of experience versus the historicizing of experience—require different "languages" with different discursive conventions, different levels of abstraction, and, as Scott and Chow's references to referentiality suggest, perhaps even different epistemologies of language. Rather than take for granted this thing called a white working-class Italian American woman, for example, as the grounds from which experience arises, feminist historians and scholars need to understand experience as the effect of subject constitution. Scholars like DeSalvo risk substituting an effect for a cause, what Spivak terms "positing a metalepsis" (204, 1987), for identities do not "cause" experience; they are the effects of having been constituted as experience's subject.

And as Scott's essay suggests, the position outlined in DeSalvo's reading of Woolf is readily accommodated by "normative" historiography. In this model of history, identity knowledges are called upon to insert bodies previously excluded from social history, which, thanks to the familiarity of the move, it readily accommodates. In this scenario, historiography is primarily a process of accretion. As Scott suggests, such a model of historiography risks taking for granted the very differences that a critical approach to history is called upon to interrogate and explain. To ground my discussion in a specific example, an anthology of essays on "Italian Americans" risks taking this category for granted and in the process naturalizing and reifying historically contingent and ideological constructions like ethnicity, race, blood, family, people, community, belonging, and heritage. In speaking of memoir as a kind of history, unsurprisingly, DeSalvo ignores, in particular, the poststructuralist critique of historiography.[6]

So why am I writing an essay on DeSalvo's understanding of memoir? One of the many things I learned from Louise was to allow myself to write my way into an essay, to figure out where I am going as I go there: "I initially have no idea of what I'm doing, of where the writing will take me, of what the essay will say, of what the language will sound like, of how it will be organized" (DeSalvo 2018, 130–33). Am I simply trying to demonstrate that DeSalvo's memoirs do not pass whatever poststructuralist litmus test I bring to them? Or is my project the mirror opposite, to prove the potential of DeSalvo's work to being read deconstructively? To

rescue Louise from poststructuralist critique? My own feminist consciousness is sufficient to recognize the highly problematic gender politics of this
antifeminist gesture of attempting to "save" a woman in distress. Perhaps
my project is underwritten by, as Martínez might put it, a gendered logic
grounded in the supposition that women writers are less theoretically astute
than men (2012, 27).

This is not even to broach the topic (a locution that of course always
signals a desire to do exactly that) of my own psychoanalytic investments
in Louise as ego-ideal/mother figure/object of desire, as well as the work of
mourning, the necessity of de-cathecting my libido from this lost object to
avoid the pathology of melancholia—that work made more difficult by the
fact that Louise and I lost track of one another, never getting to share, for
example, our mutual love of an Italy we were experiencing not vicariously
but via our own experiences of travel. Furthermore, my last contact with
Louise was a string of emails from around the time she was first diagnosed
with breast cancer that would ultimately end her life. Writing this essay
means confronting both a survivor's guilt brought on by the recognition of
my own discomfort around disease and death, and shame at my tendency
to assume that the terminally ill would prefer the "dignity" of suffering
behind closed doors, beyond the gaze of friends, as did Mario, the editor
of my first novel, who died from HIV, as did other people from that period
in my life in which I was close to Louise. These included André Mathis, a
French cabaret singer whom I accompanied on the piano, who also died of
HIV, and Geoffrey, another student of Louise's and someone with whom
I fell briefly in love after returning to New York to read from one of my
novels. In fact, Louise introduced me to Geoffrey.

In this fairy tale, however, I am both hero and villain, for what I am
saving DeSalvo from is my own poststructuralist critique; no one to my
knowledge has read her memoirs to demonstrate their reliance on the fiction
of the transcendental, humanist subject. When I begin writing this essay, I
have not reread Louise's work in years, and so I expect a phantom version
of her writing self—one particularly wedded to an unreflective identity
politics that would employ memoir as a tool to consolidate naive notions of
experience. But what that itself might have even looked like is, after reading
her work, no longer clear to me, for she is too fine a writer to adopt wholesale a "realist" epistemology to consolidate the figure of "woman." Louise's
woman is *always* divided by class, ethnicity, and even race, for example,
whether it be her grandmother (her mother's stepmother), her mother, her
sister, or herself. Identifications and desires traverse some boundaries but

not others, as when DeSalvo identifies with her grandmother, who at times literally protected DeSalvo from her father's anger and physical violence, but then joins in the fun when her friends ridicule her: "My grandmother was a God-sent protector in my house of anger and sorrow. But she was also someone I was ashamed of, that I made fun of to my friends so my friends wouldn't make fun of me because of her. As if in repudiating her I could leach out the Italian in me and become what I then thought was important" (DeSalvo 2018, 709–12).

If my essay has an argument, it is simply this: DeSalvo's Italian American memoirs evince all the contradictions of North American ethnic and immigrant writing (Chow 2022, 139). The danger all such writing faces is that it will seek to interpellate subaltern subjects in the specific Althusserian sense of hailing them as sovereign and autonomous agents. Rather than employ the position of the subaltern to deconstruct the Enlightenment subject's claims to mastery and autonomy—as Chow reminds us, "the belief that a turn to the self is emancipatory is as old a myth as the Enlightenment" (2022, 113)—ethnic memoir risks turning the marginalized subject into the subject of biopower who mistakes the enslavement that comes with what Chow has called "coercive mimeticism" for liberation (2022, 115). Italian American subjects' "We are here!" mistakes the "voluntary surrender that is, in the end, fully complicit with the guilty verdict that has been declared on them socially long before they speak" with freedom (2022, 115). For rendering the Italian American body visible requires the ethnic writer to "imitate, resemble, and become" the ethnic subject—which of necessity, in turn, requires the employment of certain stereotypes. As Chow, Tim Dean, Antonio Viego, and Scott have in different ways proposed, an engagement with the psychoanalytic critique of the subject requires that we differentiate between "losses and deficits that represent unequal distribution of social resources, including visibility and dignity, on the one hand" and those that are constitutive of the subject on the other (Dean, quoted in Viego 2007, 16). This is the problem faced by any writer who wants to juggle a post-structuralist critique of the transcendental subject—Marxist, Foucauldian, or psychoanalytic—with representing—whether, in Spivak's famous formulation, by proxy or portrait, the two often confused—the subaltern (Spivak 1990, 108). As a radical lesbian theorist, Monique Wittig put it in a particularly deadpan manner, "The question of the individual subject is historically a difficult one for everybody" (106). Louise included. Me included.

Following Slavoj Žižek's reading of Althusser, Chow calls into question the idea of the resistant ethnic subject as the subject who voluntarily challenges interpellation by hegemonic discourses of race and ethnicity. Instead, Chow foregrounds the way in which "what the subject always resists is this *terror of complete freedom* rather than the ideological, institutional process of being interpellated" (2022, 110, italics in original). In this scenario, identity results not from "imposition of rules from the outside" or resistance against such imposition, but rather a kind of "*unconscious automatization, impersonation, or mimicking,* in behavior as much as in psychology, of certain beliefs, practices, and rituals. It is such automatization, impersonation, and mimicry that, in turn, gives that identity its sense of legitimacy and security—and, ultimately, its sense of potentiality and empowerment" (110, italics in original). This "impersonation" is what Chow terms "socially endorsed, coercive mimeticism" (115). In DeSalvo's memoirs, this Italianate mimicking includes melodramatic modes of physical and emotional comportment—"in my house, we gesticulated wildly. We shouted. Threatened harm to others ('I'll kill you'), to ourselves ('I may as well kill myself')" (DeSalvo 2005, 38). Cooking as a demonstration of love and a creative, feminine, and feminist response to the daily grind of housework and women's lack of agency, including authority over one's own body; eating as an act of both physical and emotional sustenance; and the recording of her family's history in first the "Old Country" and then the United States on the one hand, and surviving sexism, deprivation of food and affection, and sexual abuse on the other: DeSalvo, her father, and per-haps even her mother are all survivors of abuse, and in the case of DeSalvo and her father, the perpetrators were other Italians.[7] And DeSalvo is quite self-conscious about the way food is compensatory for loss:

> I know I act this way, this crazy-in-the-kitchen way, because I want the food I make to be perfect. With each perfect meal I make, I can undo the past. Undo that my mother couldn't feed me, undo her fury at my grandmother. Undo my father's violence. Undo my ancestors' history. I act as if, through this alchemy at the stove, I can erase my past instead of reliving it. But reliving it I am—all the fury of it, all the battles, all the despair. And must stop reliving it. (DeSalvo 2005, 166)

Note several contradictions here to which we will return: an investment in ego psychology allows DeSalvo to imagine that her damaged subjectivity can be repaired via the act of cooking; that same investment, however, leads her superego to claim that she must cease to engage in this self-destructive behavior. But in fact, she does not. The memoir from which this is drawn is published in 2005; DeSalvo will return to these same ghosts in 2018—continuing to live all the fury, battles, and despair—when she publishes her last book, the process of aging providing her with the rationale "to tinker, to add new material, to shift the ballast of an essay" (DeSalvo 2018, 143). Cooking, ego psychology, the recording, via memoir, of her past experiences—none can actually deliver on their promises to "undo" the damaging effects of history.

As Chow suggests, to confess to being ethnic is not to escape power but to provide evidence of its productive capacities. Chow critiques the humanist understandings of self-representation as liberating by demystifying the ethnic subjects' illusion that "by referring to themselves, they are liberating themselves from the powers that subordinate them" (2002, 115). We see this illusion in DeSalvo's reading of Woolf cited above: "Rewriting history from the point of view of the victim, of the outsider," is treated as a liberating act of social justice. In light of Foucault's account of biopower and following Chow, we might instead read an ethnic memoir as "allowing such powers to work in the most intimate fashion—from within their hearts and souls, in a kind of voluntary surrender that is, in the end, fully complicit with the guilty verdict that has been declared on them socially long before they speak" (2002, 115). The idea that breaking the silence about one's ethnic condition is a form of liberation from suffering is implicit in DeSalvo's memoirs when she asks, "For how could I publish an essay that spoke of my family's past, my father's violence, my husband's adultery?" (DeSalvo 2018, 105–6). The question is rhetorical, for it is precisely of these secrets that her memoirs will speak:

> For there were, and would be, secrets in our family—that my mother's mother had died; that the grandmother I knew was her stepmother; that after her birth mother's death, my mother was abused by caregivers; that she had been institutionalized and shock treated; that my grandfather drank too much; that my father was violent; that my sister killed herself; that I was sexually abused by someone known to the family. These subjects were never discussed, much less written about. (DeSalvo 2018, 51–54)

Throughout the memoir, all of these secrets, and more, are shared.

The necessary correlative of this breaking of silence to reveal secrets is the delivery of ethnic experience: as she writes of the memories of Italy presented to her by her grandparents, "Their stories, which I believed were fabrications when I was young, were true, all true" (DeSalvo 2004, 6). One of the functions of DeSalvo's memoirs is to preserve these stories so as "to ensure that their deaths do not erase the meaning and significance of their lives" (DeSalvo 2018, 162–63). But the precondition of writing is the absence of the writing subject, and no act of writing can secure the meaning and significance of a life. Memoir is thus doomed to failure.

One of the central problems of writing "theoretically" about ethnicity is that of trying to use a language that does not "neutralize precisely the very emotional effects of injustice that persist as the remnants of lived experience" (Chow 2002, 135). Memoir implicitly suggests that the language of theory, or what Wiegman instead calls critical imagination, is not adequate to the project of recording—and presumably redressing—the suffering that accompanies being the Other. That DeSalvo has been damaged by poverty, and its attendant racialization, is clear. For, as the title of her final book suggests, DeSalvo's memoirs are a record of sorrow. They memorialize her family history, from the poverty of her grandparents to the afterlife of that poverty in the United States, an afterlife that destroyed some family members—her mentally ill mother, her alcoholic maternal grandfather, her suicidal sister—and left others permanently wounded—her paternal grandmother, her father, herself: "Deep sorrow. A yearning that will never be satisfied. I know that what I wanted, what I needed, I will never find here, and that I will have to live with this knowledge, and that learning to live with it will be another kind of education" (DeSalvo 2005, 144).

The "here" to which DeSalvo refers is Rodi Garganico, the village where her step-grandmother was born and to which DeSalvo has returned to "make a record. So my family's story would not vanish" (2005, 139). Once again, memoir is a record of its own failure, a tabulating of what psychoanalytic critics call castration, that bodily knowledge of yearnings that will never be satisfied.

Note the contradiction again, the recognition of the reparative work memoir undertakes, and its constant failure to secure its object of desire. DeSalvo's memoirist is trapped in the "Who am I?" willing and obligated to produce an identity via memoir—"Who I am, who I have become, is rooted in this beautiful place that my grandmother's family was forced to leave" (DeSalvo 2005, 168)—but aware that such a project is doomed: "the only real place I can visit is the Rodi Garganico in my memory," the Rodi her grandmother narrated to her (2005, 143). In such a formulation, memories are "more real" than reality. As for the "real" Rodi DeSalvo experiences: "I am nothing but an invader here" (2005, 144).

Whatever she might have said about Woolf, DeSalvo is far too self-critical—and far too good a writer—to assume that writing memoir is a simple transcription of "what really happened" and a naive, positivist attempt to rewrite history. In her memoirs, DeSalvo produces herself as the divided subject, who maintains two contradictory knowledges at once, who knows and does not know that language can never make good on its promise to re-present the past, to undo the wound that is life. And one of the signs of DeSalvo's recognition of this perpetual wounding is a refusal to recuperate Italy, "a land that starved my grandparents until they were forced to leave for America" (DeSalvo 2005, 192).

However ambivalent De Salvo might have felt about theory, her memoirs return perpetually not only to a personal past that will not be healed but to language and its inability to make good on its promise to repair the wound. Wiegman's phrase "critical imagination" is highly suggestive of DeSalvo's own resistance to this coercive mimeticism, this realist fallacy that proposes that writing is simply the (allegedly) transparent, linguistic transcribing of what is already present or the stripping away of the blockages to the repressed voices of the subaltern. DeSalvo's own attempts to use writing to employ personal history to rewrite social history is interrupted by her reminder that every memoir does not simply reflect but also constitutes its subjects, and those subjects will always be fractured, divided, alienated from themselves.

For, despite her own claims, memoir is not history, and DeSalvo knows this. Her endless returns to the scene of the crime—her childhood, parental neglect, the legacy of poverty and abuse—fly in the face of a model of history as accretion because, presumably, once the experiences of the subaltern have been added to the historical record, the positivist historian can move on in search of other gaps and fissures to fill in. In DeSalvo, however, there is no redemption. Which is to say that DeSalvo's memoirs are not history, even social or personal history, but literature, that way of writing that at least theoretically exceeds realist epistemologies in its perpetual return to the signifier and its opacity. The fact that DeSalvo revised some of these essays over and over, literally until she died, is proof of that perpetual return. The language of experience cannot make good on its promises to allow the subaltern to speak, and, in so doing, heal the wound that is history. So all she can do is keep speaking.

Although she insists her relatives' stories were all true, DeSalvo cannot be accused of the naivete of realism and does not treat realism as if it were nonrepresentational. Traveling to Rodi, she confronts the impossibility of delivering experience: "All I can do is conjecture, imagine, invent their lives.

My story of their story, a distortion, a misrepresentation of what they lived. But my story of their story, now a respect I must accord them—though I cannot possibly get it right, though I cannot possibly understand who they were—so their lives do not pass into oblivion. My story of their story gives me something I did not have before. It fixes me in time" (DeSalvo 2005, 143). Given my having been wounded, "all I can do" is continue to fabricate, to weave together the strands of this textile called life, to perform as a bricoleuse. "Fixes" is an interesting word choice here, for it can mean both "repairs" and "affixes." In DeSalvo's work, it is fiction—story, distortion, misrepresentation, text—rather than historicism, naive or otherwise, that allows her to locate herself temporally and spatially. And, like "fixes me," the phrase "in time" is equally ambiguous: in time for what?

Whatever DeSalvo claimed about memoir, as she writes, she invents herself as an Italian American working-class feminist. Hers is a subjectivity having been produced by experience, and writing is her way of jotting down the traces of that subjectivity. For, as she insists, memoir is never a process of simply recording one's experience but is instead a fabrication: "I initially have no idea of what I'm doing, of where the writing will take me, of what the essay will say, of what the language will sound like, of how it will be organized" (DeSalvo 2018, 130–31). This is one aspect of writing that, as Louise's student, I most hope to convey to my own. It is how this difficult essay gets written.

The idea of writing as a (thwarted) repair of the self is omnipresent in DeSalvo's writing, but this idea is always haunted by failure: "My writing life has been a series of breakings and mendings, a shattering of the writing self that was, a repairing, through writing, of something in my life that warranted understanding and that needed fixing" (DeSalvo 2018, 110–11).

Here again, we see the emphasis on fixing, on bricolage, the restitution of the fractured ethnic subject—in an act of coercive mimicry, she calls this metaphor "a very Italian way of describing the creative process"—(2018, 114) via "mending." But that mending is always provisional, for the writing life never concludes, as DeSalvo's extraordinary commitment to revision demonstrates. Even with the death of the writer, the "breaking and mending" continue in the act of reading—as this present essay demonstrates, as I break and mend the Louise I knew, did not know, and continue to know and not know. And that breaking and mending haunt my own writing life, for as I write, my memory of Louise chides me to be my bravest writing self, to meet her expectations that I be the writer that she believed me to be—an impossible project, a chasing after a lost object that can only end in failure. And will only end in my death.

That DeSalvo was no naive realist is evidenced in the many passages in her memoirs where she discusses the act of writing, emphasizing not truth but "the power of the imagination, the power of language to create a world, the power of language to forge a bond between people, the power of language to record experience and to reflect upon its significance, the power of language to make us feel as if what we do has meaning" (DeSalvo 2018, 77–79). Once more, we see the contradiction, the idea of language as a powerful tool to repair suffering and record experience, but also the recognition that such power is illusory: for language's power "to make us feel as if" is precisely that, a ruse.

One of the most powerful attempts to nudge memoir towards the kind of history Scott proposes is DeSalvo's essay on her maternal step-grandmother's process of naturalization as a US citizen. Of course, such writing will be contradictory. Bringing together the language of emotion with the abstraction of theory—signaled, in DeSalvo, via the scare quotation marks she puts around the term "racialized"—it cannot help but be so (DeSalvo 2018, 865). In this memoir, DeSalvo "theorizes" the experience of her step-grandmother to get at something of how ethnicity works in capitalism. Yet the language in which she performs this theorization is chiefly that of a rage against injustice.

According to world-systems theory, in the modern world, ethnicity supplies capitalism with one of the tools it needs to reproduce its hierarchized and spatially distributed division of labor (Wallerstein 2003). Ethnic difference provides a powerful yet flexible and adaptable way to code subjects into positions within that globalized labor hierarchy. Because commodity chains traverse state frontiers (with the corollary that different kinds of labor need to be available in different spatial locations), capitalism can allocate to different ethnic groups specific roles in worldwide labor processes by referring to alleged and allegedly shared cultural traits. Such traits make one more or less suited to particular kinds of work. When, because of competition processes, a global relocating of labor becomes necessary, ethnicity, via immigration, helps transfer certain kinds of workers—typically those lower on the hierarchy—to the places they would be most useful to the accumulation of profit. All it takes is a handful of immigrant success stories to increase this relocation of labor.

In accounts of her ethnicity, DeSalvo always emphasizes the poverty of Southern Italy, the efforts of its peoples to survive not only its peripheral role in the Italian economy but its multiple foreign invasions, and, once they arrived in the United States, the places such peoples occupied on the lower end of the labor hierarchy—as well as the way Italians were "darkened" in an attempt to tie visible biological characteristics such as skin tone to the alleged cultural traits that made one "suited" to such work. Her 2005 *Crazy in the Kitchen*, for example, begins by providing a brief description of Southern Italy that emphasizes its peripheral status, its history of repeated conquest, and the effects of the ravages of poverty on its residents. "The rich, my grandfather said, owned everything. everything. The poor, my grandfather said, owned nothing in the land where he came from, they did not even own their own shit, which was taken from them by the landlords for fertilizing the fields where the poor, like my grandfather, worked for almost nothing" (DeSalvo 2005, 4). Such poverty led both her maternal and paternal grandparents to leave Italy for the United States, whose promise of education for the children of one's children's children they found enchanting (2018, 46).

Throughout her autobiographical writings, DeSalvo emphasizes the roles of her grandparents and parents in the United States on the lower end of the labor hierarchy. She asks us to remember this historical shift in labor necessitated by both the peripheral status of the Italian south and the United States' need for workers willing to accept substandard wages, and she understands the role ethnicity plays in capitalism's division of labor: "But at this time her (my) people were believed able to build the nation's railroads, its subways, its buildings; fight its wars; mill its fabric; sew its clothing; mine its coal; stow and unload its cargo; farm its fruits and vegetables; organize its crime; play its baseball; and, of course, make its pizza, its ravioli, and its spaghetti and meatballs" (2018, 856–59).

In the aforementioned essay on her step-grandmother's naturalization, DeSalvo provides a specific instance of how capitalism can manufacture race according to its historically contingent needs. This essay, published more than once but included in her *The House of Early Sorrows* under the title "Dark White," begins with a brief account of her father's life as a child immigrant to the United States from Scafati, a village near Naples, and the prejudice he faced in his adopted country. After explaining her reason for recounting her family history—so that, thanks to sharing family stories with her children and grandchildren, their "forebearers, these people, their lives, our past, will not be forgotten" (2018, 647–48)—she moves back and forth between personal and social history.[8]

In this essay, DeSalvo weaves material she has learned about the history of Italy and Italian immigration—including both the deprivations to which *contadini* and farm workers were subject in Italy's *Mezzogiorno* and the initial brutal treatment of Italian immigrants in the United States, which featured, in the American South, lynching—with her family's specific circumstances as members of the immigrant working class. This is followed by an explanation for why her grandparents did not complain about those circumstances. In another act of coercive mimeticism, DeSalvo explains that they were "products of *contadina* culture: proud, accepting, and fatalistic" (2018, 670). She then insists that

> because they didn't recount their grievances but instead buried them, I have few stories to share about these grandparents; little has come down to me about how my grandparents and their parents lived in Italy or when they came to the United States; nothing about how they were treated or the difficulties they encountered. What little I learned about them came through story, only I was too young to know that the stories they told—about the ferocious sun, the unforgiving sea, the empty bellies—weren't stories at all. And because, unlike other migrants, these people were often illiterate, they left very few written accounts with which we can write their history. And their grandchildren are just beginning to write their stories, cobbling them together, as I have, from anecdote, research, speculation. (DeSalvo 2018, 676–81)

The passage is both startling and laudable in its contradictions, including its supplementing of history with story. What little the writer has learned about her ancestors' stories that were not stories came through story, story that, in turn, both adds to and supplies what is missing from history. Note how the refusal of language to reveal the truth of her grandparents is not repressive but productive: Because these stories that were not stories were not told, the writer must speak in the name of her grandparents; because, thanks to their silence, the writer cannot deliver to us the experience of her grandparents, she must fabricate it. And that productive silence produces three book-length works on these now told untold stories.

Additionally, what would otherwise be considered, by a realist epistemology of language, an act of injustice—speaking for others rather than allowing their experience to speak for itself—is authorized by claims of ownership; because they are my family, my people, and they (did not) tell me their stories that were not stories, I can speak for them.[9] That ownership, however, is not based on "blood" but the kinship of a particularly artificial and even accidental sort, for the woman in question in this essay is DeSalvo's mother's stepmother, described at one point by DeSalvo's father as a "mail order bride" shipped to Italy to take care of DeSalvo's mother when she was still a child (DeSalvo 2018, 694–95). In DeSalvo's memoir, then, "my people" is not a hereditary group. It risks showing the frayed edges of the category of ethnicity itself, revealing the artificial and accidental quality of any ethnic identity.

When DeSalvo's father delivers her step-grandmother's naturalization papers to her, he provides her with a story that proves to be wrong: He thinks her maternal grandparents came from a small village near Bari, but he is mistaken. "My grandfather, I learned, came from Vieste and my grandmother from Rodi Garganico, both in Puglia but at some distance from Bari" (2018, 691–92). Not only can her father not speak for himself, but when he does speak, he cannot get it right. Minus the mediating voice of the writer, the truth of experience—stitched together from "anecdote, research, speculation"—will be lost. Regardless of what DeSalvo wrote about Woolf and her investments in "telling what you remembered, and writing down what had happened to you," to tell the true story of her family, DeSalvo must engage in "the work of memory, narrative, identification, and desire" to which Wiegman alludes. Rather than the "flatlining of the complexity of experience" we would expect, given her commitment to truth telling, to find in DeSalvo, what we find instead is a richly theorized work of fiction, a story.

The most overtly "theoretical" move in DeSalvo's essay occurs, however, when she analyzes what happened to her step-grandmother. As part of the naturalization process, she is described by a low-level bureaucratic as "color White; complexion Dark," and this description is then recorded on her papers (2018, 802). First asking why, given the photograph attached to the document, her "complexion" would need to be noted, DeSalvo then insists this description is false, and her grandmother would never have provided it: "as anyone could see, her complexion was fair though the document insists that it was Dark" (2018, 811–12).[10] Fully committed to the anti-racist assumption that racial categories are ideological fictions, DeSalvo notes, "My grandmother had become 'racialized'" (2018, 865). As Wittig puts it, "what we believe to be a physical and direct perception is only a sophisticated and mythic construction . . . which reinterprets physical features (in themselves as neutral as any others but marked by the social system) through the network of relationships in which they are perceived. (They are seen as *black*, therefore they *are* black") (Wittig 1993, 104). In charting this racialization, DeSalvo provides a concrete example of how the state assists capitalism via allegedly value-neutral techniques like the gathering of demographic statistics.[11]

Furthermore, in insisting the paid functionary got her grandmother's complexion wrong, DeSalvo undermines the idea on which much ethnic memoir as positivist history is predicated—the idea that experience is a value-neutral category, a simple record of the real, whose veracity must be trusted. For, to make her argument, DeSalvo must foreground how this paid functionary "got it wrong"—although this bureaucrat "experienced" her grandmother's complexion "first-hand"—something DeSalvo herself could not have done at the time since she was not yet born.[12]

In other words, DeSalvo does not suggest that the functionary fibbed about her grandmother's complexion, that he falsified his experience to assist the state in its production of racialized subjects so as to fulfill the lower rungs of the labor hierarchy. (And, according to DeSalvo, it is not insignificant that her family was poor—her grandmother, for example, acting as the superintendent of her apartment building to get a reduction in her rent.) According to DeSalvo, "Anyone who looked at her, who truly witnessed her face on that day," would not describe her as dark" (2018, 828–29). Yet this bureaucrat did—because his experience was mediated by the kind of subject he had been produced to be, and whose own role was to produce her grandmother as the type of subject she was supposed to be. As DeSalvo rightfully concludes, her grandmother's naturalization document is material evidence that "my people's whiteness was provisional, that agents of the government were using their power to create rather than record difference in physical appearance" (2018, 848–49). But these functionaries were seeing what their experience had taught them to see: what they were supposed to see.

So who is the Louise I am supposed to see? Lately I am fascinated by this locution, the way it means both "ought to" and "assumed to," and how the agent doing the supposing is an absent subject. Being suspicious of the evidence of experience and its faith in the realist fallacy, I know there is no real Louise for me to reveal, and even to try to do so is to make her available to the machinations of biopower. But, as Chow states, theory's emotional disengagement threatens to lose the effects of suffering that memoir intends to produce. Thus, when writing about memoir's failure, Louise and

I both resort to memoir. For memoir is a narcissism justified by suffering, the narcissism that keeps the self alive. Minus that narcissism, none of us would survive life's many losses and disappointments.

What are the stakes in preserving this record of suffering? DeSalvo is forthright about the personal ones. "I want to find out as much as I can about my family before he [her father] dies" (2005, 109). But what about the rest of us? As DeSalvo suggests, "this form of memoir that honors our forebears by reimagining their lives but without romanticizing them is especially necessary during a time when ordinary people are being robbed of their ability to lead a dignified life, when their past stands in danger of being erased, when in a nation of supposed promise, the future is bleak for those, like my forebears, who work hard and long, yet try to continue, against all obstacles, to hope, to dream" (2018, 150–53). "Dark White" is an important reminder of how racial categories are historical and the way capitalism has provided itself with a lethally efficient way of creating and dispensing with groups of workers to fill the lower echelons of the international division of labor. Although she may not have intended it, Louise's account of her grandmother's racialization is an effort to fabricate the cultural memory of southern Italian Americans at a time when, for some Italians and their Italian American relatives, Africa is still too close for comfort. To the depressingly prominent Italian American supporters of Donald Trump and his racist policies, DeSalvo argues, "This was you; you were dark."

Presumably, beyond simple voyeurism, the appeal of memoir is its invitation to empathize with and learn about the cultural and historical background of its writer. Unfortunately, in the current political and social climate, it does not seem to be working. Anecdotally, Italian Americans do not care about their racialized past; reminding them that they were once "dark" does not seem to carry much weight. In this land of the systemic erasure of historical memory, their experience of their own Italian American identity is largely confined to food, family, certain card games, the few words of Italian (or dialect) they might remember from their parents and grandparents, and a naive (in the sense of unexamined) ethnic pride connected to them all.

Nonetheless, DeSalvo's account of her grandmother's racialization suggests how the performative effects of Italian American identity might be martialed in a contemporary critique of racism. It responds, perhaps in spite of itself, to Scott's call for an employment of experience that does not take Italian American identity for granted but attempts to historicize, for example, one of the techniques of power by which this "dark" identity was produced (Scott 1993, 401). And it does so without repudiating the emotional effects of injustice that haunt the subjectivity of the oppressed.

Notes

1. Not being a Woolf scholar, I am in no position to adjudicate the accuracy of DeSalvo's claims but will note that this work had a profound effect on her own turn to memoir, particularly as a mode of self-healing from the trauma of sexual abuse. On her transition from a Woolf scholar to a memoirist, which she characterized as "a significant turning point in my writing life," see DeSalvo 2018, 147–48.

2. For a biography of DeSalvo, see Giunta 2002.

3. Set in New York, my book was about a young white gay man struggling to define his romantic and sexual ethics at a time when our collective knowledge of the epidemiology and route of transmission of HIV was still limited.

4. In one of her memoirs, DeSalvo makes this connection between Woolf's work and her own memoir writing explicit: "Virginia Woolf committed herself to writing about the lives of the obscure, for she believed these lives revealed more about the history of a culture than the lives of the great and famous" (DeSalvo 2018, 144–46).

5. As Chow has it, "Presumed to be direct and unmediated, the act of referring to oneself has taken on the aura of a type of representation that can miraculously transcend the limits of representation, a type of representation that . . . is morally justifiable because it is (thought to be) non-representational (2002, 113, italics in original).

6. For a summary of this critique, see Champagne 2019, 29–49.

7. Her mother's illness led to DeSalvo and her sister being sent to spend their summers with relatives, one of whom sexually abused DeSalvo. On the abuse, see DeSalvo 2002, esp. 102–5.

8. This attempt to use language to "fix" and preserve the history of the ethnic subject is an instance of what Viego terms a "compensatory, falsely reparative critical move" that however unintentionally provides "precisely the image of ethnic-racialized subjectivity as whole, complete, and transparent, an image upon which racist discourse thrives and against which we imagine we are doing battle" (Viego 2007, 16). It is the producing of this image that Chow terms "coercive mimeticism." As I have been suggesting throughout this chapter, what fascinates me about DeSalvo's memoir is the way it both does and does not invest in the project described by Viego, the way it both knows and refuses to acknowledge the "falseness" of its reparative critical moves.

9. On the critical turn to self-referential genres like memoir and their employment of a realist epistemology of language, as an always-failed attempt to circumvent

"the crime of speaking for others," see Chow 2002, 113. As Chow argues, "The fantasy they tend to harbor is that the act of referring only to the self can finally redeem us from the fundamental and contentious binary structure of representation in which one is always (inevitably) speaking of/for something or someone else."

10. "Had she been asked, my grandmother would have said, "Sometimes fair; sometimes dark" (DeSalvo 2018, 838–39).

11. "Because my grandmother was not quite white, she was also thought to be not quite (or not very) smart, not quite (or not very) reliable, not quite capable of self-government, not quite (or not very) capable of self-control, not quite capable of manifesting the traits of duty and obligation, not quite adaptable to organized and civilized society, not quite clean enough, not quite (or not at all) law-abiding (remember the Mafia)" (DeSalvo 2018, 853–56).

12. It seems that one of the constitutive contradictions of the employment of experience is the necessity of substituting one, discounted version of experience for another. In this example, DeSalvo must reject the experience of the bureaucrat to validate her own sense of her step-grandmother's complexion—despite the fact that she was *not actually there* at the time the functionary made his determination. Her own insistence that she, and not the bureaucrat, is correct challenges the very notion of experience as the grounds of truth. Additionally, such an insistence risks undermining DeSalvo's own argument, for to claim her step-grandmother is "really" fair is to employ the racist epistemology that assumes racial differences are not only self-evident but also empirically verifiable—an idea DeSalvo herself has rightfully challenged. DeSalvo suggests as much when she argues that the problem is simply that the functionary did not look "hard" enough at her grandmother's actual complexion. Beyond this recourse to a realist epistemology, such a claim assumes that racism is not systemic but a matter of individual bad faith, for the implication is that the functionary *could* have looked and simply seen that her grandmother was "light."

Works Cited

Althusser, Louis. 1971. "Ideology and Ideological State Apparatuses (Notes Towards an Investigation)." In *Lenin and Philosophy and Other Essays*, translated by Ben Brewster, 127–86. London: Monthly Review.

Champagne, John. 1995. *The Ethics of Marginality: A New Approach to Gay Studies*. Minneapolis: University of Minnesota Press.

———. 2019. *Queer Ventennio, Italian Fascism, Homoerotic Art, and the Nonmodern in the Modern*. Oxford: Peter Lang.

Chow, Rey. 2002. *The Protestant Ethnic and The Spirit of Capitalism*. New York: Columbia University Press.

DeSalvo, Louise. 1989. *Virginia Woolf: The Impact of Childhood Sexual Abuse on Her Life and Work*. New York: Ballantine Books.

———. 2002. *Vertigo*. New York: Feminist Press.

———. 2005. *Crazy in the Kitchen: Food, Feuds, and Forgiveness in an Italian American Family*. New York: Bloomsbury Publishing. Kindle.

———. 2018. *The House of Early Sorrows*. New York: Fordham University Press. Kindle.

Giunta, Edvige. 2002. "Introduction" to *Vertigo*, by Louise DeSalvo, ix–xxix. New York: Feminist Press.

Martínez, Ernesto Javier. 2012. *On Making Sense: Queer Race Narratives of Intelligibility*. Stanford: Stanford University Press.

Scott, Joan W. 1993. "The Evidence of Experience." In *The Lesbian and Gay Studies Reader*, edited by Henry Abelove, Michèle Aina Barale, and David M. Halperin, 397–415. New York: Routledge.

Spivak, Gayatri. 1987. *In Other Worlds: Essays in Culture Politics*. New York: Routledge.

———. 1990. *The Post-Colonial Critic. Interviews, Strategies, Dialogues*. Edited by Sarah Harasym. New York: Routledge.

Viego, Antonio. 2007. *Dead Subjects: Towards a Politics of Loss in Latino Studies*. Durham, NC: Duke University Press.

Wallerstein, Immanuel. 2003. *Historical Capitalism*. London: Verso.

Wiegman, Robyn. 2012. *Object Lessons*. Durham: Duke University Press.

Wittig, Monique. 1993. "One Is Not Born a Woman." In *The Lesbian and Gay Studies Reader*, edited by Henry Abelove, Michèle Aina Barale, and David M. Halperin, 103–9. New York: Routledge.

6

Criminalizing Desire

An Intersectional Approach to Patriarchy's Monsters in Karen Tintori's *Unto the Daughters: The Legacy of an Honor Killing in a Sicilian American Family* and Juliet Grames's *The Seven or Eight Deaths of Stella Fortuna*

Mary Jo Bona and Jessica Maucione

On July 5, 1902, in the rural outskirts of Rome, eleven-year-old Maria Teresa Goretti resisted the repeated sexual advances of the twenty-year-old son of the family who owned the farmhouse she, her mother, and her siblings had lived in since the death of her father. Because she fought back against her attacker, he first choked and then stabbed her fourteen times. She died in the hospital after voicing her forgiveness of the murderer and would-be rapist. Beatified and canonized by Pope Pius XII in 1947 and 1950, respectively, Maria Teresa Goretti continues to this day to be heralded as the Patroness of Purity and the Little Saint of Great Mercy—her relics visited the United States in 2015 in celebration of accepting and offering forgiveness.

Coinciding with the exposé of sexual abuse perpetrated by clergy in the Catholic Church, the twenty-first century is likewise seeing narrative interventions that unearth some of the other violent realities committed by Italian and Italian American fathers, brothers, and husbands in traditional families. There is a robust and well-documented literary history of Italian American women's narratives that counter nostalgic romanticizing of the

Little Italys and the families that once lived in them across the United States: Such places have often served as a chronotope, enfolding members into configurations of time and space that proscribe nontraditional behavior.[1] This chapter makes a critical intervention into two post-millennial narratives: Karen Tintori's *Unto the Daughters: The Legacy of an Honor Killing in a Sicilian American Family* and Juliet Grames's *The Seven or Eight Deaths of Stella Fortuna* to argue that the generic hybridity used by the authors enables a complex and deliberate representation of gendered domestic violence in Italian and Italian American families. *Unto the Daughters* is a memoir that uses elements of fiction such as plot and dialogue to reimagine the familial life of Tintori's great-aunt, Francesca/Frances. *The Seven or Eight Deaths* is a novel that injects first-person narratorial commentary from Grames to remind readers of the biographical imperative of her story.

We place Tintori and Grames into the larger tradition of Italian American women's writing and deploy feminist intersectional theories to enlarge a critique of how the intergenerational contexts of the narratives tend to criminalize women's desire in heteronormative ways. To the extent that the post-millennial texts enact heteronormative lenses, they seem to reinscribe an Old World/New World binary imaginary that would seem to limit their critiques of gender and ethnicity under trans-Atlantic modes of patriarchy. However, by examining Tintori's and Grames's strategic insertions of extra-literary devices such as genealogical trees and photographs, we argue that such techniques trouble ideas about authenticity and afford the authors space in which to critique institutionalized patriarchy by parodying the very genres in which they write. Because these authors produce works that ultimately reconceive conventional genres, their narratives are as important as their challenges to Italian American family culture and its trafficking of women's bodies.

Guided by early theorists of photography such as Susan Sontag, Roland Barthes, and, more recently, Marianne Hirsch, we examine how Tintori and Grames frame conceptions of family identity through insertions of and references to photographs. We recognize that to examine the "intense immobility" of putatively "docile" photographs,[2] also invites us to confront and to interpret such photographic insertions, as they "furnish evidence," as Sontag states,[3] and help readers to challenge notions about an Italian American version of the family romance.[4] Thus, *how* these authors choose to narrate their stories is as important as the fact that these stories overtly represent the violent exploitation of women's bodies, which has rarely been the principal focus of Italian American narratives. That Tintori and Grames centralize violence against women in their works is truly worthy of further examination.[5]

Because Tintori and Grames tend to reify heteronormativity in their works, they reiterate a thematic focus and structural aesthetic of many earlier immigrant narratives by acceding a priori to the nation-state as violent, patriarchal, and misogynistic. However, because gendered domestic violence drives both narratives, the woman's body in their works is represented as unsafe, unprotected, and subjected to constant precarity within Italian American family space, which is largely dominated by male power. Tintori and Grames tend to frame this structural reality as a remnant—an import from southern Italy rather than a sociological phenomenon with distinctly American causes and consequences.[6] Both narratives intensively portray continued violence against Italian immigrant women and their female children decades after their original migration. Tintori and Grames represent male violence toward women as related to female children's desire to function outside normative family patterns. For example, fourth-generation daughter Karen Tintori hears her parents "*hammer*" home traditional heteronormative prescriptions for her future, and the author documents these rules as early as page 2 of her narrative in *Unto the Daughters* (our emphasis). As though unable successfully to liberate herself from what she calls her parents' "old-fashioned Italian mentality," Tintori repeats her parents' directives at the narrative's end, intensifying the edicts through an italicized list of declarative sentences: "I *was* going to college. I *wasn't* getting married until I graduated college. I *wasn't* moving out of their house until my wedding day." She concludes by saying "I bristled, . . . but I was powerless to change their plan."[7]

Such feelings of subjection bear further scrutiny. As a firstborn daughter, Tintori is demonstrably obedient, but by the time she is in college, she verbally rebels against having to perform duties solely because she was born female. When she is studying for finals, Tintori's intellectual pursuits conflict with domestic work, despite her grandmother's proverbial provocation: " 'When God gave your mother a daughter, He gave her an extra pair of hands. Now open the peas like your mother told you.' " Recognizing the way mothers both succumb to and inflict on their daughters a domestic ideology that can be both exhausting and demeaning (as it was for the author's mother, "who'd resented being loaned out as a young woman to do laundry and housekeeping for her mother's friends"), Tintori recognizes a potential future staring her in the face should she continue obeying such commands.[8] In this scene, the college student leaves her bedroom, where she is studying Shakespeare, to open a can of peas for her mother, who is cooking. She performs this quotidian duty, but momentously decides that day that she would not have any daughters. Tintori's rebellion goes even further, in fact, when she makes the earth-shattering decision to convert to Judaism, announcing her separation from two institutions that formidably influenced her development: her Italian American family and the Catholic church.

As we will demonstrate, these authors do engage in intersectional analysis, especially regarding gender and class, but omit critiquing citizenship, assimilation, nationality, as well as institutionalized heterosexuality, especially as they relate to women's autonomy. As twenty-first-century artifacts that at times resist or avoid intersectional interrogation, these texts nevertheless lend themselves well to such an analysis. Though the intellectual turn to and coining of the term "intersectionality" is fairly recent—Kimberlé Williams Crenshaw employed it first in 1989—the practice is not new. Second-wave feminists Audre Lorde, Angela Davis, and Gloria Anzaldúa, for example, had long been articulating the need to fill the epistemological and practical gaps left by binary and single-axis thinking about minoritization, marginalization, and processes of identity, power, and domination. Similar to Patricia Hill Collins and Sirma Bilge in their 2016 book *Intersectionality*, we are defining intersectionality as an epistemology that analyzes "the complexity in the world, in people, and in human experiences," since "[t]he events and conditions of social and political life and the self . . . are generally shaped by many factors in diverse and mutually influencing ways."[9] Because Tintori and Grames build on a legacy of Italian American writing in which representations of violence and criminality push against women's desire in less stereotypical ways than seen in popular novels and films, an intersectional analytical juxtaposition of their texts allows us to trace latent as well as emergent themes at the junctions of gender, sexuality, class, citizenship, and Italian American immigrant experiences.

Cover Stories

The cover of Karen Tintori's 2007 book *Unto the Daughters: The Legacy of an Honor Killing in a Sicilian-American Family* features a torn-in-half, black-and-white photo with drops of blood over it, promising to reveal hidden family secrets of murder and intrigue. The commercialized quality of the cover serves as an enticement, alluring a wider readership familiar with popular fiction and crime drama. Tintori does not disappoint her reader, but part of the allure is also a decoy: to hook readers into a narrative account that neither reads like popular fiction nor sounds like *The Godfather*. The half-torn photo becomes totemic, revealing how the author will use photographs to authenticate her aunt's life, but also to suggest appalling violence undergirding that story. A family tree and a blurb likening the book to a nonfiction version of the film *The Godfather: Part II* are followed by incorporations of material culture (including thirteen black-and-white family photos) that together frame the story as archival fact. Tintori includes an early description of the one surviving photo that includes Frances, the author's great-aunt, who was honor-killed at age sixteen by her brothers, only to provide it near the book's conclusion when readers' investment in Frances, otherwise lost to history, has presumably grown. This withholding is then followed by the sole surviving photograph of the author's murdered aunt, only recently unearthed by the author, she reports. Tintori's late insertion of her aunt's photograph, "the murdered girl," reflects Barthes's assertion that "the Photograph's essence is to ratify what it represents" and therefore authenticates "the existence of a certain being."[10] Because the memoir also functions generically as a murder mystery, this photo signifies the authorial (and authoritative) recovery of the missing, murdered body of Frances, whose erasure was nearly complete until the publication of Tintori's book. As a pieced-together and controversial family history, *Unto the Daughters* reads like autobiographical fiction with important exceptions, including Tintori's two sections that frame the memoir, the prologue and author's note, to which we shall return.[11]

By contrast, Juliet Grames's novel *The Seven or Eight Deaths of Stella Fortuna* is a work of fiction framed as family history and dedicated to the author's immigrant grandparents. The book and jacket cover design bear no photographs (except for the photo of Grames on the inside back cover of the dust jacket), but they do put forward visual claims of authenticity. The jacket cover bears realistic-looking olive sprigs—a symbolic referent to southern Italy as well as to its traditional connection to peace and friendship. As a sign, the olives also indicate something more in that they are fruit from a tree that grows well despite having to take root in stony ground. The book cover's inside bears a pen-drawn map of Ievoli, "the old Italian village," with buildings and street names and countless lush trees. The pages before the preface display "Stella Fortuna's Family Tree,"[12] a parodic gesture toward authenticity as well as a mystery—the fruit of the tree includes a question mark and a missing person, among other details—some seemingly haphazard (to be understood later), others tantalizing. Juxtaposing Tintori's and Grames's texts, both multigenerational family sagas hinging on patriarchal violence, conjures many questions: How do we indict patriarchal violence in the millennium? What shapes might contemporary public reckonings with historical silences take? And, finally, how do we meaningfully connect patriarchy's past sins to its current ones?

Patriarchy's past sins have been highlighted quite generously in Italian American literary culture, from Garibaldi LaPolla's *The Grand Gennaro* to Louisa Ermelino's *Malafemmena*.[13] In the following paragraphs, we offer an overview of early exemplars of Italian American writing, which represent female desire as fundamental to women's development and, at times, resistant to patriarchal beliefs. Female characters' desire is problematized by the institutions of family and the Catholic Church, but such desires are fully represented by women authors of early Italian American literary history, demonstrating fissures in the fabric of the mythical Italian American family, headed by the paterfamilias and supported by the obedient mother at home.

Female Desire and Italian American Women's Writing

Karen Tintori and Juliet Grames build on established traditions represented by earlier writers, including Mari Tomasi, Antonia Pola, and Octavia Waldo, and, more recently, Dorothy Bryant and Helen Barolini, whose woman-centered focus was an outgrowth of second-wave feminism, which placed female desire front and center. Mari Tomasi and Antonia Pola wrote about women's responses to immigrant realities in the new world. For Tomasi (*Like Lesser Gods*), abiding love for a husband does not prevent an immigrant wife from trying to destroy his stonecutting career in New England to save him from dying of stonecutter's disease. She fails, but her passionate anger for his work is projected outward toward the larger industry of quarrying. For Pola (*Who Can Buy the Stars?*), an immigrant woman's success depends on her financial acumen, which the mother in this narrative possesses in spades, flouting norms and establishing herself in a lucrative bootlegging business, avoiding the fate of the workers (including her spouse) in a mining town in the Midwest.

Writers who focus on second-generational responses to institutions of family and church explore the difficult development of children of immigrant parents. Octavia Waldo (*A Cup of the Sun*) and Dorothy Bryant (*Miss Giardino*), for example, grapple with the long-term effects of the paterfamilias in a changing world in which the state guards the interest of children, not solely the father as head of the family. As a result of trenchant forms of male violence in the household (from domestic abuse to incest), these authors highlight the traumatic effects of violence on female children. Thus, in Italian American literary narratives, writers have shared the family secrets in all their ignominy, giving the lie to the ethnic chauvinism endorsing the idea that the family is *soprattutto* (above all) and a place of virtue, safety, and vitality. These narratives make it clear that nothing could be further from the truth. Tintori's *Unto the Daughters* and Grames's *The Seven or Eight Deaths* are fruit from this matrilineal vine, extending an analysis into the crimes of patriarchy by centralizing their focus on female desire *despite* the paterfamilias.

As we have said, the authors' mixed-genre narratives foreground the results of approaching storytelling through an interdisciplinary lens, thereby enlarging ideas about immigrant and ethnic discourse in the Italian American imaginary. By incorporating archival documents, including photographs, interviews, and nonfictional sources, both authors blur the boundaries between fiction and autobiography, producing what we might call archival-fiction, a literary technique that overtly invites a social critique of the very institutions they are representing. However, we did see less critique than we had hoped, finding the two post-millennial texts sometimes frustrating to reckon with as third- and fourth-generation nontraditional daughters of Italian America. While the male violence inflicted on the central character, Stella, is unrelenting to the point of obscene in *The Seven or Eight Deaths*, we were unsettled by the tone of both the fictional and autobiographical voices in Grames's novel, for example. Both authors nonetheless expand ideas about female representation under auspices of extreme forms of patriarchy, influenced by postmodern shifts in representation and overt and implied intertextuality.

Tintori and Grames examine the continued effects of extreme forms of patriarchy on generations of women that followed their female ancestors. While they both pay homage to Gay Talese and nod to him in their title (Tintori) and historical backdrop (Grames), neither author mentions a creative writer from the women's tradition of Italian America. By the millennium,

Italian American women writers were on the literary map, carefully excavated and introduced in Helen Barolini's magisterial *The Dream Book*, which was republished in 2000 in a revised paperback edition by Syracuse University Press with a front-cover commendation by Alice Walker. Novels by Tina De Rosa, Helen Barolini, Josephine Gattuso Hendin, and Dorothy Bryant were all reprinted in the 1990s by the Feminist Press.[14] While Karen Tintori thanks her former editor, Rosemary Ahearn, for her advice on early drafts, did she know that Ahearn was also Louise DeSalvo's editor as well? DeSalvo's 1996 *Vertigo* broke all kinds of rules about decorum and proper sexual behavior by a working-class Italian American girl.[15] Grames names Toni Morrison's *A Mercy* as one of her personal inspirations, yet her author's note bears no mention of Carole Maso or Adria Bernardi, two writers who also engage Grames's assertion regarding Morrison's question "about what people have been willing and forced to do in order to be American" (441).[16] This omission may reflect a post-millennial authorial prerogative to forge pathways outside of Italian American feminist tradition, too, even as our own critical and scholarly impulses may be to "bring them back in."[17]

Concerning Tintori's *Unto the Daughters*, an argument for her gap can be made on behalf of the "new journalism" that developed in the United States in the 1960s and 1970s, "pushing the boundaries of traditional journalism and nonfiction writing. The genre combined journalistic research with the techniques of fiction writing in the reporting of stories about real life events."[18] Tintori's *Unto the Daughters* innovates on this genre in two ways: through a sustained analysis of how patriarchal power (epitomized by the institution of the family) continued to exert the old-world legacy of honor killing on American shores and through the author's incorporation of family photos that understate her immersion into her subject's life (her great-Aunt Frances) to convey a narrative of "normalcy," that is, of heteronormativity as a strategy of redemption for her Italian American family. Of the thirteen family photos included in *Unto the Daughters*, three are single-photo portraits of Tintori's great-grandparents, and one is a school photo of her mother. The remaining nine photos, with one notable exception,[19] comprise family members, beginning in the prologue with a photo of four generations of the Costa family, including Tintori, sitting on her great-grandmother Concetta's lap. Coupledom precedes photos of newly married couples with firstborns and after by grandparents.

As Marianne Hirsch explains, from family albums to art exhibitions, "the primary unit of interaction . . . is the couple: heterosexual courting or married couples"; all the people included in Tintori's collection are presumably heterosexual and "of the same race or ethnicity: no chances are taken."[20] Tintori's decision to include traditional family photographs is unsurprising given that her early expertise as a journalist prepared her to write moving accounts related to her Sicilian family history.[21] With the influence of new journalism and its evolution in the 1990s into what is called creative non-fiction in US writing degree programs, experimentation "with forms, styles and practices" aligned well with Tintori's focus on her family's history and the tragic consequences of male power.[22]

Let's also keep in mind that three male American writers are generally credited with beginning the new journalism movement: Tom Wolfe, Truman Capote, and Gay Talese. Each of these writers brought journalism into a new literary era, with Wolfe publishing a manifesto and anthology on the genre in 1973.[23] Talese's exposé on the Bonanno crime family of New York, *Honor Thy Father* (1971), and Capote's "nonfiction novel" *In Cold Blood* (1966) highlighted extreme examples of the abuse of power. One back-cover blurb of Tintori's book offers an interpretive preview: "*Unto the Daughters* reads like a nonfiction version of the film *The Godfather: Part II*—as if it had been told from the point of view of a female Corleone." The past-perfect tense impeccably encapsulates the hypothetical nature of the comment, since we are aware of the impossibility of that ever happening. However, Tintori put the name of her great-Aunt Frances Costa back on the genealogical tree, publishing her into history and uttering the "unspeakable" in her narrative. Her closest literary allies in this venture are the new journalists, Gay Talese in particular. While Tintori is not overtly intertextual, the publication of this work is a result of the interdependence of texts to influence each other, including resonances of Italian American and, more largely, ethnic women's narratives.[24]

Grames's *The Seven or Eight Deaths of Stella Fortuna* more overtly announces intertextual influences by virtue of the genre in which she engages: the immigrant saga, specifically from a feminist point of view. In this way, Grames shares company with a plethora of writers before her, including Helen Barolini, Amy Tan, and Sandra Cisneros, to name just three across ethnic cultures and spanning a generational trajectory from *Umbertina* (1979) to *The Joy Luck Club* (1989) and *Caramelo* (2002). Though not solely reflected in the literature of Italian America, immigrant sagas portray the transnational scope of migrating lives, using generational structures and rhetoric to examine the tangled skeins of genealogies. Certainly, the mother-text of Grames's twenty-first-century novel is Helen Barolini's *Umbertina*, a generational trilogy that places feminism at the heart of the novel. While we don't deny that Barolini's novel is flawed and agree that its strongest section is part 1, devoted to the Calabrese matriarch and reinforced by the eponymous title devoted to her, we find it important to trace the intertextual resonances that abound in *The Seven or Eight Deaths*, which we illuminate below.[25]

Just as Barolini in *Umbertina* details change through time by focusing on three distinctive female characters, she also changes genres in each part of the novel to meet the varying needs of those three characters. It must be emphasized that Barolini refused to reduce the plights of her female characters solely to their roles as women in a patriarchal culture. Nonetheless, Barolini orients her novel—both structurally and thematically—around the complicated lives of each woman, attending carefully to their positions as women who must cope with the contingencies distinct to their generation and social backgrounds.[26] Grames extends this focus on patriarchal culture in *The Seven or Eight Deaths* by centering intensively on the life of Stella Fortuna, whose suffering is highlighted by life-threatening forms of violence by her father and husband in Italy and America. Grames offers uncensored details of Stella's body in pain, beginning with a childhood trauma of burning and ending with a cerebral hemorrhage in old age. While she attempts to rewrite the progress narrative to which Barolini is engaged in *Umbertina*, Grames manages to suggest two contradictory ideas simultaneously: The author first clarifies that nothing ever gets better for Stella, yet she continues to survive the wreckage done to her woman's body, battered by violence, rape, and ten pregnancies. Unlike other suffering women represented in Italian American literature, Stella is unable to place her body "within a community of pain," mending the damages wrought by her Italian culture.[27] She is too damaged, and her voice remains unnarrated: Her wounds remain unspeakable. Her interlocutor, Grames, must recount, as Elaine Scarry explains, "the passage of pain into speech," since her grandmother, Stella Fortuna, can only express her pain through her body.[28]

Grames's table of contents, for example, is organized into recounting Stella Fortuna's deaths: "Death 5" is unsurprisingly titled "Rape (Marriage)," as throughout Stella's life she explains her animosity toward her rapist/husband through euphemism, resulting from him having done "a bad thing."[29] This marks an important feminist move, as the patriarchy's continued resilience rests in part on its continued refusal to name rape, and further, as Eve Sedgwick writes, "it matters not at all what the raped woman perceives or wants as long as the man raping her can claim not to have noticed (ignorance in which male sexuality receives careful education)." Sedgwick continues, "the rape machinery that is organized by this epistemological privilege of unknowing in turn keeps disproportionately under discipline, of course, women's larger ambitions to take more control over the terms of our own circulation."[30] This gap in naming does suggest progress—"the bad thing" that happens to Stella, unrecognizable as rape in the mid-twentieth century, is acknowledged as rape by the twenty-first-century writer. However, as will be discussed later, the novel resists extending the characterization of Stella Fortuna, who "love[s] her mother more than anything,"[31] into a critique in line with Adrienne Rich's seminal 1980 work "Compulsory Heterosexuality and Lesbian Existence." Instead, the novel potentially falls under that which Sedgwick's 1990 *Epistemology of the Closet* (quoted above) critiques as the heterosexism latent within many feminist texts.

Archival Traces in Family Tree Histories

Both authors begin their works by incorporating *the family tree* as a form of interaction with readers, who are invited to engage past histories riven with violence. Employing a form of narrative diegesis through their use of genealogical trees, Tintori and Grames set the terms for how readers might engage the figures within the pages that follow. In light of her devotion to the new journalism, Tintori presents readers with a genealogical tree that is standard fare in *Unto the Daughters*. The admirable exception, of course, is Tintori's decision to include the name of her great-aunt, Francesca Costa (Frances), the victim of her older brothers' honor killing, a girl excised from the family tree for more than eighty years. Placing Frances's name and dates onto the family tree alongside her nine siblings compels curiosity from the outset. Notably, Tintori's title, cover page, and epigraphs have preceded the inclusion of this family genealogy, so readers are prepared to read about injustice.

Tintori includes epigraphs that paint Sicily with a wicked hand. A place where truth is camouflaged and "annihilated by self-interest" (Giuseppe di Lampedusa), Sicily is a "cursed country," and only by migrating to America do "beasts" become "men" (Gavin Maxwell). On the one hand, Tintori positions Sicily as the historical backdrop that wreaks havoc in America. On the other hand, the author gives the lie to the progressive fiction that one's migration to another country changes one's taxonomy. After a decades-long quest to uncover the truth to write a victim back into a family history, Tintori prepares readers to interpret this story against the negative import of the Sicilian homeland. She also inserts a subheading before Maxwell's epigraph regarding her ancestors' migratory destination in the United States, addressing the epigraph "To Detroit" to announce implicitly that her great-uncles become monstrous in America. In addition, within the first pages of her prologue, Tintori recalls in detail her experience of nearly drowning at age thirteen in 1961 to reinforce the fact that the murder and cover-up of her great-aunt in 1920 are repeated as trauma in her own body forty-one years later.

While Tintori's nonfiction framing is stylized after new journalistic accounts, Grames situates *The Seven or Eight Deaths of Stella Fortuna* within a family tree and narrator that at once makes claims on evidence-based, journalistic accounting of Italian American family history but also seems to parody it. Grames dedicates her novel "To my immigrant grandparents, Antonette Rotundo and Serafino Pasquale Cusano, and especially the nonbiological one, Concetta Rotunda Sanelli," an opening note that functions beyond dedication to certify the author's positionality about Italian American family storytelling and exposé. The table of contents divides Stella Fortuna's life into stages and events as related to her eight deaths, "Death 1, Death 2, etc.;" categorized under four parts, "Childhood," "Youth," "Maturity," and "Old Age," and here reside the first hints at the fantastical, as the story tells of a woman who lived for more than a century despite dying seven (or eight) times. The generically obligatory family tree comes next. At first glance, Grames's tree fits the mold of a familial authenticating and organizing device—the Italian names and nicknames are bold-lettered and capitalized in a serious-looking font. Just below many of the names, however, is a tiny, italic script, including details that begin to subvert the notion of the family tree as authentication. For example, under MARIA GALLO, Stella Fortuna's maternal grandmother, it reads, *"banisher of the evil eye."* The tree also bears an early signal of the book's critique of Italian and Italian American patriarchy—at least historically, as the narrator argues later that "emigration . . . dismantled the patriarchy."[32] Under Stella's father's name, it reads *"Stella's enemy"*—the one important fact about his character for the story to come. Following the family tree, Grames's preface is narratorial rather than authorial, a move that may be experienced as generic hybridization but also may be considered parodic. It continues the stylistic mirroring of the new journalistic family memoir account, like Tintori's, balancing claims on authenticity with the admission of some creative license made necessary by *omertà*. In fact, Grames's narrator acknowledges on the one hand that "family memory is a tricky thing,"[33] and yet on the other hand establishes her ethos by framing the story she is about to relate—"the story of Mariastella Fortuna the Second, called Stella, formerly of Ievoli, a mountain village in Calabria, Italy, and lately of Connecticut, in the United States of America"[34]—as the product of years of research and parsing out of reliable sources. "Among my many sources," Grames's narrator says, "Tina Caramanico [Stella's younger sister, the narrator's aunt], is the most important," adding, "I think finally, after all these years, she wanted to set the record straight."[35] The preface closes with gratitude to her sources and, finally, a tongue-in-cheek ownership of responsibility: "Any error in fact or judgment is entirely on the part of the author."[36] The blurring of the author and narrator here, again suggestive of generic hybridization perhaps combined with parodic mimicry, seems to continue in the "Author's Note" at the book's end and inside the book's back cover under Grames's photo. The author notes that "Stella Fortuna would not exist without the larger-than-life characters among my Italian-American relatives,"[37] while her biography relates first that Grames was "born in Hartford, Connecticut [the stateside setting in the novel], and grew up in a tight-knit Italian-American family"—followed only then by details about her career.

Shame on Their Honor:
Sister Murder and Photographs That Speak

In the penultimate chapter of *Unto the Daughters*, Tintori inserts the final photo she includes in her memoir. It is the "real" wedding photo of her grandparents and includes her grandmother's sisters, Frances and Mary. This photo remained in hiding throughout the grandparents' entire lives and was substituted with a "posed, tinted portrait" that Tintori's mother had of her parents in "peasant clothing."[38] As her cousin reveals at Tintori's grandmother's funeral, the wedding picture of her grandparents in peasants' garb replaced the actual wedding photo as "part of the whole lie."[39] Piecing together all the bits of her great-aunt's story over fifteen years, Tintori permits herself to utter and show the unspeakable in her final chapter. Tintori's graphic description of the brutal killing of her aunt serves as a literary addendum to the voiceless photo of Frances with her sister Josie on her wedding day. As Barthes writes, "the Photograph's essence is to ratify what it represents," and, similar to Barthes, Tintori could not deny that her aunt "had been *there*,"[40] even though generations of the family went to great lengths to continue to obliterate the existential fact of her Aunt Frances having ever been born (see figure 6.1).

Figure 6.1. Gramma and Grandpa Mazzarino's real wedding photo.

In her final chapter, Tintori offers uncensored details of her aunt's honor killing, revealing the true reason underlying her brothers' murder of their sister: "for daring to step into her future" without their permission.[41] Lest the reader think that the brothers solely murdered their sister because she dared to elope (as her mother had done before her) with a young barber with whom she fell in love, think twice. As Tintori explains, "[h]er father, anxious to move his sons up in the ranks of the Mafia during Prohibition, promised her against her will to a prominent Mafioso twenty years her senior. . . . She blackened the family's face by spurning the Mafia, ruining her brothers' chances, and that was her sin."[42] Permitting herself to interpret the past through an intersectional lens of gender and class, Tintori suggests the lie involved in pretending the brothers are concerned about their sister's honor and their responsibility as brothers to maintain her chastity to keep wholesome the family's reputation. The brothers' violence occurred because their sister refused to be trafficked like merchandise for their monetary benefit in an ill-gotten criminal enterprise substituting old-world ideas about honor.

Later confirming this story with the much younger brother of the Costa family, Uncle Louie, Tintori offers searing details spilled in his old age: "'My brothers killed her at Belle Isle,' he told me, after she came back to say she was married to the barber. . . . [Pasquale] said Rocco 'chopped her hands off with a shovel, and tied her legs to cement and threw her in.'"[43] By detailing the grisly way Frances's brothers murdered her great-aunt, Tintori fulfills the promise she makes implicitly in the first sentences of chapter 1 of her memoir: "If not for her father's passport, defaced but not destroyed, Francesca would never have surfaced. She would have remained a woman lost to history, her story swallowed in the depths of the Detroit River off Belle Isle."[44] These sentences offer further credence for Tintori's severe aquaphobia from which she suffers and conveys in her prologue. Tintori's final chapter again recalls this childhood fear of water decades before she knew the truth about how her great-aunt was tortured and then thrown off an island in the Detroit River.

The reference to Belle Isle is also a reminder of the family's original crossing in 1914 from Sicily with the passport listing the children's names, including Francesca's name "defaced but not destroyed."[45] As Barthes explains, "The important thing is that the photograph possesses an evidential force, and that its testimony bears not on the object but on time. From a phenomenological viewpoint, in the Photograph, the power of authentication exceeds the power of representation."[46] Tintori's inclusion of the photograph of Aunt Frances and, additionally, her several references to the Costa family's passport, is a claim on authenticity, a reification of the nonfiction categorization, the brutal truth of her family's history. Tintori addresses her Aunt Frances directly in the final lines of her book, tying together great-aunt and author irresistibly: "Did you have a daughter of your own? Did you teach her how to swim?" Consenting to nonchronological conceptions of time, Tintori recognizes the haunting nature of trauma and its continuing effects on the present. Had she concluded her story here, *Unto the Daughters* would have more persuasively accounted for the harrowing effects on later generations when women's desire is criminalized, giving men license to maim, kill, and disappear their bodies.

Italian Women Warriors and Legacies of Rape Culture

Grames is not shy about centralizing rape culture in *The Seven or Eight Deaths of Stella Fortuna*. What Tintori only intimates in *Unto the Daughters* Grames elucidates in her début novel. Italian women—sisters, wives, mothers—live precariously in families with men who rape them. Such is the case in the Fortuna family, first illuminated in the family tree and then extended over four generations in fictional prose and autobiographical commentary. By the time Stella is nineteen years old and living in Connecticut with her mother and siblings, "reunited" with their father for the first time in nine years, she is in imminent danger. Physically beautiful and full-figured at a young age, Stella is a big star in small-town Calabria. Her charisma, toughness, mental aptitude, needleworking expertise, and physical strength are no guard against the ravages of patriarchy in Calabria or Connecticut. On page 5 of the novel, Grames announces Stella's childhood decision: "She'd already decided she would never marry," an interior thought repeated more than two dozen times in various incarnations throughout the novel.

Stella first experiences sexual abuse by her father when she is nine years old. Without knowing anything about sex, Stella hears and sees her father's "use" of her mother's body night after night. Accused by Antonio of being a "slut" for watching her parents' nightly fornications, Stella is then sexually abused for the first time. Her father jams his hand into her hymen, her mind and body "a murk of fear and disgust and rage and pain and fluids."[47] In 1939, after years of separation from the father, Assunta and her children finally make the crossing to America, rejoining a rapist husband and wreaking havoc on Stella's life. Stella is positioned as sexual fodder for her father's predatory eyes; her coerced marriage functions here as a proxy rape for the father, who continues to prey on unsuspecting girls his entire life, including his grandchildren.[48] It is no wonder that Grames describes "Death 5" in conjunction with marriage, as Stella has been traumatized from childhood by sexual abuse. Thus, in "Part II: Youth," Grames describes the end of Stella's single life this way: "DEATH 5: *Rape (Marriage)*," anticipating the dream sequence that frames this section. Stella's rape dream, which continues throughout her life, anticipates her first sexual experience with her husband, who rapes Stella during their honeymoon.[49]

By age forty-four, Stella's body will have been beaten and raped. She will have futilely tried to commit suicide to avoid marrying. She will survive severe assault by her father, who beats her while she lies naked, punching out two more teeth from her mouth; her husband will rape her in a Montreal hotel "where men took a woman to do the job."[50] She will endure multiple pregnancies (with ten surviving children). Having become an alcoholic, she will fall down a flight of stairs and suffer brain hemorrhaging. She will survive thirty years after the surgeon performs an experimental procedure "to relieve pressure."[51] After her lobotomy, Stella speaks truth to power, but, like Cassandra, no one believes her. Except us. Similar to Tintori's willingness to air the dirty laundry of honor killing for all to see, Grames courageously shares this previously unspeakable story with her readers. This story is as unrelenting as it is graphic; it is the story of how a woman's body becomes a ruined site of multilayered systemic oppression, beginning with male power in the family.

In contradistinction to narratives of progress and mobility for immigrants who fled poverty for a better life in America, Grames critiques patriarchy through an intersectional lens, accounting for gender, class, and nation: "In the nine years since the Fortunas had last seen Tony, Assunta and her children had been poor but free; now they were prisoners of his will and whims. Tony had all the money; he was the only one who could speak English; he controlled every aspect of their lives."[52] This control is careful in disguise. Employing a form of literary ekphrasis, Grames references two photographs before and after the Fortuna migration. Both are portrait photos of versions of the Fortuna family. These photographs, though not included in the book, serve as archival documents, extra-literary materials that tell certain kinds of stories. The existential reality of the photos themselves reinforces upstanding ideas about traditional Italian peasant families in Calabria and Italian immigrant families in America.

The first family portrait is taken after Antonio returns from the Italian army during the First World War. Taken by a portraitist from the small town of Nicastro (in the province of Catanzaro), the photo is delivered after Assunta's first Stella dies from influenza in 1918, an illness that spread "all over Europe as soldiers trickled home, one last-born misery to shred already suffering families."[53] Antonio refuses to call a doctor to attend to his daughter's raging fever, and Assunta is powerless to change his mind as he raises his fist to her. The child dies next to her mother. This is the story narrated but not told by the photograph that is delivered directly by the Nicastro portraitist, who offers condolences and waives the fee. Shifting to autobiographical commentary, Grames admits that she has seen this 1918 portrait and that its features are ingrained in her memory: "Nineteen-year-old Assunta casts the impression of a much older woman, with her full bosom and weathered face . . . Antonio, meanwhile, is a vaudeville patriarch with his square-buttoned vest and handlebar mustache. The first Stella, the lost *bambina*, is strung between them like a rosary, her Christ-like pigeon toes propped over a small standing table."[54] These kinds of family portraits were, according to Francesco Faeta, "very common" in southern Italian towns and highlighted "the nuclear family" and "the diaspora itself . . . that brings about the need to reaffirm the family through a representation that celebrates it."[55] This is the photo Stella examines in her kitchen in 1970 and that hangs by her refrigerator. Stella does not see a weathered face in her mother, Assunta: she sees youth, beauty, and strength. Grames's willingness to offer multiple interpretations of the portrait photo from the carefully staged photo of coupledom and offspring to the figure of the mother, interpreted by grandmother and granddaughter each according to her own experiences, reflects deeply on their generational positions on the family tree.

The only other studio photo taken of the Fortuna family occurs in 1940 and serves as Antonio's gesture of assimilation; however, his aspirations are defeated by his own brutality. While family photographs have the capacity to perpetuate "familial myths," as Hirsch explains, by reducing strain and "sustaining an imaginary cohesion," Grames refuses to collaborate on the "reproduction of ideology," showing resistance to this story by excluding actual photographs in the novel.[56] The photo Grames references as a verbal picture includes all six Fortunas: the parents seated in front with sons on each side and daughters "Stella and Tina standing behind them to disguise the old shoes they'd bought in Nicastro," the famed town from which the Calabrian photographer hailed.[57] No other photos remain, Grames claims, that feature the entire family. This admission is revelatory because, during this period, less expensive home cameras (Kodak) came into standard use by Americans, including those from the working class. The documentary evidence of the Fortuna family is slim indeed and similar to the erasure of all documentary evidence of the existence of Tintori's great-Aunt Frances. In Grames's story, it seems likely that this family loses interest early in making new memories, perhaps reflecting Walter Benjamin's comment that "the camera introduces us to the unconscious optics as does psychoanalysis to unconscious impulses."[58] Grames's novel attempts to construct images of a family story that refuses to shutter the history of this family's subjectivity, infected by monstrous behavior by the paterfamilias, whose brutality affected generations beyond him.

Conclusion

Karen Tintori's *Unto the Daughters* and Juliet Grames's *The Seven or Eight Deaths of Stella Fortuna* are important twenty-first-century critiques of Italian American family culture. Both authors refuse to look away from the patriarchal violence endured by women in their respective immigrant family trees. Their insertions of and references to photography serve to mediate their memories of family and, at times, resist their power to romanticize Italian American family culture. In this way, both authors use photographic images to "unfix" dominant ideologies to which family members subscribe "often unconsciously."[59]

The precepts of twenty-first-century intersectional feminist inquiry prompt us to take measure of residual, even recalcitrant, assumed heteronormativity and erasure of the American patriarchy that favors, if not requires, that erasure even as we do celebrate these contemporary feminist narratives. Stella has no use for or interest in any man in any way; she loves only her mother. *The Seven or Eight Deaths of Stella Fortuna*'s love story is a tragic one, the maternal love between mother/daughter that is disrupted and violated by the paterfamilias. The novel allows you to go there—to the queer reading—but stops short of dismantling the assumptions upholding heteronormativity. When Adrienne Rich asked the following questions in "Compulsory Heterosexuality and Lesbian Existence" in 1980, she felt that this kind of examination was "long overdue":

> If women are the earliest sources of emotional caring and physical nurture for both female and male children, it would seem logical, from a feminist perspective at least, to pose the following questions: whether the search for love and tenderness in both sexes does not originally lead toward women; *why in fact women would ever redirect that search;* why species-survival, the means of impregnation, and emotional/erotic relationships should ever have become so rigidly identified with each other; and why such violent strictures should be found necessary to enforce women's total emotional, erotic loyalty and subservience to men. I doubt that enough feminist scholars and theorists have taken the pains to acknowledge the societal forces which wrench women's emotional and erotic energies away from themselves and other women and from woman-identified values.[60]

We argue that Stella's character, and therefore Grames's mixed-genre period novel, *do* become part of the "history of female resistance" to the institution of heterosexuality that Rich began to unearth in "Compulsory Heterosexuality,"[61] but also that they belie lesser progress in the linguistics of the undertaking. In other words, there is palpable progress between the novel's mid-twentieth-century setting and its #metoo era publication in relation to its direct attendance to rape as gendered, patriarchal violence.

Our own suggestion here of a queer reading of Stella is a recognition of that which exists instead between the lines, in what remains unwritten and unsaid, just as Eve Sedgwick instructs that " 'closetedness' itself is a performance initiated as such by the speech act of a silence—not a particular silence, but a silence that accrues particularity by fits and starts, in relation to the discourse that surrounds and differentially constitutes it."[62] In our reading of these particular silences, the novel implicitly suggests that the assault of patriarchy that had been wreaking havoc on Stella Fortuna and her intergenerational female counterparts for a century continues, though for some it may have appeared to have gone underground. Tintori's conclusion of *Unto the Daughters* subtly, perhaps even cautiously, celebrates the liberated present against the iniquitous past: The author, for example, can enjoy becoming "Miss Columbus" in an Italian American (heavy on the American)[63] beauty pageant and earn a scholarship to college, where she is free to study and become anything she likes in the process. We wish to posit the possibility, too, that the photo placed here parodies the Italian American notion of progress tied to stereotypical narratives of Columbus and the righteousness of imperialist motives.

We remain concerned that these texts could suggest, instead of a critique of patriarchy that persists in the New World, literary beatifications of historical women who have endured, or unknown women who have endured, its violence to enable contemporary American women of Italian descent to fully enjoy an unrestrained freedom. In a sociopolitical sense, these literary beatifications could serve to echo the church's beatification of Maria Teresa Goretti as a symbol of forgiveness of patriarchal violence. There remains work to be done, particularly in terms of intersectional feminism that applies queer theory to disturb heteronormative patriarchy. As Sara Ahmed argues in *Queer Phenomenology: Orientations, Objects, Others*, "Compulsory heterosexuality diminishes the very capacity of bodies to reach what is off the straight line. It shapes which bodies one 'can' legitimately approach as would-be lovers and which one cannot."[64] Yet Ahmed invites us, too, to understand a "refusal to inherit, as a refusal that is a condition for the arrival of queer."[65]

If Frances and Stella are Maria Gorettis without the beatification, maybe there is no forgiveness. Instead, finally, Italian American women writers may be claiming an innovatively queer moment here through a hybridized genre and wider audience appeals (St. Martin's Press and Ecco/an imprint of HarperCollins are trade presses that publish literary fiction/nonfiction alongside more commercial releases). Ahmed instructs that "the task is to trace the lines of a different genealogy, one that would embrace the failure to inherit the family line as a condition of possibility for another way of dwelling in the world."[66] Tintori and Grames ultimately break *omertà*—the code of silence on which Italian American patriarchy depends—with the publication of *Unto the Daughters: The Legacy of an Honor Killing in a Sicilian American Family* and *The Seven or Eight Deaths of Stella Fortuna*, respectively. These Italian American women writers' refusal to inherit familial paradigms that naturalize patriarchy in their post-millennial archival-fictions therefore helps open up critical space to imagine otherwise.

Notes

1. We take the term "chronotype" from M. M. Bakhtin, *The Dialogic Imagination: Four Essays*, trans. Michael J. Holquist (Austin: University of Texas Press), 1983. For enclaves known as "Little Italys," see Rudolph Vecoli's "Are Italian Americans Just White Folks?" Vecoli argues for the intrinsic significance of the Italian diaspora and the Italian American experience.

2. Roland Barthes, *Camera Lucida: Reflections on Photography*, trans. Richard Howard (New York: Hill and Wang, 1981), 49.

3. Susan Sontag, *On Photography*, 1977 (New York: Picador, 2001), 15.

4. Marianne Hirsch, *Family Frames: Photography, Narrative, and Postmemory* (Cambridge: Harvard University Press, 1997), 41.

5. This is not to suggest that violence against women has been underrepresented throughout Italian American literary and cinematic history; to the contrary, largely because of the cottage industry spawned by Mario Puzo's novel *The Godfather* and Francis Ford Coppola's *The Godfather* trilogy, portrayals of violence against women have proliferated. Perhaps the most egregious and gratuitous example occurs in a 2001 episode of the HBO series *The Sopranos*, which films a brutal beating to death of a twenty-year-old pregnant stripper. What is of interest to us is to show how recent authors critique patriarchal violence against women, offering context for women's suffering and a critique of institutionalized patriarchy through Italian/Italian American cultural customs.

6. In fact, women as well as men lost power as a result of migration. With Italian men's experiences of emasculation, domestic violence increases within the home—and without extended family around, there is not only no protection from abusive husbands and fathers, but the institutions that replace it—the school, the marketplace, etc.—are built on what bell hooks calls "the system of imperialist white supremacist capitalist patriarchy." *Belonging: A Culture of Place* (New York: Routledge, 2009), 8.

7. Tintori, *Unto the Daughters: The Legacy of an Honor Killing in a Sicilian-American Family* (St. Martin's Press, 2007), 203.

8. Tintori, *Unto the Daughters*, 217.

9. Patricia Hill Collins and Silma Bilge, *Intersectionality* (Polity Press, 2016), 2. In addition, " 'Home Truths' on Intersectionality," Jennifer C. Nash argues that the reduction of intersectionality to synonymity with, rather than understanding it as a product of, black feminism does a disservice both to intersectionality and black feminism. " 'Home-Truths' on Intersectionality," *Yale Journal of Law and Feminism* (447–48, 2011). As feminist literary scholars, we recognize that intersectionality, as a literary analytical tool, is generative: a process by which power and identity,

violence and domination, and their relationships to one another and their shifting contexts manifest new ways of conceiving historical and contemporary realities.

10. Barthes, *Camera Lucida: Reflections on Photography*, 85, 107.

11. Tintori explained to us that she wrote *Unto the Daughters* three times as a novel, but was unsuccessful in getting it published. Her former editor at Simon & Shuster (which published her book *Trapped*) encouraged her to denounce *omertà* and write the story in first person. "So I used my journalist's head and my novelist's heart, found a new agent, and wow, Francesca's story is still garnering attention thirteen years later." Email correspondence with the author, January 12, 2020.

12. Juliet Grames, *The Seven or Eight Deaths of Stella Fortuna: A Novel* (New York: Ecco/HarperCollins, 2019), viii, ix.

13. Garibaldi M. Lapolla, *The Grand Gennaro*, 1935, ed. and intro. Steven Belluscio (repr., New Brunswick, NJ: Rutgers University Press, 2009); Louisa Ermelino, *Malafemmena* (Louisville, KY: Sarabande Books, 2016).

14. Tina De Rosa, *Paper Fish*, 1980 (repr., New York: Feminist Press, 1996); Helen Barolini, *Umbertina*, 1979 (repr., New York: Feminist Press, 1999); Josephine Gattuso Hendin, *The Right Thing to Do*, 1988 (repr., New York: Feminist Press, 1999); Dorothy Bryant, *Miss Giardino*, 1978 (repr., New York: Feminist Press, 1997). Each of these reprints includes a scholarly afterward.

15. Louise DeSalvo's *Vertigo* was also reprinted by the Feminist Press in 2002. Her follow-up memoir, *Crazy in the Kitchen: Food, Feuds and Forgiveness in an Italian American Family*, examines the effects of father abandonment on families, illuminating how Louise's father protected his mother and dismissed his father as unworthy of respect.

16. While we can reference several Italian American women writers who have published experimental narratives that challenge traditional understandings of generational time, historical chronology, and assimilative desires, we cite two here, as they are especially resonant in postmodern innovation: Carole Maso's *Ghost Dance* (1986) and Adria Bernardi's *Openwork: A Novel* (2007).

17. Forgive the *Godfather Part III* film reference in which Al Pacino playing Michael Corleone famously utters: "Just when I thought I was out . . . they pull me back in" (Coppola 1990).

18. Liz Fakazis, "New Journalism," https://www.britannica./com/print/article/411713.

19. Tintori includes a photo of herself as Miss Columbus Day. There is irony in this choice, but we are uncertain if it is self-aware. Tintori reads some irony in this, as she had become a self-proclaimed feminist and part of second-wave feminism trying to get scholarship money from a beauty pageant. But ironies abound further as the fraught history of Columbus Day continues to influence discussion of this nomenclature to celebrate a day of heritage for Italian Americans.

20. Marianne Hirsch, *Family Frames: Photography, Narrative, and Postmemory* (Cambridge: Harvard University Press, 1997), 56.

21. The first book that emerges from Tintori's family history resulted in her 2002 *Trapped: The 1909 Cherry Mine Disaster*. Tintori is the granddaughter of one of the mine workers who escaped the Cherry, Illinois, mine disaster that killed 259 men. The Cherry coal mine fire was "the worst coal mine fire in U.S history." https://www.publishersweekly.com/978-0-7434-2194-2.

22. Fakazis, "New Journalism."

23. Tom Wolfe and E. W. Johnson, eds., *The New Journalism* (New York: Harper and Row, 1973). In this anthology, the editors include journalistic reportage by such writers as Truman Capote, Hunter S. Thompson, Norman Mailer, Joan Didion, and Gay Talese. See also Marc Weingarten, *The Gang That Couldn't Write Straight: Wolfe, Thompson, Didion, Capote and the New Journalism Revolution* (New York: Three Rivers Press/Crown Publishing), 2005.

24. We are thinking here of texts published in the 1970s and 1980s such as Maxine Hong Kingston's *Woman Warrior* and Alice Walker's *The Color Purple*. Both authors complicate ideas about genre and portray characters who are told "not to tell."

25. Suffice to say: Helen Barolini's *Umbertina* does important work for Italian American writing and the immigrant saga as well: it weds Italian and American characters, themes, and topographies. A good portion of the novel is set in Italy with Italian American and Italian characters, extending the national trend of earlier Anglo Americans and their fascination with locating their ingenues in Italy. Within the novel, recursions to immigrant migrations are replaced by a fully detailed historical narrative of life in Calabria, the region from which Grames's family also originates. When we read part 1 of *Umbertina*, the documentary film came to mind, with its emphasis on historical veracity, detail, and vivid, archival footage. Of her own writing, Barolini has stated, "I am not a linguistic stylist first and foremost. It is not the words per se that engage me, but the ideas and human feelings they represent." The style of part 1 is that of the history writer, with emphasis on change through time: "I thought of showing transcultural and transgenerational change, and the losses and gains that each change implies" (Barolini, "Interview," 47).

26. William Boelhower's ordering principles of ethnic trilogies in his seminal article "The Ethnic Trilogy: A Poetics of Cultural Passage," with its emphasis on generations, offer a structurally sound method by which to read Barolini's novel, originally conceived of as a trilogy. Thus, a generic reading of *Umbertina* can be mapped out. See Bona, "Celebrating Helen Barolini and *Umbertina*," in *Italian Americans before Mass Migration: We've Always Been Here* (New York: Bordighera), 139–48.

27. Arthur Frank refers to the "*dyadic* body" as one that can empathize with "a body outside of mine, 'over and against me [;]' this other has to do with me, as I with it," allowing a suffering self to place their body within a "community of pain" (35). *The Wounded Storyteller: Body, Illness, and Ethics* (Chicago: University of Chicago Press, 1995).

28. Elaine Scarry, *The Body in Pain: The Making and Unmaking of the World* (New York: Oxford University Press, 1985), 9.

29. Grames, *The Seven or Eight Deaths of Stella Fortuna*, 431.

30. Eve Kosofsky Sedgwick, *Epistemology of the Closet* (Berkeley: University of California Press, 1990), 5.

31. Grames, *The Seven or Eight Deaths of Stella Fortuna*, 8.

32. Grames, *The Seven or Eight Deaths of Stella Fortuna*, viii, 43, ix. "The patriarchy" for Grames, then, appears to be distinctly Italian, and liberation from it only happens over post-emigration generational distance from this source.

33. Grames, *The Seven or Eight Deaths of Stella Fortuna*, xiii.

34. Grames, *The Seven or Eight Deaths of Stella Fortuna*, xi.

35. Grames, *The Seven or Eight Deaths of Stella Fortuna*, xiv.

36. Grames, *The Seven or Eight Deaths of Stella Fortuna*, xvi.

37. Grames, *The Seven or Eight Deaths of Stella Fortuna*, 442–43.

38. Tintori, *Unto the Daughters*, 231, 99.

39. Tintori, *Unto the Daughters*, 232.

40. Barthes, *Camera Lucida*, 85.

41. Tintori, *Unto the Daughters*, 233.

42. Tintori, *Unto the Daughters*, 233.

43. Tintori, *Unto the Daughters*, 234.

44. Tintori, *Unto the Daughters*, 9.

45. Tintori, *Unto the Daughters*, 9, 158.

46. Barthes, *Camera Lucida*, 88–89.

47. Grames, *The Seven or Eight Deaths of Stella Fortuna*, 84.

48. Grames, *The Seven or Eight Deaths of Stella Fortuna*, 386–87.

49. Grames, *The Seven or Eight Deaths of Stella Fortuna*, 174, 312–13.

50. Grames, *The Seven or Eight Deaths of Stella Fortuna*, 297.

51. Grames, *The Seven or Eight Deaths of Stella Fortuna*, 420.

52. Grames, *The Seven or Eight Deaths of Stella Fortuna*, 181.

53. Grames, *The Seven or Eight Deaths of Stella Fortuna*, 37.

54. Grames, *The Seven or Eight Deaths of Stella Fortuna*, 36.

55. The portrait photo Grames describes in her novel emerges from a photographic tradition established by Saverio Marra, who worked in San Giovanni in Fiore in the province of Cosenza over forty years and whose portraits of Calabrians are shown "as they were, as they wished they were, with their noble, motionless eidetic tension, with their looks, their distinctive class features . . . surfacing into the photographic memory through the need of the identification photo or the photo I would like to call *migratory or migrating* (because in fact . . . these photos migrated to the New World to remind people of their duties, their rights, their loyalties, their belonging)" (Faeta 17). For a discussion of the formal aspects of family portraits as a specific subgenre, see Rosario Perricone, "I ricordi figurati 'foto di famiglia in Sicilia,'" in *L'Italia Del Novecento: Le Fotografie E La Storia*, ed. Giovanni De Luna et al. (Torino: G. Einaudi, 2006), 167–221; Peppino Ortoleva, "Una Fonte difficile. La Fotografia e la Storia della Migrazione," *AltreItalie* 5 (Aprile 1991), https://www.altreitalie.it.kdocs/78755/00057.pdf.

56. Hirsch, *Family Frames*, 7.

57. Grames, *The Seven or Eight Deaths of Stella Fortuna*, 197.

58. As quoted in Hirsch, *Family Frames*, 10.

59. As quoted in Hirsch, *Family Frames*, 273.

60. Adrienne Rich, "Compulsory Heterosexuality and Lesbian Existence," 637–38.

61. Rich, "Compulsory Heterosexuality and Lesbian Existence," 659.

62. Sedgwick, *Epistemology of the Closet*, 3.

63. Brent Staples's recent *New York Times* opinion piece "How Italians Became 'White'" recounts the historical positioning of Italian Americans as assimilable to whiteness through the granting of the Columbus Day holiday as a way to appease Italy's government after the 1891 lynching of eleven Italian Americans in Louisiana.

64. Sara Ahmed, *Queer Phenomenology: Orientations, Objects, Others* (Durham: Duke University Press, 2006), 91.

65. Ahmed, *Queer Phenomenology*, 178.

66. Ahmed, *Queer Phenomenology*, 178.

Works Cited

Ahmed, Sara. *Queer Phenomenology: Orientations, Objects, Others*. Durham: Duke University Press, 2006.

Bakhtin, M. M. *The Dialogic Imagination: Four Essays*. Translated by Michael J. Holquist. Austin: University of Texas Press, 1983.

Barthes, Roland. *Camera Lucida: Reflections on Photography*. Translated by Richard Howard. New York: Hill and Wang, 1981.

Barolini, Helen. *The Dream Book: An Anthology of Writings by Italian American Women*. 1985. Reprint, New York: Syracuse University Press, 2000.

———. *Umbertina* 1979. Reprint, New York: Feminist Press, 1999.

———. Interview. By Carole Bonomo Ahearn. *Fra Noi* (September 1986): 47.

Bernardi, Adria. *Openwork: A Novel*. Dallas: Southern Methodist University, 2007.

Boelhower, William. "The Ethnic Trilogy: A Poetics of Cultural Passage." *MELUS* 12, no. 4 (1985): 7–23.

Bona, M. J. "Celebrating Helen Barolini and *Umbertina*." In *Italian Americans before Mass Migration: We've Always Been Here*, edited by Jerome Krase, Frank B. Pesci, and Frank Alduino, 139–48. New York: Bordighera, 2008.

Bryant, Dorothy. *Miss Giardino*. 1978. Reprint, New York: Feminist Press, 1997.

Cisnernos, Sandra. *Caramelo*. New York: Knopf Doubleday, 2003.

Collins, Patricia Hill, and Silma Bilge. *Intersectionality*. Cambridge, UK: Polity Press, 2016.

Coppola, Francis Ford, dir. *The Godfather: Part III*. Los Angeles: Paramount Pictures, 1990.

Crenshaw Kimberlé Williams. "Mapping the Margins: Intersectionality, Identity Politics, and Violence against Women of Color." *Stanford Law Review* 43, no. 6 (July 1991): 1241–1299.

De Rosa, Tina. *Paper Fish*. 1980. Reprint, New York: Feminist Press, 1996.

DeSalvo, Louise. *Crazy in the Kitchen: Food, Feuds and Forgiveness in an Italian American Family*. New York: Bloomsbury, 2004.

———. *Vertigo: A Memoir*. 1996. Reprint, New York: Feminist Press, 2002.

Ermelino, Louisa. *Malafemmena*. Louisville, KY: Sarabende Books, 2016.

Francesco Faeta, ed. *Gente di San Giovanni in Fiore: Sessanta Ritratti di Saverio Marra*. Firenze: Fratelli Alinari Spa Idea, 2007.

Fakazis, Liz. "New Journalism." https://www.britannica./com/print/article/411713.

Frank, Arthur. *The Wounded Storyteller: Body, Illness, and Ethics*. Chicago: University of Chicago Press, 1995.

Grames, Juliet. *The Seven or Eight Deaths of Stella Fortuna: A Novel*. New York: Ecco/HarperCollins, 2019.

Hendin, Josephine Gattuso. *The Right Thing to Do*. 1988. Reprint, New York: Feminist Press, 1999.

Hirsch, Marianne. *Family Frames: Photography, Narrative, and Postmemory*. Cambridge: Harvard University Press, 1997.

hooks, bell. *Belonging: A Culture of Place*. New York: Routledge, 2009.

Lapolla, Garibaldi M. *The Grand Gennaro*. Edited with an introduction by Steven Belluscio. 1935. Reprint, New Brunswick, NJ: Rutgers University Press, 2009.

Maso, Carole. *Ghost Dance*. Hopewell, NJ: Ecco, 1986.

Nash, Jennifer. "'Home-Truths' on Intersectionality." *Yale Journal of Law and Feminism* 23, no. 2 (2011): 445–70.

Pola, Antonia. *Who Can Buy the Stars?* New York: Vantage Press, 1957.

Puzo, Mario. *The Godfather*. New York: New American Library, 1969.

Rich, Adrienne. "Compulsory Heterosexuality and Lesbian Existence." In "Women: Sex and Sexuality." Special issue, *Signs* 5, no. 4 (1980): 631–60.

Scarry, Elaine. *The Body in Pain: The Making and Unmaking of the World*. New York: Oxford University Press, 1985.

Sedgwick, Eve Kosofksy. *Epistemology of the Closet*. 1990. Reprint, Berkeley: University of California Press, 2008.

Sontag, Susan. *On Photography*. 1977. Reprint, New York: Picador, 2001.

Staples, Brent. "Opinion: How Italians Became 'White.'" *New York Times*, October 12, 2019.

Talese, Gay. *Unto the Sons*. New York: Alfred A. Knopf, 1992.

Tan, Amy. *The Joy Luck Club*. New York: Penguin Books, 2006.

Tintori, Karen. *Trapped: The 1909 Cherry Mine Disaster*. New York: Atria Books, 2002.

———. *Unto the Daughters: The Legacy of an Honor Killing in a Sicilian-American Family*. New York: St. Martin's Press, 2007.

Tomasi, Mari. *Like Lesser Gods*. 1949. Reprint, Shelburne, VT: New England Press, 1988.

Vecoli, Rudolph. "Are Italian Americans Just White Folks?" In *Italian and Italian American Images in the Media*, edited by Mary Jo Bona and Anthony J.

Tamburri, 3–17. Staten Island, NY: American Italian Historical Association, 1996. Reprinted in *Italian Americana* 13, no. 2 (Summer 1995): 149–61.
Waldo, Octavia. *A Cup of the Sun.* New York: Harcourt, 1961.
Weingarten, Marc. *The Gang That Couldn't Write Straight: Wolfe, Thompson, Didion, Capote and the New Journalism Revolution.* New York: Three Rivers Press/ Crown Publishing, 2005.
Wolfe, Tom, and E. W. Johnson, eds., *The New Journalism.* New York: Harper and Row, 1973.

7

The Very Queer Truth

Ben Piazza's Italian Southerner

Douglas Steward and Tracy Floreani[1]

Though Ben Piazza's 1964 novel *The Exact and Very Strange Truth* is out of print and not widely known, it makes a significant contribution to more complex understandings of both Italian American literature and the writing of the American South.[2] Set in Arkansas and Georgia, his novel offers an intriguing negotiation of racial lines in a setting not typical for Italian American artists. Like other Southern works of the same period, Piazza's narrative relies on motifs of social alienation and the bizarre that characterize writings of contemporaries like Carson McCullers and Flannery O'Connor. His ethnically marked story, however, effectively disrupts the typically racialized mode of the "Southern grotesque" and deploys the grotesque's trope of "freakishness" to juxtapose questions of ethnic identity with gender and sexuality. In this work, the novel also relies heavily (and playfully) on the psychoanalytic concepts popular in the mid-twentieth-century period in which it was written. *The Exact and Very Strange Truth* is a novel in which "something happens to objects themselves" (40). The self becomes an object for the protagonist Alexander Gallanti, in a way that Freud theorized in his essay "On Narcissism," as he attempts to understand both his ethnic and sexual identities.

The story takes place in the 1940s, covering a span of years roughly coinciding with World War II. The narrative begins with twelve-year-old

179

Alexander accompanying his mother, who is suffering the aftermath of a stroke, and two younger siblings, Veronica and Quentin, on a plane trip from Little Rock, Arkansas, to Savannah, Georgia, so that the mother can recuperate near the ocean and her oldest son, Rudolph. The trip serves as a frame for the novel, with the bulk of the narrative composed of Alexander's thoughts as he considers his place within the family story on the nighttime flight during which he is unable to sleep. Piazza's use of alternating first- and third-person narration allows him to slip into and out of Alexander's voice for whole sections of the book to offer a narrative that goes beyond the temporal parameters of the flight. We learn about the Sicilian father's immigration and experiences with discrimination in Little Rock and of the parents' courtship and elopement, "how they had to [elope] because she was a Baptist and an Arkansas American and he was Catholic and a foreign Italian and both their families were against it" (18). And we witness key scenes in the life of the family that grew out of that elopement, such as the wartime experiences of Alexander's older brothers and the contentious and sometimes violent relationship between their eldest sister and father. In the mosaic of scenes, the narrative always returns to Alexander's nagging sense of isolation within the large family and his attempts to connect with various nonfamilial figures throughout his childhood, from African American domestic workers to a white couple he watches sleeping through a window every morning on his paper route.

In addition to the classic "Southern grotesque" elements that pepper the book, such as a lengthy description of a freak show, a story about a baby whose arm is gnawed off by a giant rat, and Alexander's gift of nicely wrapped chicken heads for a sister-in-law he hates, the novel relies on the subtler thematic grotesque that has become a trademark of much twentieth-century Southern literature. Alexander Gallanti is consistent with Alan Spiegel's now well-known exploration of the grotesque Southern character, whose physical or psychological "deformity" renders him an outcast (429). In this, the grotesque Southern character reads as an exaggerated version of the archetypal alienated Modern, one whose story often takes place among other social misfits or against a backdrop of the bizarre.

Piazza's reliance on this Southern mode is so strong that the voice in his novel at times seems to read as an Italianized version of *The Member of the Wedding* by Piazza's queer Southern predecessor Carson McCullers. Like McCullers's androgynous/tomboy protagonist Frankie, the somewhat effeminate Alexander of Piazza's novel spends much of his time with Black female domestic workers and develops ambivalent relations with them as surrogate parental figures. Socially rejected and isolated, both protagonists also make notably awkward attempts at sexual experience. Their physical features (Frankie's excessive height and "boyish" behavior, Alexander's blond hair and blue eyes) define them and cause them to be afraid of other social misfits because of their potential to mirror the protagonists' selves. To highlight the characters' sense of social isolation and fear of rejection, each story emphasizes a visit to a carnival freak show. Alexander feels drawn to Miss Minus and The Asian Duck Lady, yet simultaneously fears he may someday become a "freak," too (116). In McCullers's story, Frankie experiences something similar: "it seemed to her that they had looked at her in a secret way and tried to connect their eyes with hers, as though to say: we know you" (272). Both characters also seek to mitigate their feelings of isolation from their families and peers by inventing a revised familial unit that presumes a psychic connection with others who are ignorant of the protagonists' desires. For Alexander, this kind of desire occurs in various forms, most notably in his early childhood when he imagines himself as the "third twin" to a set of towhead twins he admires at school, and later in what he calls "the secret place of us" that he hopes to discover when the quartet of family members arrives at their new home in Savannah. These examples underscore how much Piazza's narrative is immersed in the Modernist Southern grotesque, with all its consequent racialized and psychoanalytic elements.

Alexander's exploration of self is composed of a series of scenes that highlight his misfit status in terms ethnic, social, sexual, and psychological. His narcissism is perhaps most spectacularly enacted in the analeptic passage describing the aforementioned blond-haired/blue-eyed Dukes twins, who provide Alexander such a stunning vision of what he himself lacks—self-resembling familial others—that he fantasizes he might become a part of their sibling relationship. "I was the only one in my family with blue eyes and cotton hair," he recounts at the beginning of the passage. "Since all the others had black hair and brown eyes, this was a true puzzle" (26). It is hard to say whether or not Piazza intends the reader to snicker at Alexander's naive difficulty in coming up with a possible explanation, the most obvious of which is maternal infidelity. (Piazza himself was light-complected, like other "blonde Sicilians.") Regardless, because of Alexander's incongruently Aryan features, a neighborhood girl even declares, "I sometimes wonder if you even *belong* to that family" (26). In an effort to make his features conform to those of his family, an effort that Alexander perceives to be obligatory, he douses his hair in black ink. The effect of this is to turn half of his face as well as half of his hair an unnatural black. Punishment naturally ensues, and Alexander recalls that "it took three months for my hair to get back to my cotton color, and my face was part black for some time" (26). The partial-blackface incident immediately precedes an account of his infatuation with the blond Dukes twins. Alexander never reveals to the boys his infatuation with them or the fact that he fantasizes himself as a third in their mirror relationship. Instead, Alexander observes them from a distance, secretly enjoying their self-resemblance while carrying out amazing acrobatic feats on the playground bars. Sadly, one day "they both went wrong on the bars and instead of landing on their feet, facing west, they landed on their heads" (27). Alexander laments, "There wasn't one single thing I could do or say, I just stood there and watched my three-person twin idea get all broken up. [. . .] I stopped following them around and I gave up my secret" (27). Although the exact chronology is unclear, the order in which events are narrated suggests that Alexander probably still had partially black hair and face at this time. Basically, these two events demonstrate Alexander's inability to find adequate others with whom to identify; his attempts to do so end in punishment and injury and signifiers of racial confusion. Moreover, his narrative preserves these moments as significant. In fact, in the present tense, while Alexander is remembering the blackface and Dukes twins' incidents, he is staring at himself in a mirror because he is covered in poison ivy sores. Although staring at oneself in a mirror of some kind is the archetypal posture of narcissism, Freud notes that the narcissist "has by no means broken off his erotic relations to people and things. He still retains them in phantasy; i.e., he has, on the one hand, substituted for real objects imaginary ones from his memory, or has mixed the latter with the former; and on the other hand, he has renounced the initiation of motor activities for the attainment of his aims in connection with those objects" ("On Narcissism" 74). Indeed, these are Alexander's most typical attitudes: passive observation and frustrated, imaginary identification with figures from his past. We see the Freudian concept repeated in variation throughout the novel, as with the aforementioned scene in which he fantasizes belonging through passive voyeurism on his paper route or through erotic refiguring of objects within his fashioning of an increasingly queer self, as demonstrated in later portions of this analysis.

As striking as Alexander's narcissism is his melancholia. The book contains quite a few moments of humor, but they are largely at Alexander's expense, adopting a tone through which the adult narrator pokes fun at the social awkwardness, strangeness, or naiveté of the child self. Within his present/child narrative, though, Alexander remains a morose character, and his most melancholy moments involve some form of sexual loss or frustration. Indeed, if we accept (in the traditional psychoanalytic sense) that the parent-child relationship is a sexual one, then the entire book is organized around sexual loss: The father's death serves as its first major event and turning point, and the mother's death concludes the novel. Up to the father's death, Alexander's own voice is more present within the novel. After his father's death, a third-person narrator takes over the story, with only brief relapses into first-person. Such relapses suggest that the third-person voice is also Alexander's, with the important difference that he begins to take himself as an object (again, in the psychoanalytic sense), rather than acting as a narrating subject.

Appropriately enough, the novel is packed with Oedipal, taboo, and phallic references—both subtle and overt—to Alexander's sexual fixation on several of his family members, and many focused on his Sicilian father. The father's relationship with Alexander's older sister is especially marked as symbolically incestuous, but Alexander too is the object of special physical attentions from his father that hint at an erotic bond. He enjoys, for example, a game with his father called *"ride a cock horse,"* in which the child straddles his father's ankle while the father, sitting in a chair, "gallops" the child as if on a toy horse. At one point, father and son gaze into each other's eyes and repeatedly avow their love for each other. Alexander then remarks, "I could feel his whiskers because he was kissing me. Daddy's legs were crossed and just right for *ride a cock horse*" (88). The phrase is included in a famous nursery rhyme:

> Ride a cock horse to Banbury Cross
> To see a fine lady upon a white horse.
> Rings on her fingers and bells on her toes,
> She shall have music wherever she goes.

The nursery rhyme is associated with the brazen Lady Godiva and May Day celebrations, the most prominent feature of which is the phallic May pole, a pagan symbol of spring fertility. Although the phrase *cock horse* can be innocently applied to bouncing a child on one's foot, in the context of Piazza's novel, the action of scruffily kissing Alexander while involving him in a piston-like motion endows the phrase with all of the sexual connotations of the word *cock*.

Alexander also enjoys a special kind of kiss, which his father calls a *pizzicuneddu*: "This was a kiss where I would pull his lips apart by pulling on each whisker cheek with my thumb and index finger and then kiss him on the mouth and then he would do the same to me. I don't know where he got that kiss (from Sicily I guess) but he sure liked it" (65). The unusual kiss is explicitly marked as ethnic, and the father's somewhat effete interest in flower-gardening seems, too, to mark him as ethnically different. Moreover, it is the smell of his father's flowers that leads to Alexander's first orgasm. As he lies face down on the ground smelling his father's flowers, he recounts a sensation "like a fever. It was so strong that all my thinking stopped and then I felt it happening like peeing, only with pleasure" (37).

In fact, there are several passages in which peeing, or otherwise wetting oneself, carries a sexual—sometimes incestuous—connotation. As Alexander stands naked in a river at one point, he calls out to his sister, "Come on, sister, get wet all over." After they splash around for a bit, he sees "her wet panties clinging to her skin" and suggests that they show each other their genitals, but she refuses (46). Given, especially, that one of Alexander's brothers is named Quentin, Piazza may be playfully evoking Caddy's wet, muddy drawers in William Faulkner's *The Sound and the Fury*, a text that is equally structured by incest and death, but he is certainly also evoking Freud's ruminations on the threat of (symbolic) castration as the definitive condition of sexual difference. For instance, shortly before his father's death, Alexander goes into his parents' room to caress their underclothes and try on his mother's high heels. He removes them, then looks at his penis in the mirror, hoping to see some change. (Not incidentally, while he is doing this, his father is outside tending to the orgasm-inducing flowers.) Alexander then climbs into his parents' bed and, while lying on their respective sides, says, "Now I am the mother. [. . .] Now I am the father" (109). While erotic in some respects, this gender play also hints at Alexander's identity anxieties. Framing his play within Freudian terms, the heterosexual "castration anxiety" response would be to fetishize an object that signifies "female" to stave off the homosexual impulse; however, Alexander's play works against Freud's heteronormative framework when the boy uses the object in such a way that indicates a half-hoping confrontation with his queer self (154).

Following this incident, Alexander reads that dinosaurs are extinct and learns that *extinct* is a word meaning "1) of a fire, extinguished, of a volcano no longer in eruption. 2) quenched; that has ceased to burn or shine. 3) of a person—cut off, dead, vanished. 4) that has died out or ceased to exist" (111). He then entertains a daydream ripe with taboo and the phallic symbolism of "his mother dressed in a baptismal gown standing on a big rock in a Tarzan movie jungle, holding out her right hand, holding out her right hand with the gold wedding ring on one finger, petting the snake-like head of a brontosaur as big as the rock" (111). Alexander then goes into the bathroom, and the third-person narrator describes the two bathrooms for the eight members of the household—one designated "for the boys" and the other "for the girls"—and that Alexander alternates which one he uses when no one else is in the house. On this occasion, he goes to the boys' bathroom. He gets an erection, which he touches and scolds himself for. He then picks up his father's razor and pretends to shave. Looking at himself in the mirror, he realizes that his father is standing behind him, angry that Alexander is playing with the razor, which he has been forbidden to do. His father spanks him repeatedly with the razor strap, after which Alexander has the perspicacity to realize that he would not have engaged in this punishable transgression if he had only gone into the girls' bathroom, and alternately wishes himself and his father dead (112–15). Throughout this extended scene in bedroom and bathroom we see a sort of playing at gender performances, with an erotic reward for playing at being his mother and fear and punishment for performing his birth-assigned gender.

The very next day, his father suffers a stroke and does die shortly thereafter. Following the funeral, Alexander dreams that

> he was riding up Main Street on a dinosaur, past all the places he knew. He was swinging a gold sword in the air and he was very happy. He was laughing out loud and saying, "Mr. Dinosaur, this is the best ride I ever had in my life." [. . .] Then something terrible happened and Alexander fell off the dinosaur. Everything was dark and when the light came back he saw that the dinosaur's long neck had been cut off and the gold sword was lying in the street with blood on it. Alexander ran back down Main Street yelling, "Somebody killed the dinosaur." (135)

Piazza's cumulative technique is richly, and quirkily, at work here. This ride evokes the *ride a cock horse* passage, and the image of the mother stroking the brontosaur's snake-like head ensures that its phallic form has not been lost on readers when they learn that its long neck has been lopped off in Alexander's dream. Alexander's fear of his own castration at his father's hand leads him to wish his father dead in classic Oedipal fashion. Traditionally, the fear of the father would manifest itself in a castration complex that should resolve and, eventually, conclude the Oedipal phase of child development. Alexander fantasizes himself not only the agent of his father's demise but fantasizes it in such a way that he is the agent of his father's castration, one that winkingly uses the dinosaur to symbolically validate Freud's notion of the castration complex as a "primal phantasy" and "prehistoric truth" (*Introductory Lectures*, 370). Unsure of which bathroom to go into and equally able to say, "I am the mother" and "I am the father," Alexander is unable to "evolve" and resolve his Oedipal crisis. Not surprisingly, then, Piazza understands Alexander's queerness as a function of regressive sexual development, a Freudian view that was widely promoted mid-century.

While the razor-dinosaur episode is quirky and complicated, more simple and traditional indications are also present that Piazza is evoking Freud's Oedipal theory. For instance, after the mother's (later) stroke, while performing his daily chore of massaging her legs Alexander "accidentally raised up her night gown and she was naked underneath. He didn't know what he had seen" (192). Earlier in the text we learn that the mother suffers bladder control problems and that Alexander's brother believes that babies come from the father and mother taking turns peeing into a milk bottle. The "exact and very strange truth" of the novel's title refers to the fact that Alexander's life keeps changing for the worse as his family members either die or marry, events that Alexander experiences as sexual frustrations. "Things can be one way today and tomorrow be the very opposite. That," he says, "is the exact and very strange truth" (16). For instance, Alexander wants his brother to continue to sleep in the same bed with him rather than with his new wife, and his mother's embarrassing dysfunctional urination, thematically linked to sex, anticipates her complete loss as a sexual object in death. The exact and very queer truth is that Alexander cannot give up his family members as primarily sexual objects and instead regressively "retains them in phantasy."

Alexander's understanding of his identity within the family is balanced by identification with people outside the family (like the Dukes twins) as well as all of the novel's freaks and outcasts *except*, curiously, the two white characters explicitly marked as homosexual. Mr. Claire Alphey is one such character. The owner of a bookstore next door to Mr. Gallanti's shoe repair shop, Alphey invites Alexander to come look at picture books whenever he likes; however, Alexander declares, "I didn't like him. He talked funny and stared at me like something was wrong" (79). A bartender on the same business strip makes perfectly clear what is "wrong" with Alphey when he teases Alexander, "Mr. Claire Alphey? Is he your daddy? Hmm? Why, he talks funny enough to be somebody's Momma" (69). In a book so interested in mirror images and opposites ("I am the mother. [. . .] I am the father"), we might expect Alexander to identify with Alphey's sexual inversion, but instead he is disquieted by the bookish man's queerness.

An encounter with a clearly marked queer schoolmate perhaps explains Alexander's inability to identify with other queers. Like Alexander himself, Bernie Andrews is othered because of his intelligence, "high voice," and "peculiar" way of speaking. Other boys in school "called him a freak and said he was more girl than boy" (153). But Bernie seems unfazed by the bullying and even flirts openly with Alexander. Echoing back to Alexander's fear of becoming a "freak," he repeatedly thwarts Bernie's advances at either flirtation or friendship. For instance, in one scene, Alexander is looking in the school halls for his mother while wearing his pilgrim costume for the Thanksgiving play:

> Bernie Andrews came over to him and put his hand on Alexander's shoulder: "What a magnificent looking Pilgrim you are," [said Bernie]. [. . . Alexander] moved away from Bernie. He didn't like Bernie's hand on his shoulder. [. . .]
>
> "Pilgrim, mother is mater and mater is mother so what is the matter with you?"
>
> "Did you see my mother?"
>
> "I don't know. What does your mother look like? Does she have orbs as beautiful and blue as yours?"
>
> "Oh, come on! I don't know what orbs are. Just tell me if you saw my mother."
>
> "Pilgrim, orbs are eyes and beautiful blue orbs are beautiful blue eyes. Does your mother have beautiful blue eyes like you?"
>
> "Bernie, that isn't any way to talk about my eyes. One boy doesn't say to another boy, 'Does your mother have beautiful blue eyes like you?'"
>
> "Pilgrim, you would be surprised if I told you the things that one boy can say to another boy." (154–55)

As with Mr. Claire Alphey, Bernie's overt queerness unsettles Alexander. Alphey and Bernie mirror for Alexander his own queer freakishness; however, he cannot assume the resolve of a true pilgrim in his own era. Bernie is flamboyant and hilarious as a kind of precocious Arkansas queen, already developing a skewering wit, while Alexander is merely an ersatz pilgrim.

Given that Piazza situates himself so self-consciously in the field of Southern writing, in which Black characters "endure" and serve as moral compasses, especially for sexually confused white children, it is not surprising that a Black character near the end of the novel delivers one of the more telling comments on incest and identity. Angel Jones, the Black man who offers the mother and children a ride on his wagon to the theater in Savannah to see *Gone with the Wind*, tells Alexander he does not know if the other character from their hometown with the name Jones is kin, "but then," he says, "sometimes it's hard to know who is kin and who ain't" (214). Indeed, this has been Alexander's confusion throughout the text: He feels estranged from his family at the same time that he feels a strange sexual attraction to them that he cannot give up. Yet the possible understanding he might gain about his sexuality through identification with nonfamilial queer characters does not seem to him a viable option.

The one queer character with whom Alexander *does* identify is Black and a much more adventurous pilgrim than Alexander. The son of the family's maid, Jesus Elizabeth Jones appears several times in the text. We learn, for instance, that Alexander considers *Jesus Elizabeth Jones* "the most beautiful name [he] had ever heard" (35). Jesus Elizabeth's mother had expected the boy, born on Christmas, to be a girl, so she simply combined the name she had intended for a girl with Jesus. Alexander clearly identifies in some way with Jesus Elizabeth, and, like the Dukes twins, he also seems destined to be marked by physical trauma. In an early scene in the book, when Jesus Elizabeth is still a baby, a rat chews off half of his left arm while his mother is out of the house. Although Alexander's Italian father wields just enough white authority to persuade the white hospital to treat the child, the arm cannot be saved.

Here, too, exact chronology seems less important than narrative juxtaposition. Just after we learn of Jesus Elizabeth's rat attack, Alexander moves on to his first orgasm in his father's flower garden. And just after Alexander, in his pilgrim costume, has defined a pilgrim as someone who "goes in search of a new place, a new country where everything will be perfect" (183–84), he reverts to the story of the grown Jesus Elizabeth, who leaves a note for his mother about going to Chicago. In the note, he writes, "Dear Momma, I'm sorry about it but I stole that fifteen dollars you was saving in the sugar bowl. I went to Penny's and bought a red dress and a pair of red high-heeled open toe, open heel pumps. At this very minute while someone is reading you this letter I am sitting in the back of a bus wearing same red dress and red pumps and headed for Chicago and a new and happy life" (184). This is the Great Migration undertaken with unusual flair by a transgendered pilgrim. Whereas Alexander is a failure as a pilgrim, regressing into rather than leaving behind the imperfect country of his childhood, Jesus Elizabeth has gone shopping and left behind not only Arkansas but his male identity as well. We thus encounter another of the novel's many mirror images. In the rat-attack/flower-orgasm passages, Jesus Elizabeth is traumatized; then Alexander experiences joy. In the pilgrim passage, Alexander is traumatized as Jesus Elizabeth experiences joy. Perhaps what makes the character worthy of Alexander's esteem is an ability, in Judith Butler's terms, to rise above melancholia through a "subversive and parodic" attitude about "the binary, heterosexist framework" (66). While Alexander is trapped between choosing the boy's bathroom and the girls' bathroom—and facing potential punishment for either choice—Jesus Elizabeth boldly and unapologetically chooses a path that defies the heteronormative frame.

To be sure, Black characters such as Jesus Elizabeth and Angel Jones exist in the novel to ultimately illuminate *Alexander's* queer/ethnic truth rather than their own. In this respect, they are, to quote Ralph Ellison on Faulkner's use of Black characters, "representative of those virtues of courage, pride, independence and patience that are usually attributed only to white men—and [. . .] accepting the Negro as 'the keeper of our [the whites'] consciences'" (Ellison 274). The fact that they are more courageous or wise than Alexander does little to counterbalance the fact that they repeat a long-standing pattern in which Black characters have meaning for white characters rather than for themselves. What makes Piazza's effort here distinctive is its use of Catholic imagery and the Sicilian immigrant father figure as an intermediary between white and Black. Indeed, although Alexander resembles his father so little that he inadvertently blackens his face to look more like him, there is one respect in which he does resemble his father, revealed when he describes his father's ethnicity involving a love of "God only knows what secret and forbidden pleasures" (20). Slavoj Zizek has suggested that this may most fundamentally be what the racial or ethnic Other designates: the one we believe has access to secret and forbidden pleasures that we want ourselves—whoever *we* may be (155, 168–69). And what is the place of the father in Piazza's novel? Death and incest. If the place of the ethnically marked father is death, and this is the place of forbidden and secret pleasures—the bliss of the death drive—then it perhaps makes sense that two of the most important Black characters in the novel bear sexless names that are "beyond" death: Angel and Jesus. It is surely not accidental that the name of Jesus Elizabeth's single mother is Mary. Jesus Elizabeth's unusual name,[3] in particular, draws special attention to a peculiar, somewhat breathless comment that Alexander makes early in the text while he is still the novel's first-person narrator: "I feel so separate from everybody and I just want somebody to be with and get up close to get up so close that there isn't even any space at all between us and we can feel each other breathe and our skin is like one skin and very warm together. Everybody is asleep and dreaming their own dreams but I am not asleep. Maybe I am dead, maybe everybody is dead and we are on our way to Jesus" (32). Strikingly, this passage functions as the novel's core expression of Alexander's alienation, and "Jesus" surely means something complex and queer in the context of this story. The Jesus of Piazza's novel, toward whom Alexander thinks (perhaps *hopes*) the family may all be on their way, is Black, has secret and forbidden desires, and wears a red dress and red high heels. He has only one arm but the most beautiful name ever heard. He may be kin to an Angel, but it's hard to say who *is* kin and who ain't. It would be easy to read this passage as thesis ("I just want somebody to be with") and antithesis (but "Maybe I am dead"). We suggest, though, that the second statement is a development of the first. In Alexander's mind, Jesus and his father have both crossed a line beyond which lie the secret and forbidden pleasures of sexual union, the pilgrimage he himself does not have the courage to undertake. In Piazza's novel, this lack of courage is consistently linked to Alexander's inscrutably Aryan features. The Sicilian father and Black Jesus are both associated with dark, secret, forbidden pleasures, while Alexander is upset when Bernie flirts with him by drawing attention to his blue eyes, signifying his whiteness.

By the end of the novel, Alexander's Anglo-Southern mother has also died, passing away in the theater while she and her children are watching *Gone with the Wind*. In the midst of the pageantry of a mythologized antebellum South, the other anchor of Alexander's Oedipal and ethnic identities ceases to exist. Alexander ultimately cannot find the "secret place of us" that he had dreamed about, regressing instead back into his narcissistic childhood, where the narrative remains entrenched.

Notes

1. This article began as a collaboration between Doug Steward and Tracy Floreani some years ago, but the intent to complete the project was curtailed by Steward's untimely death on November 5, 2020. Floreani has published elsewhere on Ben Piazza's novel and has brought her work together with the only known copy of Steward's draft for posthumous publication. See Tracy Floreani, "The Very Strange Truth: Ben Piazza's Italian Southerner," *Essays on Italian American Literature*

and Culture, ed. Dennis Barone and Peter Covino (New York: Bordighera Press, 2012): 54–61.

2. *The Exact and Very Strange Truth* was Piazza's only published novel, after which he focused his career on acting. He worked regularly on Broadway and in television and film until his death in 1991. Born Benito Piazza in 1933 to a Sicilian father and Southern Baptist mother in Little Rock, Arkansas, the story is clearly based, in part, on his own experiences.

3. "Elizabeth," too, has religious connotations. It means "consecrated to God" and was the name of the mother of John the Baptist. In this respect, Jesus Elizabeth's name marries the Catholic and Baptist elements in the novel just as Alexander's parents do. Of course, it is also the name of more than one famous queen.

Works Cited

Butler, Judith. *Gender Trouble: Feminism and the Subversion of Identity*. Oxfordshire, UK: Routledge, 1990.

Ellison, Ralph. "The Shadow and the Act." In *Shadow and Act*, by Ralph Ellison, 273–81. New York: Vintage, 1964.

Faulkner, William. *The Sound and the Fury*. 1929. Reprint, New York: Vintage, 1990.

Freud, Sigmund. "Fetishism." In vol. 2 of *The Standard Edition of the Complete Works of Sigmund Freud*, trans. James Strachey, 152–57.

———. *Introductory Lectures on Psychoanalysis*. In vol. 16 of *The Standard Edition of the Complete Works of Sigmund Freud*, trans. James Strachey, 243–463.

———. "Mourning and Melancholia." In vol. 14 of *The Standard Edition of the Complete Works of Sigmund Freud*, trans. James Strachey, 239–58.

———. "On Narcissism: An Introduction." In vol. 14 of *The Standard Edition of the Complete Works of Sigmund Freud*, trans. James Strachey, 69–102.

McCullers, Carson. *The Member of the Wedding*. In *Complete Novels*. 1946. Reprint, New York: Library of America, 2001. 459–605.

Piazza, Ben. *The Exact and Very Strange Truth*. New York: Farrar, Straus and Giroux, 1964.

Spiegel, Alan. "A Theory of the Grotesque in Southern Fiction." *Georgia Review* 26 (1972): 426–37.

Strachey, James, trans. *The Standard Edition of the Complete Psychological Works of Sigmund Freud*. London: Hogarth, 1957.

Zizek, Slavoj. "Love Thy Neighbor? No, Thanks!" In *The Psychoanalysis of Race*, edited by Christopher Lane, 154–75. New York: Columbia University Press, 1998.

From Page to Stage

Italian Americans and Italian Canadians

8

Queer Intimacies in
Italian Canadian Literature

Domenico A. Beneventi

While there has been a substantial body of critical and creative work in Italian Canadian literature on gender and sexuality questions since it emerged as a recognizable canon in the 1980s, especially in terms of writing by women,[1] works by and about gay, lesbian, and queer subjects have been relatively few.[2] The popular success of Steve Galluccio's 2002 play *Mambo Italiano* (Galluccio) and the subsequent 2003 film by Émile Gaudrault has raised the visibility of the "invisible" homosexual within the traditional Italian Canadian immigrant family structure and explored questions of self-hatred, secrecy, and eventually—acceptance—that rely largely on stereotypes about both homosexuality and Italian ethnicity for its comedic effect. But this popular success has elided other queer narratives by Canadians of Italian descent. This chapter explores two such recent texts, Salvatore Antonio's play *In Gabriel's Kitchen* (2006) and Christopher DiRaddo's novel *The Geography of Pluto* (2014), looking specifically at how these authors use, imagine, and narrate queer spatialities and temporalities in their works; in other words, how do queer characters represent alternate mappings of the city and the intimate space of the home as they negotiate a queer standpoint in counterdistinction to the heteronormative spaces in which they dwell? Furthermore, I explore how a queer temporality manifests itself in moments of past-oriented, negative affects of "feeling backward," as Heather Love has suggested (2007),[3] of a static *presentism* linked to moments of corporeal intimacy that attempts to freeze the present moment, and as a future-oriented utopic horizon that is never actualized (Munoz 2009). These works repeatedly link physical space with the space of the queer desiring body itself–an imbrication between bodily affect, memory, and the space of the city, with its familiar haunts, bars, spaces of queer encounter–or in the secret spaces of the home.

Furthermore, I want to suggest that in Antonio's play and, to a lesser extent, in Di Raddo's novel, the schism between queer Italian Canadian youth and the previous generation emerges not only from the difficulties around the disclosure of sexual identity—the proverbial "coming out of the closet," but from a more fundamental schism between what Sarah Ahmed has described as a queer phenomenology[4] and what Edelman suggests subtends heteronormativity: the promise of the child, "an erotically charged investment in the rigid sameness of identity that is central to the compulsory narrative of reproductive futurism" (21). *In Gabriel's Kitchen* questions Italian Canadian performances of hegemonic masculinity (Connell), particularly that of the patriarch—Paolo—whose immigrant fantasy of class mobility is invested in the figures of his two male children—Marco and Gabriel—who come to symbolize the promise of a heteronormative futurity and the continuation of the family name.[5] But, the play asks, what happens if the immigrant child is queer?

First staged at Buddies in Bad Times Theatre in Toronto, a preeminent venue for queer theatre in Canada, *In Gabriel's Kitchen* tells the tale of the Montesanto family, who live in Woodbridge, a middle-class Italian immigrant enclave on the outskirts of Toronto. Concetta and Paolo Montesanto and their sons, Marco and Gabriel, are a typical Italian immigrant family that has struggled toward the comforts of middle-class existence in Canada, instilling in their sons a sense of Italian heritage, tradition, and morality informed by their religious belief. Much of the play takes place in various parts of the Montesanto household; the first-floor kitchen is where most present-day action occurs, whereas the unfinished basement is the obscene space in which scenes from the past between Gabriel and his first boyfriend, Matt, take place. Through this temporal and spatial disjunction, the audience comes to understand that the Montesanto family is still reeling from the loss of their son Gabriel, who commits suicide when his family rejects his homosexuality. The drama unfolds in the conflicts between Marco, who has left the family home to live in Vancouver, and his parents, who refuse to face the realities of their son's death and the idea that they were in part responsible for the suicide of eighteen-year-old Gabriel.

Christopher DiRaddo's *The Geography of Pluto* describes the coming of age of Will Ambrose, a young geography teacher who tries to negotiate various relationships, the most significant of which are those he has with Max, his boyfriend; Angie, his best friend who is a lesbian; and his mother, a librarian who works at the Atwater Library. The novel traces Will's development from a young man living at his mother's house to discovering his homosexuality and eventually discovering the larger gay community in Montreal. As the plot progresses, Will is confronted with various forms of loss—the loss of his relationship with Max and the loss of his mother after her long battle with illness.

In the following pages, I explore how the queer characters in the works of Antonio and DiRaddo open up spaces of "utopic longing" (Munoz)—both real, physical, and lived spaces (such as the immigrant home, the city, and the suburb); and imaginary spaces on which memory, affect, and life narratives are written. I want to show that in their desire to negotiate a space of belonging in the city and the family, the queer protagonists imagine and experience time and space in ways that are different from the heteronormative and ethnically prefigured surroundings in which they dwell.

"Darmi la forza di non vedere":
Silencing and Epistemology of the Ethnic Closet

In *Epistemology of the Closet,* Eve Sedgwick argues that the idea of the proverbial "closet" as the socially constructed pact through which non-normative gender and sexual identities hang, ambiguously undisclosed, is essentially "initiated as such by the speech act of a silence—not a particular silence, but a silence that accrues particularly by fits and starts, in relation to the discourses that surrounds and differentially constitutes it" (3). This is particularly true in the case of immigrant communities wherein old-world values are often informed by religious beliefs and patriarchal power structures: Silence maintains the fantasy of heteronormative familial order and social closure while enclosing queer individuals in prescriptive identities that do real psychological harm. Indeed, silence is centrally operative in both *In Gabriel's Kitchen* and *The Geography of Pluto* as strategies of negotiating queer identities and intersectionally navigating the expectations of ethnic continuity and tradition. In Di Raddo's novel, the protagonist, Will, feels "Silly, lying to my mother at this age" about his sexual identity, and when he is watching TV and a gay film comes on, he quickly turns it off for fear of her reaction. It is only once his mother is gravely ill, and he fears losing her, that he comes out to her in "fits and starts": "unprepared and unscripted, sitting on the edge of her hospital bed, tripping on the words as they came out" (71). The silence and silencing of Gabriel in Antonio's plays is central to the drama and leads to his suicide and the subsequent silence of each member of the family in acknowledging the traumatic moment in which Marco finds his brother hanging from a supporting beam in the unfinished basement—the rosary that had "miraculously" saved him from being run over by a truck as a child reappearing around the young man's neck as an accusation against his family. Ironically enough, it is through silence rather than utterance that the "truths" of the family are revealed, as Antonio states in his production notes: "When a (silence) occurs, in the script it is usually a shared non-verbal scene, where a certain truth has been revealed, or a certain belief has been destroyed. Silence is the most uncomfortable, terrifying shift that can occur in this script. It has an element of danger to it, in that no thing and no one, is safe" (xiii). If the play veers between moments of "heightened drama and quiet desperation" (vi), silence plays a crucial role in both maintaining familial harmony but *also* pointing to the moments of rupture, hesitation, and truths too painful to be expressed. Silence represents the discomfort of truth, the negative affect that reveals not only the very structures of heteronormative discipline but also their possibility of rupture and reversal: In other words, the silences at the heart of the play occur not only in terms of the epistemology of the closet and the silencing of Gabriel's desire and identity but also in the silencing of the members of his family.

Furthermore, the silence of the play's three non-queer characters as "epistemological performances" reveals the truth of their own complicity in the tragedy: "the fact that silence is rendered as pointed and performative as speech, in relations around the closet, depends on and highlights more broadly the fact that ignorance is as potent and as multiple a thing as there is to knowledge" (Sedgwick 4). The refusal to hear or acknowledge queer identities in *In Gabriel's Kitchen* and, by extension, the whole of the Italian Canadian immigrant community is a performative gesture intent on maintaining the fantasy of heteronormative and patriarchal order, something the play explicitly stages as Concetta, symbolically looming over a moment of queer intimacy between her son and his partner, refuses to see in her injunction to God to inure her to blindness. Moments of seeing and not-seeing/recognition and misrecognition repeatedly occur throughout the play: Paolo (not) recognizing his son for who he truly is; Concetta refusing to imagine seeing her son in moments of intimacy with Matt yet suppressing what she already knew of him when he was a child ("*fa che tutto ciò che vedo in lui non sia quello che ho intuito essere*"); Marco seeing, in a traumatic and indescribable moment, the dead body of his brother ("I kept blinking, blinking—blinking crazy like, like if I keep shutting what I'm seeing maybe—when I look again it won't be real—WHAT am I seeing—God—my baby brother" [91]), but also Gabriel being seen by his lover as art, as beauty, in the character of Concetta, that easily recognizable trope of the nurturing yet suffering Italian immigrant mother symbolically looming over a moment of queer intimacy between her son and his partner in which she refuses to *see* and calls upon God to curse her with blindness.

The indeterminacy of meaning in moments of silence (both Gabriel's and his family's) opens up the play to a queer *episteme* that reconfigures the space of familial domesticity and familial relations to a variety of inter-pretations. Thus, as David Oiye mentions in his introduction to the play, "The world in which the story plays out on stage is one where anything is possible; visitations, the conjuring of the departed or the holy, fantastic understandings, spiritual transportation, and unbridled personal truths" (ix). This magical-realist element in the play suggests the possibilities opened up by queer spatialities and temporalities—a queer phenomenology that con-stitutes an alternative to the heteronormative space of the family, of public and private identities, and the regimented temporalities of the heterosexual world. In the following pages, I examine how both the play and the novel construct alternate spatialities and temporalities, arguing that these become necessary for the protagonists to escape from the normative and explore their own emerging queer identities.

Queer Geographies

A queer geography implies self-erasure, silence, longing, subterfuge, doubled meanings, subtle glances, and secret languages of the body: Indeed, domestic space, public space, and national space have denied or marginalized queer subjects until very recently.[6] Queer spaces such as the gay village, for instance, are often still seen as morally suspect, as a space of libertinism and free sexual exchange that endangers the heteronormative regimentation of public and private spaces and bodies and the codification of the "closed" familial structure defined by heteronormative monogamy.[7] Their main characters want to belong but cannot do so fully, and thus long for a utopic space of queer sociability and escape from a heteronormative society in which their queer acts, bodies, desires, and utterances are not seen as abnormal or perverse. This desire for escape is expressed in spatial and temporal terms in the works I am considering here, as is the case for much contemporary gay or queer writing. As Munoz writes in *Cruising Utopia: The Then and There of Queer Futurity,*

> Queerness is not yet here. Queerness is an ideality. Put another way, we are not yet queer. We may never touch queerness, but we can feel it as the warm illumination of a horizon imbued with potentialities. We have never been queer, yet queerness exists for us as an ideality that can be distilled from the past and used to imagine a future . . . Queerness is that thing that lets us feel that this world is not enough, that indeed something is missing . . . Queerness is essentially about the rejection of a here and now and an insistence on potentiality or concrete possibility for another world. (1)

That queer utopic longing for a space of escape is both a rejection of the "here and now" and a projection to an imagined possible future expressed, in these two texts, in geographical and cosmological terms. If the queer protagonists in *The Geography of Pluto* and *In Gabriel's Kitchen* explore, discover, occupy, and even create heterotopic sites of queer sociability, they also attempt to reconfigure the inescapable temporality that has been given them in the desire to stop time in some way in turning inward to the body as the site of utopic pleasure. In DiRaddo's novel, that escape is seen in Will's desire to explore the hidden world of the gay village and in the symbolism of the eponymous Pluto itself—a "queer" kind of planet that is not quite what it seems, lingering on the outer margins of the solar system, dark and mysterious. But, as Will's best friend remarks, "the powers of Pluto are transformative. They're associated with rebirth and renewal, beginnings as well as endings" (101). For Gabriel, escape comes in imagining an ultimately impossible future of queer domesticity within the immigrant family home—projecting the queer couple out to a future *not yet here* within the space of his family's unfinished basement in the middle-class Toronto suburb of Woodbridge. This utopic queer horizon is also symbolized in the unfinished model of the solar system that Gabriel and his lover Matt work on for a class project: "The unfinished basement kitchen. Lights slowly rise to reveal MATT and GABRIEL on the concrete floor . . . they are naked, lying beside each other on a blanket . . . on the other side of them rests the nearly completed model of the universe. A contraption with painted Styrofoam planets attached to coat-hanger wires that extend out from a base. A few planets are still not in place" (56). This unexpected adjacency of queer bodily intimacy and the easily recognizable exercise of creating a model of the solar system (attuned as it is to a very heteronormative educational space) suggests that the young couple are striving toward a queer phenomenology (Ahmed) through the joint construction of a queer domesticity shaped by affect and eros. Gabriel and Matt inhabit a queer heterotopic space where they remain unseen by the Montesano family, where the laws of physics may be slightly altered, and where their sexuality is not seen as aberrant. The building of this alternative queer space occurs amid sensual touching of bodies—the creation of new worlds and celestial bodies; "the space between them is charged" (36). Gabriel's proclamation that they just need to get to work in "building the universe" (35) invokes the religious symbolism of the Christian God's Archangels, Gabriel and Matt(hew) as divine messengers remaking the (heteronormative) world brought into being by Concetta, both earth-mother and Virgin Mary who conceives, through a Divine anointing, the salvific figure of the child: "Concetta alone on top of the table. She grabs her stomach in pain, a flash, she exhales. She reaches into her apron pockets and comes out with two handfuls of flour. She throws them onto the table before her. She takes in a deep breath and exhales. A huge mound of dough (the size of a small child) falls from above landing before her" (51). Just as Matt and Gabriel get to work making a universe "orienting" (Ahmed) its objects in their own image, in another time and place, Concetta creates a world out of her own body—in her children, but also in the love, care, and nourishment of motherhood, seen in the repeated scenes in which Concetta attempts to feed her family as a way not to face the truths that must be faced. Standing alone atop the family's dining table—a symbol of the happier days of the past but also the elevated space from which Gabriel hangs himself—she writhes in emotional and physical pain as she contemplates her son's suicide, refusing to see his disappearance. We see in this remarkable scene competing spatial and temporal configurations—where the heteronormative (religious) domesticity of Concetta and Paolo looks toward a hopeful futurity through the figure of the child (Edelman), while Gabriel's projects himself toward an as-of-yet undefined queer domestic futurity with Matt (Munoz).

Spatial metaphors are also seen throughout DiRaddo's novel. The recurring images of maps (maps of the city, the mappings of the body's geography as both Will and his mother undergo medical tests, and so on) show Will's quest to create a coherent spatial narrative of his life trajectories. When discussing the breakup of a lesbian couple, Mel and Genevieve, with his friend Angie, she explains the relationship in spatial terms: "Come here, she said, and pulled me towards a map of the city on the subway wall. See, she pointed to an intersection of streets that made up the corner of Drolet and Rachel: 'This is where she lives'" (25), signaling that the couple lives in the hip Plateau Mont-Royal district of the city. Angie's role here becomes that of a guide to a remapping of not only the city, but also its queer communities, dispersed from the gay-male identified space of cruising bars and cafés of the village to the more hidden lesbian and queer social spaces of the Plateau and Mile-End neighbourhoods farther north.

The finger on the map becomes a waypoint, a shift in the narrative of the relationship. This incites Will to examine the map for himself to figure out his own "points of interest" (26), which "charted the years of my life as if they were just another feature on a crowded transit map . . . where my mother lived—and where I had grown up—and then I saw all the lost hours at Max's place . . . how many times had I biked those streets in between his home and mine" (26). These itineraries follow Will's own emotional journeys as he fans out all over the city searching for community. The desire to know his queer itinerary extends out over the whole city and inward to the geographies of the heart and the emotions. The map is "used to help us locate our position, chart journeys, tell us about a specific time and place. But I feel lost in all of this emotional geography" (109). When Will begins dating Max, he fantasizes about giving him an old electrocardiogram of his own heart: "The printed graph was proof of my heart; the only tangible evidence of its tiny, intricate workings . . . This is how my heart looks, I'd think. Nothing more than a thin black line on a red road to somewhere" (109). Body and city intermingle here, calling to mind Elizabeth Grosz's notion of the urban body as "a two-way linkage that can be defined as an interface" in which body and city are not separate entities but mutually define each other. DiRaddo goes on, "It's a cliché to call a city boulevard an artery, but I could clearly see the metaphor on the map. Blue and Red lines thrown across the black and being like a person's circulatory system, the bus stops and metro tunnels spread out from a central hub. All these horizontal, vertical, and diagonal lines taking people in all directions, and I felt immobile, trapped beneath them as if by some invisible net" (26).

Will is constantly attempting to create an inclusive narrative of the city that would include both the home that he grew up in and the queer space of the gay village where he meets friends and lovers. It is a geography of illicit desires and self-discovery that had until now been hidden from view, a heterotopic space in the city: "I knew nothing beyond the three outposts of my life: home, work, school. Now a whole new area had been unearthed, one of lingering glances and vibrant character that, at night, morphed into a riotous fete the scope of which I had never thought possible" (95). As a teenager, Will hides his sexuality from his mother. When they are home watching TV one night and he comes across "what appeared to be a bunch of men parading around in full-length gowns" (11), he quickly changes the channel despite being "completely mesmerized" by this first image of queer sexuality on screen. His best friend, Angie/Angela (10), was "a tomboy, slim and athletic with long black hair that she kept in a ponytail. I never saw her in a dress or anything the slightest bit feminine" (11). Even though Will's mother knows that Angie is a lesbian, she insists on calling her by her birth name "out of respect for her parents" (18), a "subtle way of feminizing her, the verbal equivalent of applying blush to the cheeks of this boyish girl" (18). Similarly, names indicate a queering of identity—a self-fashioning that subverts gender and sexual norms, identities, and expectations—Izo, which is short for Isabelle (23). By insisting on calling her son's best friend by her gender-specific given name, Will's mother subtly hints at the schism between heteronormative sociality and domesticity and the more fluid identities possible in queer spaces and social circles that the protagonist explores throughout the novel.

The space of Max's apartment, despite its disarray, becomes a queer space-time that subverts the heteronormative discourses outside its walls—a privileged, utopic space of intimacy: "Sleeping with Max that first night made me feel like an outlaw. For here I was, his naked accomplice, taking part in the one thing that had estranged him from his family. It was exactly what I had wanted—a conspiracy of two. As I fumbled around his body, becoming more acquainted with its crooks and corners, I felt the history of desire in both of us" (64). DiRaddo's novel suggests ways in which the queer body inheres in the spaces of the city, lingering on its peripheries, sometimes out of sight, sometimes all too visible. Here, temporality is inscribed in and through the body, as a private history blooms in the singular space of queer intimacy. Certain locations in the city resonate with memory and emotion—for instance, the pain that is felt when remembering time spent in certain places with an ex-partner.

The emotional geography of love also creates a map on and in the body:

> The first time you fall in love your brain creates a pathway, one
> with a juicy dose of dopamine at the end. It's like walking in a
> tall field of grass. Your first time through you leave an imprint,
> a trail of parted blades that bend straight at the ground. It
> leaves a mark so that the next time you find yourself before it
> you know how to get to the other side . . . it took becomes a
> kind of map—a worn-down blueprint of memories we spend
> the rest of our lives retracing. (116)

When Will and his friends go to a gay strip club, they are fascinated by
the sculpted male bodies that dance before them: "They are on a field trip,"
Will jokes, "They are on an archaeological dig" (32). Here again, the novel
attempts to enumerate and understand the various cultures, subcultures, and
countercultures of the city, excavating its hidden spaces and populations that
are normally shunned and marginalized. It is ironic that though Will is a
geography teacher with a wandering spirit, he has never traveled beyond
Ottawa. Will is caught by the past and by his failed relationship with Max:
"when I closed my eyes I could still feel his gravitational pull across time
and space, holding me within his orbit" (41). For Will, geography and
desire are inextricably linked. He learned of the city of Regina "because
that is where Shaun Findlay was from. Shaun Findlay, whose body was like
the Prairies, his chest as flat as Saskatchewan, overlain with rolling wisps
of golden hair" (43).

The city's physical space is also a symbolic space imbued with social,
cultural, and religious discourses that mark the bodies and behaviors of its
residents. When Will finds himself in Shaun's apartment in Westmount,
he noticed the cross atop Mount Royal that "glared at me disapprovingly
through the windows of Shaun's large Westmount apartment" (44). Shaun
tells Will about his place of origin by tracing a map on the carpet on which
they lay together: "showing me where it was by tracing a map of Canada
with his index finger on his living room's plush carpet floor" (45). As in the
previous scene where Angie situates Mel and Genevive's relationship, Shaun
traces out his narrative trajectory from the Prairies to this spot in Montreal.

In both these works, domestic space is intimately linked to both Italian
Canadian identity and, in a troubled way, to gay identity. Will grows up
in his mother's home in the Plateau Mont-Royal neighborhood of Montreal, and with the growing awareness of his sexuality, he decides to paint
his room to reflect his emerging identity: "I had stripped it of artifice. It
was plain, fresh, and ready to be plied with whatever I chose" (16). When

he moves out to his apartment, he describes creating a space for himself that is "small but comfortable" (4), that is as much a home to him as the "space on the other end of the phone line" (5), his mother's apartment. The house, as Gaston Bachelard has shown in *The Poetics of Space,* is rife with symbolic associations: It is the repository of memories, objects, and life narrative, but also psychological truths: "In it the values of intimacy are scattered" (14). Antonio's play is about the meaning of home—who belongs and who does not belong in the home. It is revealed that Matt also has no sense of home, for his family moves every few years due to his father's work. As Bachelard notes, the "intimacies" of home space are "not easily stabilized," as, far from being a space cut off from the discourses of public space, private space also reflects the external discourses of the public—here, heteronormative discourses around the aberrant nature of homosexuality is present in the loving home itself—a form of uncanniness that Will in DiRaddo's novel attempts to mediate by creating a second barrier within his mother's home—his room.

When Will is invited to a party atop the Olympic Stadium's tower, he stops a moment to look out over the city, taking it all in an encompassing view that connects all the places that have meaning to him—his mother's apartment, his own, the village, and Max's place, where he spent so much time. He remembers and imagines his ex-lover beside him, equating the textures of the city with the body of his lover: "I could feel Max beside me his heat, and the softness of his body that my fingers circled as if they were my own, tracing along his limbs as if they were a city map" (129). As he traces a path back to Max's apartment at the foot of the Olympic Stadium, he is met with or imagines the faces of the residents staring at him with disapproval: "I felt spooked by these streets, hated by them and their shops as they looked at me with distaste and judgment, threatening to tell me and making it abundantly clear how unwelcome I was . . . silent disapproval of who I was and what I was doing" (131). It is not clear here if Will's sense of alienation is due to his queer identity, his social class, or his ethnic and linguistic identities, for the Hochelaga-Maisonneuve neighborhood just south of the Olympic stadium is traditionally working-class and French-Canadian, and as an English-speaking Anglo-Montrealer of Italian origin, he has no history here.

As a high school geography teacher, Will teaches his students about the characteristics of cities, "stuff like population density, neighbourhoods, and city services" (20). Will's occupation demonstrates his fascination not only with the textures of the urban—its various populations, ethnicities, modes of embodiment, ways of interacting, and so on—but also with the lifelong pursuit of his narrative that would tie together the disparate parts of his life in different parts of the city: the Jean Talon market—symbol of his Italian heritage and his familial bond, the gay village—the space of sociability, desire, effect—and the French working-class east end of the city, where his lover Max is from. He assigns his students a class project in which they will "imagine and create their own city on another planet (20), mirroring Will's own desire to affectively remake or the city from a queer point of view, much as Gabriel attempts to do so in terms of the domestic space of Woodbridge. Transiting through the city, whether on foot, on his bike, or using the subway system, becomes a strategy for semantically recoding the city, creating personal paths and trajectories that call to mind Michel de Certeau's definition of walking and "pedestrian speech acts":

> The act of walking is to the urban system what the speech act is to language or to the statements uttered. At its most basic level, it has a triple enunciative function: it is a process of *appropriation* of the topographical system on the part of the pedestrian (just as the speaker appropriates and takes on the language); it is a spatial acting-out of the place (just as the speech act is an acoustic acting-out of language); it implies relations among differentiated relations . . . [walking is] a space of enunciation. (98)

The novel is shaped by these increasingly far-flung queer deambulations across the city—from the starting point of the familial home to its various neighborhoods, and as Will treads his own paths, making his own symbolic connections between place and memory, a new language or grammar of desire, queer sociability, and affect of the city emerges. As mentioned earlier, the desire to escape the confines of a heteronormative urban landscape drives Will underground to explore the city's various gay bars, discos, and cafés—seductive spaces that are fictionalized as answering to unexpressed desires. The Sky Bar is the "heavenly body we circled like satellites" (5) when Will and his friends go out to the gay village to drink, while Pluto, the eponymous heavenly body that the protagonist identifies with, is associated with the ancient Roman God of the Underworld, a space associated here with the "unseen" world of a morally suspect gay nightlife, but also "transformative"; as the much more worldly Angie explains, "the powers of Pluto are . . . associated with rebirth and renewal, beginnings as well as endings" (101). This queering of celestial bodies is also reflected in Will's pedagogy, as he tells each student that they must design their ideal imaginary city on another planet, reflecting the underlying theme of queer spatiality and a longing for a space of one's own—a "queer utopic projection into a future that is "not yet here."

If DiRaddo's novel uses the geography of Pluto to imagine a queer space that is "not yet here," in Antonio's play, that utopic longing is imagined as a remaking of the universe in the eponymous kitchen of the play's title—one yet unfinished. According to the playwright's notes, the most important aspect of the staging is the "incompleteness" of the basement space: "Plastic sheet wrap, insulation uncovered sockets, dust in the air. Everything suggests the eeriness of a space abandoned in mid-construction" (xvii). The wood-framed unfinished walls and low ceiling height decorated with hundreds of naked light bulbs create a sanctified atmosphere, a "cathedral of light," which is the queer obverse of the Catholicism that defines the family. Furthermore, the cathedral light of Gabriel's queer space catches the debris of familial domesticity: "the sad ruins of an emptied family life: hundreds of broken plates, empty picture frames, donated bags of clothing, broken mirrors, etc. (xvii). The play opens with a symbolic reenactment of the moment of familial trauma as all four members of the family stand "in almost religiously neutral poses" on a large family dining table as Gabriel loses his footing and lurches forward and then back, disappearing into the darkness of the stage. This bodily emptiness and erasure link the first scene to the second, as it takes place in a classroom with Matt presenting the class project he worked on with Gabriel, whose chair stands empty.

This crucial scene between Matt and Gabriel also has religious over-tones intersecting with questions of queer authenticity. At one point, Matt compliments Gabriel's name, saying it is "a beautiful name," and begins reciting "Gabriel's Message," the Christmas carol about the Annunciation to the Virgin Mary by the archangel. Figuratively, Gabriel is the archangel whose self-sacrifice breaks open the unspoken truths that bind the family together, and the revelation at the end of the play that Marco found his brother hanging with his childhood rosary around his neck becomes a damn-ing indictment of the religious morality that shapes the Italian Canadian heteronormative family and pushes their queer son to suicide.

The space of the basement, like the model of the solar system that Gabriel and his lover work on, is unfinished, as of yet undefined, an ambiguous space of intimacy that suggests Munoz's queer horizon, but also a failure or stalling of heteronormative social order in its inability or refusal to account for queerness in its midst and the failures of the promise of the child (Edelman). As Matt and Gabriel contemplate the open possibilities of the bare space of the unfinished kitchen, they project themselves into a queer narrative futurity that overlays the heteronormative space of Italian Canadian domesticity with a new form:

MATT (laughing): "Our little kitchen?" This basement?

GABRIEL: Sure, why not? We just have to use our imagination a bit to make it all work, you know?

MATT: You lost me.

GABRIEL: Like, it's actually kinda good that there's nothing here, you know? No walls or stuff.

MATT: What, you don't like walls?

GABRIEL: No, it's just like . . . if it's empty. It makes it easier for us to lie here and imagine what it could be like. (81)

For Gabriel, such a utopic space is out of the question, for his homosexuality is rejected by his family. Therefore, he must create a utopic and ultimately tragic space to which he can escape. The staging of the play creates a heterotopic space in which past and present, heterosexual and homosexual realities are interlaced: Scenes of present-day familial conflict are interspersed with earlier happier days of familial harmony, just as the heterosexual space of the immigrant household (the family kitchen) is inflected by the imagined and actual spaces of homosexual desire in the unfinished basement below. Thus, for instance, the playwright stages a scene of sexual intimacy between Gabriel and Matthew while lingering over them is Concetta, praying in Italian for her son's salvation from a shameful homosexual future. The tragic moment at the heart of the play is alluded to in several moments of foreshadowing in which Gabriel is seen to lunch forward into space, as, for instance, when Matt tells him to jump into his arms as a show of trust, or when Gabriel and Matt are standing on a bridge as they discuss people who commit suicide by jumping down into the ravine below. This alludes to the scene of revelation in which Marco finds his younger brother hanging from an exposed pipe in the family's unfinished basement: "Gabriel loses his balance, falls forward a step, and quickly flails back, hands in the air, falling onto his back" (3).

Queer Temporalities

The heteronormative organization of time is linked not only to the day-to-day regimentation of activities, work, leisure, and so forth, but also to the larger understandings of time in terms of the life narrative of birth, marriage, the bearing and care of children, and the passing on of wealth, knowledge, traditions, and lore to the next generation: "The time of inheritance refers to an overview of generational time within which values, wealth, goods, and morals are passed through family ties from one generation to the next. It also connects the family to the historical past of the nation and glances ahead to connect the family to the future of both familial and national stability" (Halberstam 5). We can see in both *Geography of Pluto* and *In Gabriel's Kitchen* evidence of queer temporalities or, rather, resistance to or rejection of the temporal patterns, habits, and conventions of the heterosexual world. Time in these works stands still, is momentarily suspended, or is denied in the desire for an escape to a different time—a utopic future, a troubled/troubling narrative past in which queer youth feel stunted by the heteronormative scripts placed on them.

In terms of the temporality presented in the play, it is divided between the "present" moment of a family mourning in the aftermath of the suicide of Gabriel, interlaced with scenes from a past in which the eponymous character is struggling with coming to term with his own sexuality (three years earlier): the play's narrative continually switches back and forth between past and present, while the monologues of Paolo, the father, take place "in a chronological vacuum" (xvii). This temporal schism, while fairly common in terms of theatrical narrative and the revelation that comes at the moment of crisis in a play, is further complicated by a circular queer temporality in which the two lovers attempt to escape temporality altogether in their desire to stop time itself in moments of intimacy. In DiRaddo's novel, when Will and Max meet again after their breakup, they hesitantly spend an evening together, at the end of which Max invites Will back to his apartment. It is then that Will notices the clock over Max's sink, "which perpetually read 4:37": "There were no batteries in it; Max hated the ticking sound . . . it became an apt metaphor for how I felt when I went there. Time stood still, minutes would turn into hours, the lost time replaced by music and sex. I would look out the window, surprised that the morning had arrived" (63). Here, queer time is defined by the freedom to live at night, unbounded by the strictures of familial obligation, inured to the edicts of productive time, and a utopic projection not toward a possible future but in the here and now of bodies, sensation, and sexuality. It is that sort of queer temporality with Halberstam speaks: "what has made queerness compelling as a form of self-description in the past decade or so has to do with the way it has the potential to open up new life narratives and alternative relations to time and space . . . Queer subcultures produce alternative temporalities by allowing their participants to believe that their futures can be imagined according to logics that lie outside of those paradigmatic markers of life experience—namely, birth, marriage, reproduction, and death" (n.p.).

When Max breaks off with Will, time stands still; he finds himself alone in his apartment, unable to move forward, frozen in a queer temporality: "In the stillness of my apartment the only things that moved were the hands of the clock in the hallway, reluctantly dragging me with them into the future" (120). The passage of time signals for Will a coming into his own in terms of his acceptance of himself as a gay man, an emotional and physical transformation that is measured through and by the body: "it takes seven years for the body to regenerate, for its cells to divide and its tissues to be replaced" (81). As with the play, we can see here how queer temporalities hinge upon the embodiment, affect, desire, and eros, and in that sense continually conflict with the normative temporalities of which Halberstam speaks.

In Gabriel's Kitchen evokes not only the realities of being queer in a traditional immigrant home but also the immigrant family's refusal to see and accept their queer offspring. Silence, denial, suppression—these define both Paolo, Gabriel's father, who has lost himself in work and watching television after the death of his son, and Concetta, who refuses to confront the reasons for Gabriel's suicide and obsesses about how she will be seen by her neighbors.

Finally, the domestic space of the immigrant household, much like the space of the city and the nation, is a heterotopic space inflected by Old World and new world languages, cultures, and moral positions, but also defined by the power dynamics of rigid gender roles and normative heterosexuality that in effect demands real or imaged forms of temporal and spatial displacement or escape into a utopic future for queer subjects.

Notes

1. See, for instance Domenica DiLeo and Gabriella Micallef, eds., *Curragia: Writing by Women of Italian Descent* (London: Women's Press Literary, 1998); Marisa de Franceschi, ed., *Pillars of Lace* (Montreal: Guernica Editions, 1998).

2. See groundbreaking work on queerness and Italian Canadian literature by Michela Baldo: Michela Baldo and Olivia Fiorilli, "Queering Temporalities in Italian Drag King Archives," *Lambda Nordica* 21, no. 3/4 (2016): 56; Michela Baldo, "Familiarising the Gay, Queering the Family: Coming Out and Resilience in *Mambo Italiano*," *Journal of GLBT Family Studies* 10, no. 1/2 (2014): 168–87, https://doi.org/10.1080/1550428X.2014.857493.

3. "We need a genealogy of queer affect that does not overlook the negative, shameful and difficult feelings that have been so central to queer existence in the last century" (Love 127).

4. "Phenomenology can offer a resource for queer studies insofar as phenomenology emphasizes the importance of lived experience, the intentionality of consciousness, the significance of nearness or what is ready to hand, and the role of repeated and habitual actions in shaping bodies and worlds" (Ahmed 544).

5. "A father builds a house for his family. That house is a symbol of him. It gives his family shelter and warmth and protects them from bad things—it keeps them in . . . and one day, after his wife has brought forth his children—to carry on the name, and to support them in old age—he stands in front of a building and says: this is for you. Everything . . . everything . . . is for them: That is a father" (68).

6. Initial research in queer geographies sought to describe the hidden places of LBGTQ+ sociability, such as George Chauncey's *Gay New York: Gender, Urban Culture, and the Making of the Gay Male World, 1890–1940* (1995) and *Mapping Desire* by David Bell and Gill Valentine (1995). Queer theory and postmodern geographies ushered in new intersectional approaches to the links between gender/sexuality and spatiality. See, for instance, Elizabeth Grosz's *Sexuality & Space* (1996), Michael Warner's *Publics and Counterpublics* (2002), Dianne Chisholm's *Queer Constellations: Subcultural Space in the Wake of the City* (2005), and more recent work by Halberstam, Munoz, and Ahmed cited elsewhere in this chapter.

7. In *A Queer Time and Place: Transgender Bodies, Subcultural Lives*, Halberstam writes: "Queer uses of time and space develop, at least in part, in opposition to the institutions of family, heterosexuality, and reproduction. They also develop according to other logics of location, movement, and identification" (1).

Works Cited

Ahmed, Sara. "Orientations: Toward a Queer Phenomenology." *GLQ* 12, no. 4 (2006): 543–74.

Antonio, Salvatore. *In Gabriel's Kitchen by Salvatore Antonio*. Toronto: Playwrights Canada Press, 2007.

Bachelard, Gaston. *The Poetics of Space*. Translated by Maria Jolas. Boston: Boston: Beacon Press, 1994.

Baldo, Michela. "Familiarising the Gay, Queering the Family: Coming Out and Resilience in Mambo Italiano." *Journal of GLBT Family Studies* 10, no. 1/2 (2014): 168–87. https://doi.org/10.1080/1550428X.2014.857493.

Certeau, Michel de, and Steven Rendall. *The Practice of Everyday Life.* Berkeley: University of California Press, 2011.

Connell, R. W. *Masculinities.* Cambridge, UK: Polity, 2017.

Baldo, Michela, and Olivia Fiorilli. "Queering Temporalities in Italian Drag King Archives." *Lambda Nordica* 21, no. 3/4 (2016): 56.

DiLeo, Domenica, and Gabriella Micallef, eds. *Curragia: Writing by Women of Italian Descent.* London: Women's Press Literary, 1998.

DiRaddo, Christopher. *The Geography of Pluto.* Toronto: Cormorant Books, 2014.

Edelman, Lee. *No Future: Queer Theory and the Death Drive.* Durham, NC: Duke University Press, 2007.

Franceschi, Marisa de, ed. *Pillars of Lace.* Montreal: Guernica Editions, 1998.

Galluccio, Steve. *Mambo Italiano.* Vancouver: Talonbooks, 2004.

Émile Gaudreault, dir. *Mambo Italiano.* Montreal: Equinoxe Films, 2004.

Grosz, Elizabeth. *Volatile Bodies: Toward a Corporeal Feminism.* Bloomington: Indiana University Press, 1994.

Halberstam, Judith. *In a Queer Time and Place: Transgender Bodies, Subcultural Lives.* New York: New York University Press, 2005.

Love, Heather. *Feeling Backward: Loss and the Politics of Queer History.* Cambridge: Harvard University Press, 2007.

Muñoz, José Esteban. *Cruising Utopia: The Then and There of Queer Futurity.* New York: New York University Press, 2009.

Sedgwick, Eve Kosofsky. *Epistemology of the Closet.* 1990. Reprint, Berkeley: University of California Press, 2008.

9

Daughter-Mother Borderlands in Contemporary Italian American and Italian Canadian Theater

Colleen M. Ryan

In 1985, Helen Barolini published *The Dream Book: An Anthology of Writings by Italian American Women*,[1] arguably the first anthology of Italian American women's writing, which contains sections of poetry, prose (memoir, fiction, and nonfiction), and one example of ethnic women's theater. Could there exist only one women's play, I wondered? Were there more examples of Italian women's plays out there, just hard to find? Or was there something particular about the dramatic genre that made it either less attractive or less accessible for women writers? Maybe the embodied, performative nature of theatrical writing became too real and thus strayed too far from the "stuff" of dreaming—that space where women's subjectivity could take shape?[2]

In support of her anthology's title, Barolini explains that the "dream books," used in early Colorado mining settlements, were vessels for women's creative thinking. "For every day [these displaced Italian women] had their book of dreams to help them navigate the uncertainties" that they faced, physically and emotionally, in a new and distant land.[3] Whether the fruit of their curiosities or fears, hardships or pleasures, these dreams helped women articulate their desires—desires that may have conflicted with *the* Dream, which, according to Richard Gambino, "had colonized Italian Americans and diminished their ability to explore and understand their identity crisis creatively."[4] In these "dream books," the Italian female community in Telluride collected memories and impressions, bits of history (i.e., "[there] erupted a powerful war of the European powers") and fragments of folklore to give order and coherence to the signs and symbols that were marking their journeys, shaping their identities, and foretelling, perhaps, the future direction of their lives. Therefore, like the early twentieth-century Italian women who regularly turned to their dream books for hope and advice, I turn to my "original, tattered and much thumbed" volume by Barolini to interpret the meaning of the near absence of women playwrights in our flourishing canon of ethnic writing to better understand the exemplars that women playwrights of Italian descent have or don't have today.

Introduction

Italian American women writers have been active and engaged as artists and scholars contributing to the ever growing canon of Italian American and Italian Canadian studies for more than a century. Having broadened, nuanced, and diversified the portrayal of Italian women in North America, these writers recount their triumphs and tribulations and their tales of displacement, belonging, and exclusion quite differently from their male peers. While both the production and study of their fiction, poetry, and memoirs have been consistent and fertile over the last fifty years, explorations of Italian American women's playwriting has been minimal, and analytical attention to this form of ethnic and gender-distinct artistry has been faint. Still, in the seventy-plus years since World War II, and in the fifty-plus years since the last large waves of Italian emigration, so much has happened in the life of Italian women in their North American cultures of destination. Growing numbers of women began working outside their homes, finishing high school and earning degrees in higher education, achieving legal equality, exploring their sexuality, using contraceptives, and exercising the right to divorce or to terminate pregnancies. How, then, did such dramatic, performative, and national changes affect women's rights and roles in the Italian family? And how have women playwrights captured gender conflicts and family dramas related these changes on stage? When grouped together, do these playwrights "form something cohesive" and "have a specific resonance?"[5] To further echo Barolini, could it be possible in these plays "to recognize the transcultural and transgenerational complexities of who we are, where we've come from, and what the journey has been?"

What follows is an analysis of five plays written and performed between 1980 and 2012: three in the United States and two in Canada. Focusing on the trajectory of the daughter-mother bond, in each instance we shall note 1) a cultural border crossing through the mother's body and personal narrations, and 2) an object in the mise-en-scène that functions as a connection to the mother's own story and personal longings. An analysis of the daughter-mother border and umbilical object in each play reveals that the daughter must acknowledge the mother's personal history and generational truth as "other" from her own to distinguish her voice and assert the value of her own journey. Furthermore, to forge constructive bonds with her origins and ancestors, the daughter must identify and occupy an intermediary conceptual and cultural space that permits critical awareness and autonomy in the development of her personhood.

Daughter-Mother Bonds

"That a daughter never relinquishes her primary attachment to the mother," writes Adalgisa Giorgio, "is a widely accepted psychological/psycholantyic notion, which is borne out of women's narratives of different cultures."[6] In the specific case of Italian women writers, Giorgio affirms, the daughter often experiences her mother as indifferent, particularly when compared with the attention and care she shows for her husband and sons. In her struggle for attention and affection, the daughter then remains "irremediably bound" to the mother.

In the mid-seventies, Adrienne Rich denounced the lack of attention to mother-daughter bonds across centuries of scholarship as a "silent tragedy." "The cathexis between mother and daughter—essential, distorted, misused—is the great unwritten story. Probably there is nothing in human nature more resonant with charges than the flow of energy between the two biologically alike bodies, one of which has lain in amniotic bliss inside the other, one of which has labored to give birth to the other. The materials are here for the deepest mutuality and the most painful estrangement."[7] The tension resulting from this contemporaneous attraction and hostility challenged the status quo of patriarchal approaches to literature and gradually became "the most feared, the most problematic, and the most potentially transforming force on the planet."[8] Subsequently, as feminist thinkers in North America and Europe engaged psychoanalysis and poststructuralist theories to probe the political significance of mother-daughter ties, Italian American scholars began affirming women's voices, validating their trajectories, and celebrating their contributions in both public and private spheres.

Even if, since the late seventies and eighties, female friendships and love relationships (beyond the maternal and heterosexual) have earned a central place in feminist discourses at large, these topics remained relatively marginal within Italian ethnic and diaspora studies. Only in recent decades, thanks to longevity and advancement of queer, feminist, critical race, and other theories, intergenerational female relations and multidimensional female subjectivities have become a vital part of Italian Americana's critical discourse, too. In her seminal work on contemporary Italian women writers, Patrizia Sambuco underscores this fact by inverting (this fact via the priority she gives to daughters) the order in this phrase: "daughter-mother relationships."[9] Sambuco situates her work at the crossroads of European and American feminist theory, positing that the daughter's "search for her own sense of identity" is intricately connected to the mother and her body. Building specifically on Irigaray's invitation to perceive the mother as other and beyond the dominant framework of patriarchy, Sambuco maintains that only from this alternate perspective can the daughter-narrator begin to experience her mother differently. Furthermore, she finds this "re-imagination and refiguration of the mother and of the relationship" crucial because "it takes place only at the level of literature, dreams, and fantasy."[10]

In the transnational context of Italian American women's writing, Mary Jo Bona has established that "mothers and daughters have deeply mattered in the narrative lives of Italian Americans."[11] Thanks to the influence of second- and third-wave feminism, Bona notes, Italian Americans have begun to explore the desire that binds mothers and daughters with less taboo or shame, "for only then can strong women influence through love and respect the futures of their daughters, inviting independence and creativity within a refashioned family institution."[12] This refashioned family institution, however slow its formal recognition may be, develops in parallel to enduring gender roles and family traditions among Italian Americans. Today, the young adult daughter figure provides a unique opportunity to zoom in on the perpetuation of gender roles and attitudes toward sexuality in both critical and constructive ways.

In the still more specific case of Italian American and Italian Canadian theater by women, the daughter's attraction and devotion to her maternal roots constitutes an equally vital, transgenerational trope. Whether belonging to the second, third, or fourth generation, these daughters feel the push-pull of an "umbilical connection" that keeps them physically and emotionally bound to their (fore)-mothers across space and time.[13] This chapter offers a survey of five plays written by women of Italian descent in the United States and Canada—Michele Linfante's *Pizza* (1980), Chris Cinque's *The Scrub* (1982), Theresa Carilli's *A Thorough Cleansing* (1997), Mary Melfi's *My Italian Wife* (1996), and Michaela Di Cesare's *Eight Ways My Mother Was Conceived* (2012). This selection intends to offer a panorama spanning several decades and across two diasporic destination countries to identify red threads of continuity in the theatrical genre of ethnic women's writing. Moreover, this selection allows us to move beyond traditional, patriarchal, and heteronormative family paradigms to consider the contemporary Italian American daughter more intentionally and inclusively.

Daughters Discerning Subjectivity

After World War II, America's culture of self-determination remained a largely male-gendered and economically driven concept for Italians. In most cases, "getting ahead" or "making a better life" still entailed providing for the family by means of a steady job, a nicer home, and more possessions. However, the women's liberation movement led to more explicit, pronounced, and equitable dreams for women from all ethnic backgrounds.[14] It is not that the daughters of these decades did not *also* aspire to greater educational, financial, and social autonomy and sustained consumer activity, but that their concepts of success and self-betterment were different. As per this sampling of stage plays, the young women's fulfillment requires self-knowledge, self-love, and self-affirmation beyond the traditional cultural framework, passed down through generations and in the close-knit domestic sphere.

Though Italian American daughters have often felt disappointment or resentment toward their mothers for not treading more fulfilling paths before them, the young adult daughters in the plays examined here make inroads in their personal lives over time, not by rejecting their mothers outright or completely, but by consciously narrating their own stories and forging their selfhood through difference. As Suzanna Walters notes, to "surpass the mother" is to lose the continuity with that history, which is often the history of the victims and the violated, but is one that (like any legacy) we "surpass" at our peril.[15] For Jane Moss, in her work on Spanish women's theater, this peril is one of lost intimacy; it causes "walls of jealousy, misunderstanding, scorn, and silence which must be broken down if women are to liberate themselves."[16] In the current selection of plays, I trace the daughters' agency along broken barriers between daughter's and mother's agency and desire—that is, at the points of potential "border crossings" into the (m)other's world and in a theatrical object that powerfully conjoins, without conflating, the emotional truths of both women.

Five Plays (1980–2012)

As stated, it is not easy to find published theatrical works with clear Italian ethnic discourses written by men or women. What follows is an examination of five plays with different ranges of Italian cultural inflections written by women in the United States and Canada in relatively recent decades.

Michele Linfante wrote *Pizza* (1980) for her San Francisco women's theater collective. In this one-act piece, thirty-something Grace wants to forget the stifling, working-class environment of her family's pizza parlor in Patterson, New Jersey.[17] Grace feels shame and despair for the poor and restricted life her family leads. Though she also fears hurting her mother, Grace musters the courage to move away—first to New York City and then to San Francisco. When, years later, her aged mother, Lena, plans a visit out West, Grace begins to panic, as if she had never left the pizza parlor. She is afraid of being lured by the responsibilities associated with the old world of Patterson and, thus, losing the new world or new life she has created. As she prepares mentally for a guilt-inducing visit with a mother now stricken with Parkinson's disease, Grace calls the suicide hotline, orders a pizza for delivery, and then reconnects with Lena in a new, dreamlike way.[18]

Similarly, in Cinque's *The Scrub* (*Growing up Queer in America, pt. III*, 1982), Angel encounters her mother, Lou, after many years of separation. When the scene opens, Lou has just arrived in Minnesota from Florida[19] and doesn't know that her daughter will recount their personal history in a theatrical monologue that day. As the play within a play then ensues, Angel gives birth to the memory of her mother by making her disembodied and marginal voice emerge from backstage. This disembodied voice fosters multiple levels of reflection for both the characters and audience to understand how, after years of great closeness, Lou abandons her daughter to "come out" as homosexual.

In parallel, and somewhat ironically, Lou is horrified by the public staging of their drama, which is sure to trigger pain and reveal hypocrisies. Consequently, Lou refuses to "come out" onstage and can only exist for Angel via flashbacks and onstage-to-backstage techniques that Cinque uses to highlight the women's similarities. Lou, like Angel, is queer. She was once loved by and loved another woman—an older cousin named Sandry, who was burned to death in the Florida scrub in a hate crime condemning homosexuality. Angel, now in her twenties, wants to honor her pledge to "never leave" her mother. She goes back to the pace of her mother's world to focus on similarities rather than differences between them. In this way, Angel hopes, they might forge a mutual sense of emotional availability.[20]

A Thorough Cleansing (1997) by Theresa Carilli also features a daughter in exile from both the family home and a relationship with her mother, Tessie, who had banished Frances for coming out as a teen.[21] Opening with a recurring nightmare in which the mother shoots the daughter dead in a laundromat washing machine, the play depicts the mother's rejection as a total annihilation of the daughter-subject. Moreover, because Tessie is obsessed with cleanliness—so much so that she had to take a day job when Frances was a child just to stay busy and tame her compulsive cleaning—the washing machine satirically connotes the mother's her ability to saturate, set spinning, and entomb the daughter. In hyperbolic terms, the dream may signal the mother's will to cleanse her daughter's sins or even cancel her whole identity.

At the same time, we learn that Tessie was at the pinnacle of a depression over an impoverished and unhappy marriage. So, another hypothesis for why she breaks with Frances completely is because it became impossible for Tessie to see herself reflected in her daughter and, thus, to live vicariously through what a normative daughter's future might have held for both (i.e., marriage, children, etc.). Ousted and broken, then, Frances moves to the West Coast to slowly build a life for herself through a series of jobs, an advanced degree program, and then a career as a college professor. It is only many years later, upon the occasion of potentially life-threatening surgery, that Tessie reappears in Frances's hospital room. During this visit in a sterile environment, mother and daughter try to get reacquainted, but Tessie cannot endure tender moments. She eschews the intimacy Frances proposes and overrides it with the importance of cleaning, as if the "shine" she might generate could rekindle a lost dream.

Mary Melfi's *My Italian Wife* (1996) represents the daughter-mother relationship somewhat differently, as we don't have a biological daughter and mother onstage during the comedy. Instead, we have references to an absent, first-generation immigrant mother (enjoying a cruise, symbol of the American Dream); and allusions to the first-generation daughter Rita's status as mother to her much younger (and second-generation) sibling.[22] The dramatic dialogue reveals that the late-forties teacher, Rita, practically raised her late-twenties sister, Paula, while their parents toiled tirelessly to make ends meet.

In *The Italian Wife*, the force of the daughter-mother bond is rendered via the mother's conspicuous absence, Paula's much younger age, and Rita's intermittent migrant memories. Specifically, Rita recalls recalls her arrival in Canada at age six with Mamma, and she voices the feelings of ineptitude and nonbelonging that she has internalized ever since. Intergenerational female relationships are also explored through Rita's relationship as a fill-in mom. Though married with children like Rita, Paula acts like a tagalong "kid sister," oblivious to their family's earlier hardships and fully assimilated as a Canadian. While Rita and her yet older husband, John, are like parents to her, Paula seems impervious to Rita's ethnic- and gender-specific discourses on the subjects of love, work, sex, virtue, and marriage.

In the last selection, *Eight Ways My Mother Was Conceived* (2012), actress-playwright Michaela Di Cesare treats the enduring cult of virginity among third- and fourth-generation Italians.[23] Remarkably, the twenty-something autobiographical character (Michaela) employs twelve different voices to conjoin four generations of female storytelling around her mother's immaculate conception in 1961. Shrouded in this family myth and held to the strict standard of proper courtship and virginal marriage, Michaela desires, but fears, intimacy, is ignorant about sexual pleasure, and dreads an unwanted pregnancy. After her boyfriend of three years proposes, she seems to be "on the right track" for her family. But when he leaves Michaela shortly after the engagement, both anxiety and shame set in. Michaela's return to the dating scene, however, marks the start of a critical examination of the stories that dictate her sexual mores. A trip to Italy and a breakthrough conversation inspire a new chapter in the daughter-mother relationship and catalyze Michaela's personal development.

Daughter-Mother Borderlands

Gloria Anzaldúa conceived the conflictual nature of borders in a way that combined the geographic, ethnic, political, and cultural realities giving shape to her identity. Though she developed her theory in the specific context of the US-Mexico divide, her borderlands concept has been adopted in numerous and interdisciplinary ways to more broadly denote places that are "safe and unsafe" and that "distinguish *us* from *them*."[24] The "narrow strip along a steep edge" she describes in *Borderlands/La Frontera* allows us to imagine a tenuous position and anxiety-filled experience of hybridity, as if abyss or danger lay on either side. For Anzaldúa, moreover, a borderland is "a vague and undetermined place created by the emotional residue of an unnatural boundary."[25] Whereas the two territories once adjoined fluidly, the political and social borders imposed on border spaces have made them disruptive and disorienting. They are not native or intuitive spaces to those who live there. Addressing borderlands critically, therefore, is a problematic exercise, for as much as the confluent zone may present opportunities to examine, and negotiate tensions, a synthesis or resolution between the two may be impossible from various perspectives. At best, Anzaldúa suggests, "the lifeblood of two worlds" merge to form a third culture—"a border culture."

The daughters in the Italian American and Italian Canadian plays under consideration all live along a precarious line dividing their mothers and themselves—their mothers' historical eras, homes, morals, beliefs, and behaviors—with their own. These physical and emotional distinctions bespeak ideological differences about individualism and equality and can intimate extreme emotional states such as matrophobia,[26] alienation, and other modes of distress or disdain. The stage set for Linfante's *Pizza*, for example, portrays the clear but contiguous separation between Grace's present/solo life and her family-centered past. One set is a run-down 1950s pizza parlor in New Jersey and the other a modest, contemporary apartment in San Francisco. However, the interplay between the two settings shifts from a concept of rigid separation to a more open and fluid border space. Through a combination of lighting and musical effects, pizza boxes, and props, even a connecting door, Linfante's text plays on fantasy and reality to convey the possibility of movement between mother's and daughter's separate, but still emotionally connected, worlds. In *Worlds Together, Lives Apart Mothers and Daughters in Popular Culture*, Suzanna Walters points out that "an opposition is often set up between the mother trapped in 'old' ways, whose life has not been fulfilled, and the 'new' and 'modern' daughter who is liberated or at least sees the possibilities for liberation and growth."[27] Having to come of age in the seventies, the daughter Grace will be put to the test. She will have to assert herself, even when her mind and memory play tricks on her, to *not* return to the previous time (decades) and space (the family pizza parlor) that constrained her. Fortunately, from the West Coast, she understands that her past is safely contained in the box. She has the power to decide what dimensions her mother can take as she ensure her own progress towards the future.

Cinque's *The Scrub* reflects a similar flexibility of movement among different places in time, in settings that simultaneously connect and separate

Lou and Angel, mother and daughter, over thirty years. Cinque opens the scene with old home movies of Lou and her love object, Sandry, projected onscreen. The silent videos from the 1930s Florida setting, coupled with Angel's subjective voice-over, conjure the mother's adolescent memories and detachment, since Angel has no firsthand knowledge of the events. Under this aura of temporal, spatial, and emotional distance, the lights come up. We are now in the present with Angel, a monologue performer, who will enmesh her coming-of-age story with that of her mother through a series of costume changes, diegetic music changes, and vocal input from Lou from offstage. Indeed, the most conspicuous representation of ongoing separation between mother and daughter, after twenty years spent in different parts of the country, is Lou's unwillingness to come out onstage.[28] Though she agreed to travel across the country to see Angel, she did not agree to speak publicly, so Lou either shouts from the wings or phones (from backstage) Angel, who is onstage, to speak. This interplay of intimacy and physical distance characterizes the play, as does the metatheatrical use of the backstage or wing spaces from which the mother's words rise up or voices over, as if a force from the past were bleeding into the daughter's world and threatening her autonomy and healing.

The most experimental of the plays at hand, then, *The Scrub* presages Mary Jo Bona's compelling conviction in *Queer Daughters and their Mothers* that "experimental daughters seek their mothers in frequently circuitous ways." "Their narratives are often multi-perspectival," Bona writes, "innovating on genre and style while interrogating the notion of representation itself." *The Scrub*, indeed queers the notions of time and space through its fluid interplay of the mothers' past and present, the daughter's past and present, confusing moments of maternal bliss with deeply traumatic events.

Likewise, Carilli's *A Thorough Cleansing* (1997) portrays a great emotional distance between a mother and daughter, Tessie and Frances, despite their attraction and/or need for one another. This is most notable through their dialogues; each woman's speech runs parallel to the other's, as if the daughter and mother existed on two different discursive planes. That is, Tessie generally speaks in a monologue or solo-track fashion about cleaning as she compulsively dusts, polishes, or emphasizes the value of cleanliness. Two exceptions to this fixation on tidiness are Tessie's expression of regret for not leaving her abusive husband and Tessie's shunning of Frances for being gay.

Frances instead engages her mother with genuinely interrelational intentions. Frances's contributions are sincerely dialogic, on a dual-track that seeks to accommodate Tessie's otherness through active listening and thoughtful speech. Furthermore, Frances empathizes with her mother's marital disappointments, shows quiet compassion for her obsessive-compulsive disorder, and expresses a sincere hope that Tessie can accept who she is. To the contrary, however, Tessie's staunch refusal of Frances' identity drives an insurmountable wedge between the two. Once banished from her home, Frances moves to San Francisco to navigate life on her own. She finds employment, goes to graduate school, and eventually becomes a professor.

In *My Italian Wife*, the protagonist, Rita, is also a daughter who articulates her selfhood through a career in teaching. 10 In Melfi's play, the absent mother is on a cruise, leaving the older daughter Rita to assume the maternal position vis-a-vis the younger, Paula. The daughter-mother borderland is thus expressed through absence and presence, similarity and difference. Rita, like her mother, is a first-generation Italian woman in Canada, but her sister Paula was born long after the family settled. In addition, Rita is sometimes present to Paula as a mother and other times she is absent, acting as a jealous wife/older sister. At times the two women, aged thirty and fifty-something, are both unsettled wives and daughters of Italian immigrants. Other times, they are rivals and emotionally or generationally distinct. While Rita takes pride at several points in the play for having raised Paula while their parents were busy working, Rita also resents her sister's lack of historical memory and attention to their ethnic-immigrant origins.

Pleasant and harmless though she may be, Paula is spoiled, insouciant, and floundering. She is a housewife with three children and unhappily married. Unlike Rita, Paula does not carry the indelible mark of the first-generation hardship—the ineradicable memory of the journey, the challenges of settling and assimilating, and the recurrent discourse about "a better life" ahead. Close by blood yet distant in mannerisms and mentality, the playful yet brooding Paula represents the second generation whose identity involves a conscious distance from their forebears and their dreams. As Paula flirts with her much older brother-in-law, John, and complains about her stifling marriage, Rita, by contrast, is serious, discerning, somewhat insecure, and often frustrated.

In the absence of a real mother with whom to either interrelate or from whom to "grow up" and distinguish herself with intention, Rita embodies both mother and daughter—she *is* the borderscape. As such, she functions unhappily, if not untenably, as the overachieving Italian wife-mother-daughter-and-sister all in one. The distance between "mother-daughter," Rita, and daughter, Paula, thus, articulates the ways in which the second-generation daughter is fully detached from the immigrant experience, yet nonetheless bound to and emotionally dependent on the "maternal foremother" still influenced by her memory of alienating experiences. And Paula's sexual subjectivity becomes a primary marker of their difference.

In *Eight Ways My Mother Was Conceived*, sexual agency is the catalyst driving Michaela to notice the border between herself and her maternal forbears, too. Her blind subscription to ancient family values comes to light during first her breakup experience. Since she had been told she would only ever be allowed to bring one boy home to meet the family—"one, and only one, boyfriend was ever to pass the threshold of our home, and once he did, there was no turning back!," she tragically imagines her life to be in some way over.[29] After a while, however, when her boyfriend rejects her, Michaela begins to suspect she has had flawed female role models. For example, once she leaves the family home to attend university, Michaela realizes that she is ignorant about sex and has been internally paralyzed by her family's long-standing beliefs about virginity. Not only is young Michaela unable to enjoy sex or closeness with a partner, but she actually fears she could conceive, as her Nonna Bettina did, without having intercourse—that is, "immaculately." "I never questioned the story growing up," Michaela cries. "I didn't even question it long after I had grown up. In my naïve view of the world, it all made sense and I liked believing in this picture of true love and chastity."[30] So when Michaela unexpectedly desires a new boy, Gabriel, she all but panics during intimacy and blurts out: "I can't have sex with you, ever!"[31]

The scrutiny that Michaela brings to bear on her family legend denounces the oppressive stronghold that such gender-specific inventions have had on women for centuries. Consequently, Michaela's naming and facing the "Virginity Complex" plaguing Italian Canadian daughters marks the first step in unmasking her family's hypocrisy and drawing a boundary between the cultural control her forebears sill vert her own burgeoning desires, which she plans to embrace. Furthermore, wishing to address the cause at its root right away, Michaela leaves Toronto for Calabria to visit her great-grandmother, Anna, since the "Immaculate" Nonna Bettina, who had migrated to Toronto, is now dead. Thus, the woman-to-woman conversation that takes place constitutes both border crossing and personal boundary setting, through which Michaela will unravel the mythological grip of virginity on her psyche and begin to face love and sex more freely.

The daughter-mother borderland in the selected plays therefore represents emotional peril and possibility. If the daughter stays unscrupulously entwined in the mother's subjective experience (hardship, trauma, disappointment, shame, or fear), she risks stunting her own growth and acting codependently rather than independently in her own sphere. If instead the daughter casts a critical lens on the borderland, where the women's cultures, memories, and present-day desires overlap, she is able to regulate the measure of the mother's "lifeblood" that flows into her own. In this way, the daughter turns the intergenerational "edge" or precipice into a threshold—a new and original territory in which she can shape her selfhood both consciously and selectively.

New Daughter-Mother Bonds through Umbilical Objects in the Texts

Essential to the daughter's self-awareness and self-fashioning in each play is an "umbilical object," which somehow brings the past to life for both women in the present. These objects are used as theatrical devices to denote a flow of energy between the mother and daughter, which, like an umbilical cord, must eventually give way to an autonomous life or being. In Linfante's *Pizza*, for example, the cardboard pizza box is an inanimate object with very specific ethnic and working-class connotations. It functions as a metonym, we learn, for Grace's dysfunctional family history. Connecting divergent geographical spaces and moments in time—Grace's East Coast childhood in the 1950s and her West Coast adulthood in the 1970s—the pizza box elicits a very strong emotional reaction in Grace. Whereas she once helped her mother, Lena, make and deliver the boxed pizzas in the family business (1950s), Grace now (1970s) has such boxes delivered to her home to provide a therapeutic revisitation of her past. The first time this occurs, Lena is visiting Grace from out East. This will be the women's first meeting after many years and since which time Lena has developed Parkinson's disease.

The box now sitting on her "modern" coffee table, proffering the sights, sounds, and smells of her childhood, places Lena's ethnic, gender, and class-distinct origins back in the center of her West Coast domestic space. The presence of the pizza, whether commanded consciously or not, impels her to reckon with her mother's overbearing personality, her unhappy marriage, her attraction to an overtly sexualized showgirl named Pearl (who lived in their building) and to the general the dysfunction of her family's past. Opening the box just a smidge, Grace hears the fifties song "Life Could

Be a Dream" and then slams it shut. Unable to believe that the music was seeping from the box, she opens it a second time but quickly shuts it again when the song resumes. Life, then, does become a dream, as the story of Grace's childhood at ages ten, fifteen, and twenty, respectively, unfolds on the other side of the stage.

When the California present-tense time frame resumes, Grace suddenly fears that nostalgia and guilt will quite quickly consume her hard-earned state of good mental health. As a girl, Grace was ashamed of her mother's lack of ambition and of the fact that her mother found her ugly—good for a Jimmy Durante imitation and to make others laugh. In the present, however, she feels susceptible to the memories of her mother's presence and female friends and the sense of community the family pizzas represent. Destabilized by the waft of her confusing past that emanates from the box, Grace calls the suicide hotline (where she used to work), hoping to give the pizza away.

> *(As she hangs up from this call, the doorbell rings. It is the pizza lady with another pizza for her. She is shaken, not wanting to cry, trying to look tough. She crosses her arms in front of the pizza box and looks down at the culprit pizza box.)*
>
> GRACE: For six lousy dollar you'd think they'd at least sell you a pizza that makes you forget. (*To the pizza box*) People pay to forget. Who wants to remember anything anymore? Who wants to feel anything anymore? [. . .]
>
> *(She goes through an elaborate strategy of trying to sneak a piece of pizza out of the box. As if stealing something . . . As she raises it to her lips, we hear the strains of the first lines of "Mama," a sappy Italian American song that Connie Francis used to sing. A look of comic despair and defeat crosses over her face through this first bar of music, and as he opens the box to replace the slice of pizza the second "Mama" swells out.)* (Barolini 289).

The stage notes emphasize how the pizza box connects the daughter to her mother across great distances in time and space. Now a self-sufficient adult and independent, Grace can decide what to do with the slice—ingest it or contain it in its "memory" box space. The addition of comic operatic additions and facial expressions further satirizes the anxiety Grace experiences over her aged mother's arrival.

Indeed, the cardboard object wields mystical powers that engender oneiric scenes from Grace's past. The three main childhood sequences that follow (visible on the other side of the stage) allow Grace to revisit her relationship with her mother, the female figures that once surrounded them, and her mother's crippling illness. With a fresh set of critical but compassionate eyes, Grace slowly realizes that the past cannot swallow her up and that she is now in control. A healthy subject in her own right, she can choose to let her mother into the stage left scene of her present-day life and even allow their shared connection to occupy a central place in her home.

Cinque's umbilical object in *The Scrub* carries a similar dreamlike quality and aura of mystery. The object, this time, is a conch shell much like the one that Sandry, mother Lou's adolescent lover, shares with Lou in the opening sequence—the very one in which the deaf Sandry could magically hear. The large, beautiful shell containing the powerful ocean's sounds richly symbolizes the adolescents' shared secrets, burgeoning sexuality, and the allure of hopes and dreams. Later in life, at what seems to represent Lou's maternal peak, she gives the shell to her daughter Angel. Mesmerized by the simple splendor of this gift, mother and daughter bond passionately over it. In this intimate and vulnerable moment, Lou makes Angel, her surrogate love object, vow that she will never leave.

(During the following taped conversation between the young LOU and her 6-year-old daughter, Angel takes off her boots and robe and puts on a black, satin slip)

Lou: Here, honey, this is for you.

Angel: Oh, mama, it's so beautiful. What is it?

Lou: It's a shell.

Angel: I know but what kind of shell?

Lou: Some kind of conch shell.

Angel: Conch. Is it magic?

Lou: You can hear the sea.

ANGEL: Where'd you get it?

LOU: Someone give it to me. Its's special, now it's yours.

ANGEL: Am I special mama?

LOU: Yes darling, you listen to it and you can hear me saying through the roar "My little Angel, child of God, heart of my heart."

ANGEL: Oh mama, you talk so pretty. I hear the roar. I hear you talking under it.

LOU: Don't ever leave me, little girl.

ANGEL: I never will.

The stage notes reveal a costume change that transforms the grown woman, Angel, into a sexual object of the past (black satin slip), confusing her identity with the memory and lure of Sandry. Then there is an abrupt shift from memory mode (Angel at age six) to the daughter-mother, onstage-backstage tension in the current day, still on the subject of abandonment and also violence.

ANGEL: And I wouldn't have left, not ever. A girl loves no one so much as her mother.

LOU: (*off stage*) O puhleeze

[. . .]

ANGEL: Then she blames you. Then she drives you away with sticks and curses . . .

LOU: As God is my witness . . .

ANGEL: . . . *takes back her beautiful gifts* [emphasis added]

LOU: I only used a belt, not a stick . . .

Angel: But don't be sad.

Lou: . . . as was my right . . .

Angel: I've made my way.

Lou: . . . my obligation to drive out what is unspeakable . . .

Angel: Sure. I know what exiles know.

Lou: . . . to cast out the evil that blocks the doorway into the kingdom.

Angel: I know what it is to be cast out from where you lived. I took that long last lingering view, adieu, my wicked mother, adieu.[32]

Lou, we learn, withdrew the symbolic conch shell that had connected daughter and mother through its magical seawater sensations. As an extension of that same object, Lou suddenly withdraws herself and her love from that relationship for a reason that becomes evident in the following scene. After a "normal" adolescent period of experimentation with mustaches and male clothing, Angel realizes she is gay and tells her mother so, resolutely. While on the surface this appears to be a conservative refusal of her homosexuality, the daughter's truth mirrors the mother's own same-sex love for Sandry. While Lou upheld her love to be pure, however, Angel's is coded and categorized as a disgrace.

Angel therefore unlocks the borderscapes with her assertive subjectivity. She changes the significance of the vaginally shaped conch shell passed from mother to daughter. Now she who possesses it may love a similar object and not secretly but openly and confidently. Lou's unresolved crisis at the end of the play therefore derives from the fact that Angel has by now "surpassed" her cultural example and has successfully nurtured an authentic identity.[33]

In her work on "experimental daughters," Mary Jo Bona studies the way queer daughters seek their mothers "in frequently circuitous ways."[34] "Their narratives," Bona writes, "are often multi-perspectival, innovating on genre and style while interrogating the notion of representation itself" (137). In "The Scrub," Cinque compellingly engages multiple spaces (indoor and outdoor), costumes, times frames, and media (old home movies and pho-nograph playing within the stage scenes, for instance) to question whether more traditional modes of playwrighting can amply reflect her subjective experience and her critique of heteronormative sexuality. By confusing time frames, generations, textualities, and sexualities, through the conch shell prop, Cinque shows the mother-daughter borderland to be a potentially subversive concept whereby one can denounce the constraints of patriarchy on motherhood and call "the female figure of the lover and the artist, which each daughter recognizes in her own mother" (137) into being.

More amusing, at least at first, in her choice of umbilical objects is Theresa Carilli. She uses a mop and rag combination to create melodramatic tension in the daughter-mother borderscape of *A Thorough Cleansing*. Dusting and cleaning are the only way Tessie knows how to envision womanhood and be a mother to Frances. Indeed, teaching Frances to conquer every cobweb is tantamount to another mother's reassuring hug or still another mother's sharing her favorite recipe. Carilli's humor (comedic) turns humoristic (*umoristico*—in the Pirandellian sense) though because that which initially makes us laugh soon prompts a profound reflection and then a contrasting sentiment of pity. By the time Frances is eight years old, cleaning has so completely consumed Tessie's life that it becomes her only source of identity and existential fuel. Cleaning is a panacea for pain, a coping strategy for depression, and a correc-tive for unbearable truths such as her husband's gambling and her daughter's homosexuality. For Tessie, cleaning generates hope that something bright might emerge if one works tirelessly and incessantly for it.[35]

A traditionally female-gendered object associated with domestic work in patriarchal spaces, the dust mop cleverly conjoins mother and daughter in this play. Tessie passes down her mop-torch, if you will, as if it were her only legacy.

(In the background, a scratchy recording of Judy Garland singing "Life is Just a Bowl of Cherries" can be heard.)

Tessie *hands the mop to* Frances

Tessie: You've gotta reach (*stretching*) You've gotta get every corner. You miss a corner and a cobweb grows. Reach!

One notes the flow of energy between the two women, even during a flashback, as a younger Frances responds to Tessie's compulsive thoughts and activities. And the slapstick moments such as a mop on the girl's head remind us of the child's perspective and the author's intended element of absurdity:

(Shyly, FRANCES *stretches and reaches until the mop head slips out and falls on her head)*

TESSIE: You didn't do it right, let me show you.

TESSIE *fixes the mop and pushes Frances aside.*

TESSIE: You see. You do it in time to the music.

*(*TESSIE *cleans to the music while singing)*

TESSIE: You work, you save, you worry so . . . See. That how to do it. The bedroom is never clean until the ceilings are done. Especially the corners.

TESSIE *hands the mop to* FRANCES *and* FRANCES *moves to the music while mopping.* TESSIE *nods her head in approval*

TESSIE: That's it. You see. Do it again.[36]

In this moment of umbilical potential or cleanly fusion, the dramatic tension rises. Tessie denounces Frances's non-normative sexuality while "mopping frantically," as if she could wash away any trace of it. She wants to erase the version of her daughter that doesn't reflect the "pristine" family

TESSIE: I was watching you with Jean the other day. *(She looks down and mops frantically.)*

FRANCES: Yeah.

TESSIE: I didn't like what I see.[37]

In this daughter-mother moment, Frances courageously confirms that she is gay. Tessie reacts violently. She throws a plant against the wall, as if she had been personally betrayed by her daughter, and then casts her out completely:

TESSIE: No child of mine would ever, could ever do anything like that. I should have never let you go to college. That's where you got those silly ideas. I should have never bought you that truck when you were a child. Never (*horrified*) YOU DISGRACE ME!

FRANCES: Please . . . please try to understand. When you went through all those problems with dad, I tried to understand.

TESSIE: Understand? Understand what? That you are a promiscuous disgrace? (*furious*) GET OUT OF HERE. GET OUT OF HERE NOW. [. . .] And don't come back. Do you hear me Don't you ever come back here again! No child of mine. . . .

FRANCES: PLEASE. . . .

TESSIE: GET OUT![38]

The primal bond with the mother has by now grown harmful for Frances both mentally and physically. The daughter must clearly demarcate her border and dissolve the umbilical connections, even if, years later, when Frances has an operation, the borderland between the women's cultures and identities reappears.

A decade later, Tessie travels to visit her daughter in the hospital out West, wearing an awful old getup that had belonged to her daughter back in the day. Upon arriving, she hangs beer-can Christmas lights from Frances's father around the hospital room as if to restore the aura and class-distinct tone of their Italian American family. Before long, then, Tessie resumes her routine: she gets on a chair and starts cleaning. Lacking the desire or strength to deal with any of her mother's obsessions in her current postoperative state, Frances lets Tessie fuss about her. At one point, Tessie asks about Frances's college teaching, and, as in the past, Frances accepts her mother's interest in her sincerely. In return, she tries to engage Tessa, inviting her to open up and reveal some personal things.

FRANCES: [. . .] Talk to me.

TESSIE: There's nothing to say.

FRANCES: But I'm your daughter. TALK TO ME.

(TESSIE takes a cloth and scrubs the wall)

TESSIE: When you get depressed, it means you haven't done enough cleaning. If you want something, it means you haven't gotten down on your hand and knees long enough and scrubbed until every tile shines.

FRANCES: (*pleading*) The flowers are dying and you still won't talk to me. (*slowly*) Come. Talk to me. Tell me who you are.

(Slowly TESSIE walks over to her daughter and takes her hand)

TESSIE: I will. I will tell you. (*pause*) The key to cleanliness is to get all the cobwebs. Once you've cleaned all the cobwebs, then you dust. It becomes easier to dust when the cobwebs have settled. After dusting, you vacuum. And after you've vacuumed, you can polish.

(Lights go to black)[39]

However unsuccessfully, Frances allows Tessie's cleaning to assume new meaning, with the potential to transport her to new levels of compassion and broader life perspective, given her illness and the austere hospital setting. Though the lights go down without resolution here, Frances in the finale is no longer as hopeless as she was earlier in the play ("When your mother doesn't love you, you get sick").[40] She no longer feels oppressed by her mother's emotional limits because by now, she has indeed "made her choices." Frances's hands don't sting "from blood and dirt" or crack "from the ammonia on them." Rather, they "hold a pen," as if to guarantee her creative identity and self-expression.[41]

In contrast to domestic cleaning objects and routines that conjoin daughter and mother in Carilli's play, in *My Italian Wife*, Mary Melfi appropriates an iconic, civic "object" to connect her mother and daughter figures conceptually: It is a large statue, intended for theatrical use, of Lady Liberty. Whether we consider the primal bond the one between Rita (daughter) and her absent mother or between Rita (mother surrogate) and Paula (her twenty-year-old younger sister), the statue represents the migrant memory that continues to impact both generations of daughters.

A form of collective memory, migrant memory as used here refers to how Rita and her family remember their past and how they pass it down from generation to generation. If understanding a country's memories means "grasp[ing] something essential about their national identity and outlook,"[42] Rita's interactions with the quintessential emblem of the mass migration can signify not only intergenerational tensions but also "racial, ethnic, and class differences or other socio-political contextualizations" that continue to shape Italians' self-perception and the ability of the ethnic subject (even generations removed from migration) to disengage, grasp, evaluate, empathize, and individuate.[43]

In act II, Rita's former student, Carlo, carries the large Statue of Liberty onstage for a play within the play. It is to serve as a time/place reference for the futuristic *Start Trek* convention show in which Carlo acts. However, when temporarily placed beside the Romano sisters, Rita and Paula, Lady Liberty becomes a paradoxical rendering of the American/Canadian Dream. At first, Rita's husband, John, and Paula hide behind the statue and playfully put words in her mouth. But Rita, who looks upon the statue seriously, responds differently. Her defense of Liberty's solemnity in the excerpt that follows demarcates a divide in the sisters' experience and affirms that Rita's childhood voyage to Canada from Italy was a traumatic experience.

JOHN: (standing behind the Statue of Liberty) Woof, woof.

PAULA: (standing behind the Statue of Liberty) Give me your tired, your poor, your huddled masses.

JOHN: Give me your money!

RITA: Don't make fun of Miss Liberty. She's sacred. Like the Madonna. Holy and good. I wish my mom and I had come through New York and I could have seen this lovely lady and been comforted. When new docked in Halifax, the place was enveloped in a thick fog. I remember walking down the gangplank, holding onto my mother's hand. Suddenly, the string on my shoe broke; the button holding it down and popped off. I got on all fours and started looking for that button. My mom was furious, I guess she was worried I might be trampled to death.—who knows? She picked me up and dragged me to the receiving station without a world. She could have said something like: My little bambina, don't worry, your daddy is a shoemaker. He will fix your strap. But she didn't. I felt like an orphan. And still do.[44]

For the remainder of the play, Rita will be inspired to reflect on how this collective memory passed down from her mother has unconsciously remained a lifeline, driving many of her decisions and explaining her frustration when she gets turned down for a higher-level job in school administration.

> PAULA: So, you did apply to be a vice principal again and were turned down? That's it!
>
> RITA: I should've entered the interview room with a cardboard suitcase. That's all they saw—someone right off the boat—someone so eager to work, she would drive the hourly wage down.
>
> PAULA: You have all of the qualifications!
>
> RITA: If you're an immigrant, the rules are different. It's a race for them; an obstacle course for us.
>
> PAULA: What's the reason they gave?
>
> RITA: I was too nice![45]

Rita has to disrupt the umbilical energy and emotional influence that the migrant memory has on her to embrace her own subjectivity. At forty-eight, she still hesitates to articulate her own dreams for fear of being singled out and pigeonholed as an uneducated immigrant who cannot attain prominent leadership positions:

> RITA: I have a Master's degree in English and still, as soon as I make a little mistake, I panic. I'm worried I can't speak English. It's not my language. I'm back in Halifax, walking down the debt the game playing with my shoe in my hand, limping towards the receiving station.[46]

What is more, even though she knows there is no new migratory voyage before her (nor will she be setting out on the Starship Enterprise with Carlo to learn Klingon). And although, logically, she knows here is no other "new world" to which she will need to assimilate, Rita remains anxious about her sense of belonging. She is convinced that her Italian identity will stigmatize her even after death.

> RITA: It's never over. Once an immigrant, always an immigrant. I wonder when we leave this world, for the next, is it over then? Or do we still have one more border to cross? [. . .] Will *i nostri nonni* be greeting us, making us feel welcome; or do we have to start all over again, like immigrants just off the boat? Will we have to learn a new language, Angel language? [. . .] Will the Madonna be there or is it Miss Liberty that will hold our hands and re-assure us—everything's fine?

In what constitutes her last lengthy musing, Rita effectively conjoins the migrant memory with the primal maternal bond through image of a mother carrying an unborn/newborn child toward an unknown destination with the intention of planting new roots there. "Everyone will be free because this is the place we all came from, *la terra vecchia*, the place we all immigrated from but forgot, the place where we booked passages inside our mother's wombs. Will finally be back home, returnees—carrying presents—pearls of wisdom—for those we left behind."[47] Recalling the mystery and excitement that shroud pregnancy and birth, Rita reflects on Lady Liberty and the symbolism of "America" and the journey from darkness to light that each immigrant hopes to make in their life. Though the journey guarantees neither freedom nor wealth, it does, according to Melfi, allow the returnees to amass knowledge and wisdom to add onto and alter the migrant memory and to nurture the next generation. Rita, the combined daughter-mother, embodies the borderland concept, constituting a third, "other," intergenerational being whose subjectivity midway through the journey of life is fueled by the desire for new beginnings. Rita wishes to free herself from both mothering and daughtering and to reinvent herself as an educated, ethnically identifying female in a leadership position. Ironically, however, the *My Italian Wife* title destabilizes the feminist potential, as it posits the older, non-Italian husband's perspective as the interpretative frame for Rita's quest.

Likewise, in *Eight Ways My Mother Was Conceived*, Michaela longs to experience life more freely within her still traditional, twenty-first-century Italian Canadian community. Though fully assimilated as a third-generation daughter, Michaela is still susceptible to the laws and values of patriarchy that aim to contain and control women's sexuality. Much like Melfi's protagonist, Rita, therefore, Di Cesare's autobiographical Michaela must slay the cultural demons that loom large in her psyche and inhibit her self-realization. Specifically, Michaela must unambiguously dispel the myth of the immaculate conceptions and disavow the Virginity Complex broadly espoused among her kin. More generally, however, she must face a history of violence and oppression toward women in her family, culture, and beyond.

Through her family's well-maintained folklore, Michaela learns that virginity is something girls "have" and that it is a treasure—something prospective lovers can "take," that rapists can "steal," that bad (French!) girls give away at the arcade, and those good girls guard with their lives.[48] But is it not also a curse? Does it not cast a negative spell that stymies healthy sexual development or squelches the self-determination of women, she wonders? As long as this superstitious and manipulative lore flows undisturbed between mother and daughter, persisting in 2010 from countless generations past, virginity remains a core value and source of family honor.

As a result of this sustained patriarchal belief, Michaela experiences anxiety when she starts to date. She is confused by her first boyfriend's sterile behaviors in her regard. She wonders why, after months, he has not kissed her. Is he afraid of her mother's *malocchio*? Is there something she did to displease him? Even if he approached her, though, she would not dare get hot and heavy, says Michaela, because no-penetration pregnancies are "a real problem" in her family.[49] So, rather than boost her confidence and curiosity as a sexual subject, dating and desiring a boy make Michaela spin.

The "Virginity Complex (VC)" effect only worsens when Michaela's second boyfriend enters the scene. As Gabriel proves attentive, consistent, and capable of a loving relationship, Michaela cannot embrace him. Noting his erection one night, Michaela confesses both her desire and her dread. How can the miraculous pregnancies she so gravely fears be?[50] Inverting the classic immigrant journey, the fully assimilated and cosmopolitan teen returns to the Calabrian hill town of her ancestors to unravel the Complex that impedes her emotional well-being. The truth, however, proves traumatic, as Michaela learns that her grandmother was raped: "he trick her, he grab her, and he force her."[51]

This violent news abruptly dissolves the shroud of innocence around the Virginity Complex and catalyzes a new information flow between daughter and mother on the subjects of womanhood and sexuality. This watershed moment occurs when Michaela's mother arrives in Calabria to assist Michaela in her research. For the first time, Michaela and her mother talk candidly and conceive one another as sexual subjects with similar vulnerabilities as well as similar dreams. To Michaela's surprise, her mother underscores the importance of a loving sex life in which she will know physical fulfillment and exercise agency. Michaela is further astounded when her mother suggests that Gabriel would make a good husband for three reasons: "He's gorgeous. He's well-mannered. And he has a big package."[52]

> MICHAELA: Mommy! Oh my God! What the—why would you say that?

> MICHAELA: (as Mother): Because it's important! Your father and I had sex before marriage. That's how I knew he was perfect in every way. We still have great sex, actually. It gets better with age. You get to know each other's bodies so well.

> MICHAELA: Mommy, you just saved my life in the most disgusting way possible.[53]

The brazen comment is nothing less than a peace offering between women and an invitation to Michaela to travel confidently in the "new world" of womanhood. By exposing her authentic thoughts and her personal history to Michaela, Maria loosens the contours of their daughter-mother relationship, allowing for mutual agency and, consequently, a more genuine adult relationship with her daughter.

By choosing to handle female sexuality differently than the other members of their family, Maria helps Michaela reckon with "the unfelt or unregistered forces of unconscious and cultural life that inform sexual experience."[54] Maria's willingness to quash family myths and admit her hypocrisy enables Michaela to recalibrate the value system she inherited from at least three generations before her in Canada and Italy. Though their patriarchally grounded heteronormative standards have been firmly anchored in Michaela and Maria, the "discoveries" and "opportunities" that lie before both women have the potential to transform their subjectivity and foster dreams.

At the end of this monologue, in truth, Michaela makes the galvanizing decision to pursue a graduate degree in Toronto. After a brief standoff with Maria who, at first expresses disapproval and despair, the two women start singing Gloria Gaynor's *I Will Survive* at the top of their lungs. What suddenly strikes Michaela is the great and grave responsibilities women face in raising children, especially daughters:

MICHAELA: [. . .] She's worried about me. About who will be there for me. She wants to know that I'll survive. It's a huge responsibility bringing a girl into the world. If I was holding a baby girl in my arms, I would want her to believe that the world would never break her heart. Because I'd want to believe above all else that I'd never let her get hurt. That's probably what my grandmother vowed as she held my mother close on their transatlantic journey. And that's probably what my mother wished as she helped my tiny wrinkled hand through the hole in the incubator. After all, she gave me a gift. She told me stories. And I would do that too. I would tell my daughter all those stories. But one day, I'd hand her a pen and I'd say, "Here baby, it's your story now. Nobody can make a happy ending but you.[55]

Like Rita, Frances, Angel, and Grace before her, Michaela moves on from a crucial daughter-mother encounter to pursue different professional and creative activities. Moreover, as she grows in awareness of herself as a worthy, respectable, self-standing, sexual, and compassionate human subject, she will no longer need her mother's approval to journey confidently and genuinely in her womanhood and her profession. Endowing herself with the power to pass the pen rather than the pain, De Cesare scripts a new and positive example for daughter-mother borderlands wherein she can consciously and selectively embrace her past and nurture anxiety-free relationships with the people and values she wishes to keep.

Conclusion

While the canon of Italian American women's writing has taken root and flourished over the last half-century and is rich with poetry and prose—fiction and nonfiction—recounting women's diasporic and intergenerational experiences, the theater remains an underexplored genre of women's artistic self-expression for Italian Americana, especially since the second postwar period.[56] Nonetheless, the small number of theatrical works produced and/or published by second-, third-, and fourth-generation women constitutes a largely uncultivated but powerful resource for understanding Italian women's paths to self-realization.[57] The performative and physicality qualities of theatrical storytelling endow women's stories and experiences with corporeal awareness of their female legacies.

Contemporary women playwrights of Italian descent portray the mother-daughter borderlands as a problematic space to which each woman is drawn and yet where neither woman can serenely settle or stay. In this space, the mother seeks to imagine herself as somehow "other" than her present reality suggests, and the daughter critically encounters the mother's quasi-magnetic emotional pull. The borderland also imposes a culture-specific set of expectations and values in which the daughter feels alone and trapped. At the same time, the current selection of plays reveals that the daughters do not wish to fully flee from the border to which their mothers are attached. Perceiving some ineffable element of themselves in their mothers, the daughters do not work to renounce them completely. Instead, the playwright-daughters engage a symbolic umbilical object to simultaneously negotiate a revised bond, one that the daughter can help shape and to which she can ascribe her own meaning.

In the works selected for this study, then, the umbilical objects represent more than the flow of genetic coding; they also imply the transfer of cultural values that endure despite assimilation. While these connections are initially essential for keeping the daughter alive, they can also suffocate their emergent subjectivities. The solution the playwrights, taken together, propose is to not truncate the ties to their origins completely but to exercise their rights and faculties to reconceive the daughter-mother borderland so as to ensure their own ability to dream.

Notes

1. Theresa Carilli is another pioneer in the scholarship of Italian American theater. In her guest-edited volume of *Voices in Italian Americana* (1997–1998), Carilli collected ten plays. Four of these were by women: Chris Cinque's *The Scrub*, Paola Corso's *Flash Light*, Theresa Carilli's *A Thorough Cleansing*, and Serena Anderlini-D'Onofrio's *Open Couple*.

2. Adalgisa Giorgio, *Writing Mothers and Daughters: Renegotiating the Mother in Western European Narratives by Women* (New York: Berghahn Books, 2002), 122. "Since [mother-daughter] recognition is a two-way process, the daughter's longing for maternal recognition must be accompanied by her ability to recognize the mother as an individual. Since this can only happen within the register or reality, and not fantasy, the daughter's search for maternal recognition goes hand in hand with a process of seeing the mother in her reality, which means seeing her in the reality in which she functions and by which she has been produced, and discovering her individuality beyond the maternal role."

3. Helen Barolini, *The Dream Book: An Anthology of Writing by Italian American Women* (New York: Shocken, 1985), xiii.

4. Ibid., 25. Such defensiveness, affirms Gambino, "prevents one from achieving a creative and productive vision of oneself and one's relationship with others, it imposes a psychological burden of intolerable weight."

5. Barolini, xiii. "A more difficult question, though, was not only why we are isolated and few, but whether there was any reason to suppose that, if grouped, we formed something cohesive and had, in fact, a specific resonance as Italian American women writers."

6. Adalgisa Giorgio, "The Passion for the Mother: Conflicts and Idealisations in Contemporary Italian Narrative," in *Writing Mothers and Daughters: Renegotiating the Mother in Western European Narratives by Women* (New York: Berghahn Books, 2002), 120, https://hdl.handle.net/2027/heb.08657. "Womanhood has been erased by motherhood, and motherhood has primarily meant generating and nurturing the male child. [. . .] Within this set-up, the daughter has no independent status: she is trained to become the mother/wife of the son/husband. Any Italian daughter searching for autonomy and individuality must negotiate this powerful maternal imaginary. Centuries of patriarchal religious and lay discourses have made the Italian mother an ambivalent figure who simultaneously encompasses authority and subordination, chastity and sexuality, the sacred and the profane. In particular she is a figure who, although overpoweringly present within the family, is invisible in public life."

7. Adrienne Rich, "On Motherhood and Daughterhood," in *Of Woman Born: Motherhood as Experience and Institution* (New York: Norton, 1976), 225–26, 236. See also Marianne Hirsch, "Mothers and Daughters," *Signs* 7, no. 1 (1981): 201.

8. Ibid., 236. It is important to note, however, that the binary positions of "for or against the mother" and "repeat or reject the mother" initially polarized and paralyzed vital debates.

9. Patrizia Sambuco, *Corporeal Bonds: The Daughter-Mother Relationship in Twentieth-Century Italian Women's Writing* (Toronto: University of Toronto Press, 2012). The reference is apparent starting with the title and is used throughout the book.

10. Sambuco, 6–7. In the introduction, Sambuco references "The Bodily Encounter with the Mother," in *The Irigaray Reader*, ed. Margaret Whitford (Oxford: Blackwell, 1991), 43.

11. Mary Jo Bona, "Mothers and Daughters," in *A Routledge History of Italian Americans*, William Connell and Stanislao Pugliese, eds. (New York: Routledge, 2018), 398.

12. Bona, "Mothers and Daughters in Italian American Narratives," in *The Routledge History of the Italian Americans* (New York: Routledge, 2018), 398.

13. By "umbilical connection," I intend a bidirectional symbiotic linkage with physical and/or psychological-emotional implications. I discuss this with examples further on.

14. As the titles of Helen Barolini's *The Dream Book* (New York: Schocken, 1985) and Rita Ciresi's *Sometimes I Dream in Italian* (McHenry, IL: Delta, 2000) attest, dreams represent a place of self-knowledge and self-expression for Italian American women. In Barolini's touchstone anthology, writing embodies the dream. It is the concretization of individual and collective voices that had either been silenced by power structures of patriarchy or considered unworthy of critical attention.

15. Suzanna Danuta Walters, *Worlds Together, Lives Apart: Mothers and Daughters in Popular Culture*, 156. See also Kim Chernin, *The Hungry Self: Women, Eating, Identity* (New York: HarperCollins, 1985).

16. Jane Moss, "In Search of Lost Intimacy: Mothers and Daughters in Women's Theatre," *Modern Language Studies* 21, no. 1 (Winter 1991): 3. Centuries of patriarchal domination have erected barriers between women, walls of jealousy, misunderstanding, scorn, and silence, which must be broken down if women are to liberate themselves, reclaim their matrilineal heritage, and create their own culture. Since the 1970s, women playwrights and theater groups have often focused on the difficult mother-daughter relationship in their efforts to dramatize the social and psychological situation of women, their sexuality, interrelationships, and language. By examining a group of mother-daughter plays, we will see how women's theater professionals have used the stage to spotlight this key issue in the feminist critique of patriarchy and create distinctive forms of dramatic feminist discourse.

17. Michele Linfante is a playwright and theater artist from Patterson, New Jersey, established in the San Francisco Bay area, part of the Lilith theater company, for which she wrote "Pizza" in 1980. She also co-wrote other works produced there and at theater festivals in the United States and abroad. She currently resides in Sonoma County, California.

18. Linfante wrote *Pizza* in 1980. It is a one-act about her relationship with her mother. It first appeared in Rick Foster, *West Coast Plays 6* (New York: Methuen Drama, 1981), and then in Barolini's *The Dream Book* (1985).

19. Chris Cinque is a self-taught artist residing in Minnesota but is originally from Jersey City, New Jersey. A former ELL teacher and theater artist, Cinque describes her work this way: "The tools of visual art are different from those of theater, but my impulse remains the same: to find out how we as outsiders—women, queers, feminists—can find our place in the world and history, and to express it in as dynamic a way as possible. My plays examined the conflict between myself as an outsider and my connection to history. For example, in my trilogy of one-woman plays, 'Growing Up Queer in America,' I used Dante's 'Divine Comedy' as a frame for the character to find and understand her place in a hostile world."

20. See http://www.mnartists.org/chriscinque. See also Janice Arkatov, "Chris Cinque's Monologue Piece 'Growing Up Queer in America' Opens Saturday at the Ensemble Studio's Downstage Theatre," *LA Times*, August 28, 1988.

The Minnesota-based actress-writer uses Dante's "Divine Comedy" as a metaphor for her own lesbian journey. "I always felt at a disadvantage because I'm not from one place," Cinque said. "My father's from New Jersey, my mother's a native Floridian. So we always had this North-South thing. And we moved around a lot; I could never fit in. Then being a lesbian—that was like the final straw." "It's very difficult," she added. "The social pressures are just immense. It's not uncommon to hear women say, 'I thought I was the only one.' Being a lesbian is very isolating and very frightening, especially when you're a 15-year-old girl in the South, being raised a Catholic—and told there's only one way to be: marry and have children and stay a Catholic. I knew I wasn't that, but I didn't know what I was. And everything I'd heard about lesbians was so horrifying [. . .] When I first did this show (in Minneapolis and Washington) last year, I had an amount of paranoia. I mean, my name and my picture and the word *queer* were all over town on posters. It's coming out in a very big way."

21. Theresa Carilli is a professor emeritus of communication at Purdue University Calumet. Carilli has published two books of plays, *Familial Circles* (2000) and *Women as Lovers* (1996), and she wrote her one-act "A Thorough Cleansing (1997)," for the special theater issue of Voices in Italian Americana, which she edited in 1998. Carilli is co-editor of four volumes on gender and sexuality in the media: *Locating Queerness in the Media: A New Look* (with Jane Campbell, 2017); *Queer Media Images* (with Jane Campbell, 2013); *Challenging Images of Women in the Media* (with Jane Campbell, 2012); *Women and the Media: Diverse Perspectives* (with Jane Campbell, 2005); and *Cultural Diversity and the U.S. Media*, 1998, co-edited with Yahya Kamalipour. In addition, Carilli has written numerous poems, short stories, scholarly articles, theater scripts, and a monograph titled *Scripting Identity: Writing Cultural Experience* (2008), based on her theatrical work with students. For further information, see https://www.encyclopedia.com/arts/educational-magazines/carilli-theresa-1956.

22. Mary Melfi was born in 1951 in a small mountain town in the Molise region of Italy. In 1957, she immigrated with her family to Montreal, Quebec, where she attended the local English schools. Since receiving degrees from both Concordia and McGill, she has published numerous public books of poetry, prose, and works of nonfiction and children's books. Her most recent book, *In the Backyard, Relearning the Art of Aging, Dying and Making Love* (Toronto: Guernica, 2018), addresses the challenges of losing a spouse and dating life after age fifty. Mary Melfi's plays, "Foreplay," "Sex Therapy," and "My Italian Wife" are all satiric looks at love, sex, marriage, and, in the latter, ethnic identity. See https://books.google.com/books/about/Office_Politics.html?id=QOO3b3jKewgC and http://www.italyrevisited.org/aboutauthor.

23. Michaela Di Cesare is a playwright-performer with a master's degree in drama from the University of Toronto. She has worked with the Centaur Theater in Montreal that produced her award-winning *In Search of Mrs. Pirandello* (2016) and *Successions* (2017). Di Cesare has worked with a variety of theaters in Montreal and Toronto and has performed her one-woman show *Eight Ways My Mother Was Conceived* in different Canadian cities and New York. One recent play, titled

Extra/Beautiful/U, won first place (Pam Dunn Award) in the 2017 Write on Q competition. Di Cesare also works in film and TV. Her credits include *The Bold Type, Mike, Fatal Vows, Psych Out, A Stranger in My Home*, and *Sex & Ethnicity*.

24. Gloria Anzaldúa, *Borderlands/La Frontera: The New Mestiza* (San Francisco: Aunt Lute Books, 1999), 3.

25. Ibid., 3.

26. Rich, "On Woman Born," 236. "Matrophobia can be seen as a womanly splitting of the self in the desire to become purged once and for all of our mothers' bondage, to become individuated and free. The mother stands for the victim in ourselves, the unfree woman, the martyr."

27. Suzanna Danuta Walters, *Worlds Together, Lives Apart: Mothers and Daughters in Popular Culture* (Berkeley: University of California Press, 1992), 157.

28. The double entendre is intentional here since Angel's rendering of Lou's story intimates homosexual love between the adolescents Lou and Sandry.

29. Michaela Di Cesare, *Eight Ways My Mother Was Conceived* (Toronto: Playwrights Guild of Canada, 2012), 7.

30. Ibid., 6.

31. Ibid., 19.

32. Chris Cinque, *The Scrub: Growing Up in America Pt. III*, in *Voices in Italian Americana*, ed. Theresa Carilli (1998), 121–24.

33. Ibid., 121.

34. Mary Jo Bona, "Queer Daughters and Their Mothers: Carole Maso, Mary Cappello, and Alison Bechdel Write their way Home," in *Mamma: Interrogating a National Stereotype*, ed. Penelope Morris and Perry Wilson (New York: Palgrave, 2018), 187.

35. Merritt Y. Hughs, "Pirandello's Humor," *Sewanee Review* 35, no. 2 (1927): 181. "They are a bundle of contradictions which poignantly stimulate that conflict of emotions (*il sentimento del contrario*) which Pirandello insists is the essence of the sense of humor. Humorists—both authors and readers—he believes, are always poised in an unstable equilibrium between laughter and sympathy."

36. Theresa Carilli, *A Thorough Cleansing*, in *Voices in Italian Americana* 9, no. 2 (1988): 201.

37. Ibid., 207.

38. Ibid., 207.

39. Ibid., 213–14.

40. Ibid., 208.

41. Ibid., 213–14.

42. Henry Rodeiger and Andrew DeSoto, "The Power of Collective Memory: What Do Large Groups of People Remember—and Forget?," *Scientific American*, June 28, 2016, https://www.scientificamerican.com/article/the-power-of-collective-memory/.

43. Suzanna Danuta Walters, *Worlds Together, Lives Apart: Mothers and Daughters in Popular Culture* (Berkeley: University of California Press, 1992), 157.

44. Mary Melfi, *My Italian Wife* (Toronto: Guernica, 1996), 96.

45. Ibid., 105–6.

46. Ibid., 129.

47. Ibid., 130.

48. Di Cesare, 4.

49. Ibid., 3–4. Di Cesare uses "It's a real problem" as a satiric catchphrase throughout the play to indicate things that she, as a child, considered difficult or inappropriate or awkward from her mother's perspective (i.e., people thinking Michaela was black, having too much going on in her mind at any one time, or girls speaking explicitly about their body parts).

50. Ibid., 22.

51. Ibid., 27.

52. Ibid., 30.

53. Ibid., 30.

54. Muriel Dimen, "Sexual Subjectivity," *Wiley Blackwell Encyclopedia of Gender and Sexuality Studies* (vol. 16, 2016), 2207. See also Muriel Dimen and Virginia Goldner, "Gender and Sexuality," in *American Psychiatric Association Publishing Textbook of Psychoanalysis* (Washington, DC: APA Publishing, 2011), 133–52.

55. Di Cesare, 33.

56. I would like to acknowledge Emelise Aleandri's groundbreaking work on the early immigrant theater and Pellegrino D'Acierno historical overview of theater in the Italian American context. See Emelise Aleandri, *The Italian American Immigrant Theatre of New York* (New York: Arcadia, 1999) and Pellegrino D'Acierno, *The Italian American Heritage: A Companion to Literature and Arts* (New York: Routledge, 1998).

57. There are relatively few women filmmakers who explicitly self-identify as Italian American. Nancy Savoca's is one such example. Her films *True Love* (1989) and *Household Saints* (1993) treat daughter-mother relationships, and later works such as *24-Hour Woman* (2003) and *Union Square* (2011) explore female relationships beyond the family and Italian ethnicity. Helen De Michiel's *Tarantella* (1996) focuses explicitly on the daughter-mother relationship and the crossroads between psychological oppression and vital forms of creativity.

Works Cited

Aleandri, Emelise. *Italian-American Immigrant Theatre of New York City*. New York: Arcadia Publishing, 1999.

Anzaldúa, Gloria. *Borderlands/La Frontera: The New Mestiza*. San Francisco: Aunt Lute Books, 1999.

Arkatov, Janice. "Chris Cinque's Monologue Piece: *Growing Up Queer in America* Opens Saturday at the Ensemble Studio's Downstage Theatre." *LA Times*, August 28, 1988.

Barolini, Helen. *The Dream Book: An Anthology of Writing by Italian American Women*. New York: Shocken, 1985.

Bona, Mary Jo. *By the Breaths of Their Mouths: Narratives of Resistance in Italian America.* Albany, NY: State University of New York Press, 2010.

———. *Claiming a Tradition: Italian American Women Writers.* Southern Illinois University Press, 1999.

———. "Mothers and Daughters." In *A Routledge History of Italian Americans,* edited by William Connell and Stanislao Pugliese, 385–403. New York: Routledge, 2018.

———. "Queer Daughters and Their Mothers: Carole Maso, Mary Cappello, and Alison Bechdel Write their Way Home." In *La Mamma: Interrogating a National Stereotype,* edited by Penelope Morris and Perry Wilson, 185–214. New York: Palgrave, 2018.

Bonomo Albright, Carole, and Christine Palamidessi Moore. Introduction to *American Woman, Italian Style: Italian Americana's Best Writings on Women,* edited by Carole Bonomo Albright and Christine Palamidessi Moore, 1–12. New York: Fordham University Press, 2010.

Carilli, Theresa. *A Thorough Cleansing.* In *Voices in Italian Americana,* edited by Theresa Carilli (Special Issue 1998): 130–44.

Chernin, Kim. *The Hungry Self: Women, Eating, Identity.* New York: HarperCollins, 1985.

Cinque, Chris. *The Scrub: Growing Up in America Pt. III.* In *Voices in Italian Americana,* edited by Theresa Carilli (Special Issue 1998): 50–66.

Ciresi, Rita. *Sometimes I Dream in Italian.* McHenry, IL: Delta, 2000.

Connell, William, and Stanislao Pugliese. *A Routledge History of Italian Americans.* New York: Routledge, 2018.

D'Acierno, Pellegrino. *The Italian American Heritage: A Companion to Literature and Arts.* New York: Routledge, 1998.

Di Cesare, Michaela. *Eight Ways My Mother Was Conceived.* Toronto: Playwrights Guild of Canada, 2012.

Dimen, Muriel. "Sexual Subjectivity." *Wiley Blackwell Encyclopedia of Gender and Sexuality Studies.* Vol. 16, 2007.

Dimen, Muriel, and Virginia Goldner. "Gender and Sexuality." In *American Psychiatric Association Publishing Textbook of Psychoanalysis.* Washington, DC: APA Publishing, 2011.

Egelman, William. "Traditional Roles and Modern Work Patterns: Italian-American Women in New York City." In *American Woman, Italian Style: Italian Americana's Best Writings on Women,* edited by Carole Bonomo Albright and Christine Palamidessi Moore, 78–86. New York: Fordham University Press, 2010.

Gabaccia, Donna. "Italian-American Women: A Review Essay." In *American Woman, Italian Style: Italian Americana's Best Writings on Women,* edited by Carole Bonomo Albright and Christine Palamidessi Moore, 307–32. New York: Fordham University Press, 2010.

Gambino, Richard. "Gender Relations among Italian Americans." In *American Woman, Italian Style. Italian Americana's Best Writings on Women*, edited by Carole Bonomo Albright and Christine Palamidessi Moore, 110–20. New York: Fordham University Press, 2010.

Giunta, Edvige, and Joseph Sciorra. *Embroidered Stories: Interpreting Women's Domestic Needlework from the Italian Diaspora*, edited by Edvige Giunta and Joseph Sciorra. University Press of Mississippi, 2014.

Giorgio, Adalgisa. *Writing Mothers and Daughters: Renegotiating the Mother in Western European Narratives by Women*. New York: Berghahn Books, 2002.

Hirsch, Marianne. "Mothers and Daughters." *Signs* 7, no. 1 (1981): 200–22.

Hughs, Merritt Y. "Pirandello's Humor." *Sewanee Review* 35, no. 2 (1927): 175–86.

Linfante, Michele. *Pizza*. In *The Dream Book: An Anthology of Writing by Italian American Women*, edited by Helen Barolini, 270–96. New York: Schocken, 1980.

Melfi, Mary. *Foreplay & My Italian Wife*. Toronto: Guernica, 1996.

Messina, Elizabeth G. "Narratives of Nine Italian-American Women: Childhood, Work, and Marriage." In *American Woman, Italian Style: Italian Americana's Best Writings on Women*, edited by Carole Bonomo Albright and Christine Palamidessi Moore, 78–86. New York: Fordham University Press, 2010.

Moss, Jane. "In Search of Lost Intimacy: Mothers and Daughters in Women's Theatre." *Modern Language Studies* 21, no. 1 (Winter 1991): 3–15.

Parrino, Maria. "Education in the Autobiographies of Four Italian Women Immigrants." In *American Woman, Italian Style: Italian Americana's Best Writings on Women*, edited by Carole Bonomo Albright and Christine Palamidessi Moore, 57–77. New York: Fordham University Press, 2010.

Rich, Adrienne. *Of Woman Born: Motherhood as Experience and Institution*. New York: Norton, 1976.

Roedigger, Henry, and Andrew DeSoto. "The Power of Collective Memory: What Do Large Groups of People Remember—and Forget?" *Scientific American*, June 28, 2016. https://www.scientificamerican.com/article/the-power-of-collective-memory/.

Sambuco, Patrizia. *Corporeal Bonds: The Daughter-Mother Relationship in Twentieth-Century Italian Women's Writing*. Toronto: University of Toronto Press, 2012.

Schimanski, Johan, and Stephen Wolfe. "Entry Points: An Introduction." In *Border Poetics De-limited*, edited by Johan Schimanski and Stephen Wolfe, 9–26. Hanover: Wehrhahn Verlag, 2007.

Smith, Judith. "Italian Mothers, American Daughters: Changes in Work and Family Roles." In *Proceedings of the Tenth Annual Conference of the American Italian Historical Association*, edited by Betty Boyd Caroli, Robert F. Harney, and Lydio F. Tomasi, 206–221. Toronto: American Italian Historical Association, 1978.

Treese, Lorett. "'Why It's Mother': The Italian Mothers' Clubs of New York." In *American Woman, Italian Style: Italian Americana's Best Writings on Women*, edited by Carole Bonomo Albright and Christine Palamidessi Moore, 32–48. New York: Fordham University Press, 2010.

Walters, Suzanna Danuta. *Worlds Together, Lives Apart: Mothers and Daughters in Popular Culture*. Berkeley: University of California Press, 1992.

Whitford, Margaret, ed. *The Irigaray Reader*. Oxford: Blackwell, 1991.

List of Contributors

Domenico A. Beneventi is professor of comparative literature at Université de Sherbrooke, Canada. His research interests and publications focus on Canadian and Québécois literature, urban writing, and gender and queer studies. He is co-editor of *Contested Spaces, Counter-narratives, and Culture from Below in Canada and Québec* (University of Toronto Press, 2019) and *La lutte pour l'espace: Ville, performance, et culture d'en bas* (Université Laval Press, 2017). In 2017, he was visiting professor of Canadian studies at the University of Kiel, Germany. He also collaborated on the recent Queer Canadian anthology *Here and Now: An Anthology of Queer Italian-Canadian Writing* (2021).

Mary Jo Bona is SUNY Distinguished Professor Emerita of Women's, Gender, & Sexuality Studies and English at Stony Brook University. A specialist in the field of Italian American/diaspora studies, multiethnic American literature, and feminist literary studies, her authored books include *Mothers, Mobility, Narrative: Maternality in US Literature*; *Women Writing Cloth: Migratory Fictions in the American Imaginary*; *By the Breath of Their Mouths: Narratives of Resistance in Italian America*; *Claiming a Tradition: Italian American Women Writers*, and a book of poetry, *I Stop Waiting For You*. Bona is also editor of *The Voices We Carry: Recent Italian American Women's Fiction* and co-editor (with Irma Maini) of *Multiethnic Literature and Canon Debates*. Bona is the series editor of Multiethnic Literatures for State University of New York (SUNY) Press.

Ryan Calabretta-Sajder is associate professor and section head of Italian studies, associate director of gender studies, and director of international and global studies at the University of Arkansas, Fayetteville, where he teaches courses in Italian, film, and gender studies. He is the author of *Divergenze in celluloide: colore, migrazione e identità sessuale nei film gay di Ferzan Özpetek* with Mimesis editore; editor of *Pasolini's Lasting Impressions: Death, Eros, and Literary Enterprise in the Opus of Pier Paolo Pasolini* with Fairleigh Dickinson University Press; and co-editor of *Italian Americans on Screen: Challenging the Past, Re-Theorizing the Future* with Lexington Books (2020). His research interests include the integration of gender, class, and migration in both Italian and Italian American literature and cinema. In spring 2017, he was awarded one of four Fulbright Awards for the Foundation of the South to conduct research and teach at the University of Calabria, Arcavacata and in fall 2024 he was the Tiro a Segno Fellow at New York University. He is currently working on two authored, book-length projects, one exploring the Italian American gay author Robert Ferro, who died of AIDS complications in 1988, and the second on the Algerian-Italian author Amara Lakhous. Currently, Calabretta-Sajder is past-president of the American Association of Teachers of Italian (AATI) and the founding and current editor of *Diasporic Italy: Journal of the Italian American Studies Association.*

John Champagne is professor emeritus of English at Pennsylvania State University at Erie, the Behrend College. His research focuses on the representation of gender and sexuality in modernist film, art, and literature. He is the author of six books, including *The Blue Lady's Hands* (Lyle Stuart, 1988), *When the Parrot Boy Sings* (Meadowland Books, 1990), *The Ethics of Marginality, A New Approach to Gay Studies* (University of Minnesota Press, 1995), *Aesthetic Modernism and Masculinity in Fascist Italy* (Routledge, 2013), *Italian Masculinity as Queer Melodrama: Caravaggio, Puccini, Contemporary Cinema* (Palgrave, 2015), and *Queer Ventennio: Italian Fascism, Homoerotic Art, and the Nonmodern in the Modern* (Peter Lang, 2018). Champagne publishes in scholarly and creative venues, including *Modern Italy*, *boundary 2*, *College English*, *Kenyon Review*, and *Journal of Homosexuality*. As a Fulbright recipient, he spent the 2006–7 school year teaching American studies in Tunisia at the University of La Manouba. His forthcoming book is *The Italian Vice: Italy and the Invention of Modern Male Homosexuality* (Palgrave Macmillan).

Francesco Ferrari graduated in Italian studies from the University of Bologna (Italy). He recently finished his PhD in Italian studies in the Department of French and Italian at the University of Illinois at Urbana-Champaign. His research examines the notion of nostalgia in Italian culture between the nineteenth and twentieth centuries. By adopting the perspective of affect theory and new materialism, he focuses on the interactions between things-feelings-individuals and the role played by nostalgic objects in envisioning alternative forms of futurities.

Tracy Floreani is Professor Emerita of English and former director of the Jeanne Hoffman Smith Center for Film and Literature at Oklahoma City University. She served four years as president of MELUS (2021–25) and has worked for the National Endowment for the Humanities. Her research focuses on multiethnic American literature since World War II and includes the monograph *Fifties Ethnicities: The Ethnic Novel and Mass Culture at Midcentury* (State University of New York Press, 2013) and the edited collection *Approaches to Teaching the Works for Ralph Ellison* (MLA, 2024). She is currently completing a biography of Fanny McConnell Ellison and continues recovery work on Ben Piazza's only novel.

Alan J. Gravano is assistant professor and Writing Center director at Rocky Mountain University of Health Professions. He was awarded a Fulbright Lectureship in Italian-American Studies at the University of Calabria from October 2022 to January 2023. He is a former MLA Delegate Assembly member (2017–20), the Committee on Contingent Labor in the Profession (2018–21, chair 2020–21), and past president of the Italian American Studies Association (2015–21). He serves on the MLA LLC Italian American (2022–27; 2024–25, acting secretary; 2025–26, acting chair). He contributed "Reassessing the Topography of New York City in Don DeLillo's Fiction" to *Don DeLillo in Context* (Cambridge University Press, 2021) and "Enoch 'Nucky' Thompson as the Anti-Hero in *Boardwalk Empire*" to *The Neglected Works of Martin Scorsese* (Bloomsbury, forthcoming 2025) and published "CNN's Searching for Italy: Stanley Tucci as Foodways Icon" and "Chef/Cook, Influencer, Mixologist, Travel Host: Stanley Tucci as Everyman" in *Italian Americans in Film and Other Media* (Palgrave, 2024). He co-edited *Italian Americans on the Page: Re-Reading the Classics and Examining Underexplored Subjects* (State University of New York Press, forthcoming 2025). Finally, he is the new editor-in-chief of the journal *Italian Americana*, published by the University of Illinois Press.

Jessica Maucione, PhD, is professor of English at Gonzaga University, where she also serves as Powers Chair of the Humanities, interim director of Native American studies, and co-coordinator of the Underrepresented Minority

Post-doctoral Fellowship Program. Her scholarly publications combine critical race theory with space and place theory applied to popular media and literature. Maucione's publications include articles and book chapters on space and place and critical race theory and pedagogy, Nic Pizzolatto's *True Detective*, Sylvester Stallone's *Rocky* series and Ryan Kyle Coogler's *Creed*, Leslie Marmon Silko's *Almanac of the Dead*, Karen Tei Yamashita's *The Tropic of Orange*, Edward P. Jones's *Lost in the City*, Don DeLillo's *Cosmopolis*, and John Fante's *Ask the Dust*. She has a forthcoming article on Mohsin Hamid's *Exit West* and Louise Erdrich's *The Future Home of the Living God*.

Colleen M. Ryan is vice provost for faculty at Tufts University. Ryan is the author of various books and articles on Pier Paolo Pasolini, Italian cinema, Italian women writers, Italian American film and literature, and teaching foreign languages through theater. For more than three decades, she has taught at the intersection of film, literature, gender, sexuality, and ethnicity studies. Ryan has served on the executive teams for the American Association of University Supervisors and Coordinators, Italian American Studies Association, and American Association of Teachers of Italian, and holds a Distinguished Service Award from the latter.

Bryan M. Santin earned his PhD in English from the University of Notre Dame in 2017. As an assistant professor of English at Concordia University Irvine, he teaches courses in American literature, world literature, and composition and rhetoric. His research interests focus primarily on twentieth- and twenty-first-century American literature and politics. His scholarly writing has been published or is forthcoming in the academic journals *American Quarterly* and *Religion & Literature* and the edited book collection *William T. Vollmann: A Critical Companion* (University of Delaware Press, 2014).

Douglas Steward held a PhD in English from the University of Kansas. He taught American literature and literary theory at Truman State University and Franklin and Marshall College. He held the position of associate director of programs and director of the ADE for the MLA until his untimely death in 2020. His research focused on the intersections of queer and critical race theory and the state of affairs of the humanities in higher education.

Index